OXFORD STUDIES IN DEMOCRATIZATION

Series Editor: Laurence Whitehead

. . . .

DEMOCRATIZATION

OXFORD STUDIES IN DEMOCRATIZATION

Series Editor: Laurence Whitehead

. . . .

Oxford Studies in Democratization is a series for scholars and students
of comparative politics and related disciplines. Volumes will concentrate
on the comparative study of the democratization processes that accompanied
the decline and termination of the cold war. The geographical focus of
the series will primarily be Latin America, the Caribbean, Southern
and Eastern Europe, and relevant experiences in Africa and Asia.

OTHER BOOKS IN THE SERIES

Democratization
Theory and Experience

. . . .

LAURENCE WHITEHEAD

OXFORD
UNIVERSITY PRESS

OXFORD

UNIVERSITY PRESS

Great Clarendon Street, Oxford OX2 6DP

Oxford University Press is a department of the University of Oxford.
It furthers the University's objective of excellence in research, scholarship,
and education by publishing worldwide in

Oxford New York

Auckland Bangkok Buenos Aires Cape Town Chennai
Dar es Salaam Delhi Hong Kong Istanbul Karachi Kolkata
Kuala Lumpur Madrid Melbourne Mexico City Mumbai Nairobi
São Paulo Shanghai Singapore Taipei Tokyo Toronto
with an associated company in Berlin

Oxford is a registered trade mark of Oxford University Press
in the UK and in certain other countries

Published in the United States
by Oxford University Press Inc., New York

© Laurence Whitehead 2002

The moral rights of the author have been asserted
Database right Oxford University Press (maker)

First published 2002

British Library Cataloguing in Publication Data
Data available

Library of Congress Cataloging in Publication Data
Data available
ISBN 0–19–925327–7 (Hbk.)
ISBN 0–19–925328–5 (Pbk.)

1 3 5 7 9 10 8 6 4 2

Typeset by Hope Services (Abingdon) Ltd.
Printed in Great Britain
on acid-free paper by
T. J. International Ltd.,
Padstow, Cornwall

Acknowledgements

Francisco Franco, Augusto Pinochet, and Antonio Salazar were among the first to stir my interest in the question of democratization. So I begin with a small tribute to a minor unintended side effect of three long careers bent on the obliteration of awkward ideas. In more academic terms, it was the Latin American Program of the Woodrow Wilson Center for International Scholars that first gave me the opportunity to develop this interest. I owe special thanks to Abe Lowenthal, the first director of that programme, who entrusted me with the role of coordinating what became the 'Transitions from Authoritarian Rule' project. It was through his introduction that I came to know Guillermo O'Donnell and Philippe Schmitter, and the long roll call of distinguished scholars whose names appear often, both in that publication, and in the bibliography of this one. Many of them became long-term friends as well as mentors and sparring partners.

This volume reflects the many influences and activities that have flowed from that initial project over the ensuing twenty years. I became Editor of the 'Oxford Studies in Democratization' series in 1995, and I owe a special debt to Dominic Byatt who turned my often sketchy suggestions into a stream of serious academic publications, many of which have, at least indirectly, influenced the arguments presented in this volume. He also gently pressed me to complete this long overdue book, and he arranged for Amanda Watkins, Gwen Booth and Jane Robson to provide the support and advice I needed to finish the job. John Crabtree and Rebecca Vickers also helped me along, and my indefatigable secretary at Nuffield College, Sarah McGuigan, went well beyond the call of duty in her efforts to bring order to my jumble of draft chapters.

In fact most of the chapters in this book are updated and modified versions of journal articles and conference papers that have been in production over the past five years. For example, chapter one is partly based on an article that first appeared in the *Journal of Political Ideologies* in 1997, and that owes an intellectual debt to that Journal's editor Michael Freeden, as well as to Andrew Hurrell, Mark Philp, and Jerry Cohen. Chapter two began as a presentation at the Juan March Institute in Madrid in 1996, and saw first light as one of their working papers, before appearing (in severely condensed form) in the *Journal of Democracy* in 1999. Among the acknowledgements owing for that chapter I would highlight the intellectual influence of Guillermo O'Donnell (who started me reading about ancient Greece). Chapter three is derived from a paper first commissioned by Robert Fine and Shirin Rai for a conference on civil society at Warwick University, and subsequently revised for publication under their editorial supervision. Chapter four began as a LASA conference paper, which was then taken up by Jennifer McCoy at the Carter Center and that has also been influenced by the work of, among others, Andreas Schedler. Chapter five started out as a closing paper at a conference on Political Corruption organised by Eduardo Posada at the Institute for Latin American Studies in London. It developed as I became involved in various activities of Transparency International, partly thanks to Peter Eigen and to Gillian Dell of their Berlin headquarters. Chapter six is derived from a panel at IPSA organised by Lourdes Sola and myself in 2000. Between us we are in the process of publishing a full book length study of 'the delicate balance' between monetary authority and democratic legitimacy, which includes much more detailed work on the Brazilian case. A Portuguese version of this book will be published in Sao Paulo in mid-2002, and (thanks to Leslie Bethell and the Centre for Brazilian Studies at Oxford), an expanded and updated English version should soon follow. Chapter seven also benefited from the work of the Centre for Brazilian Studies, while the main impetus came from an initiative promoted by the government of El Salvador and by the British Embassy there. They funded a conference on citizen security in El Salvador held in September 2001, which has generated a forthcoming volume in Spanish which contains its own extensive acknowledgements. Chapter eight is based on lectures on comparative method for the Politics Graduate Studies Committee at Oxford. These, in turn, derive from various exercises in 'paired comparison' that I have carried out since the mid-1990s. Jorge Heine started me on this course when he organised two conferences on the Chile/South African comparison, and Ted Newman followed up by commissioning a conference paper from me on the Colombia/Mexico comparison. In a parallel exercise Larry Diamond and the National Endowment for Democracy enlisted me to work on an East Asia/Latin American large regional comparison, which will be published by Johns Hopkins University Press in the second half of 2002. Chapter nine was originally commissioned by Amparo Menéndez-Carrión, and appeared in Spanish in a volume she edited in 1999 for the Fifth Chilean Congress of Political Science. Finally, Chapter ten made its first appearance as a paper on 'the state of the art' at the International Political Science Association conference in Quebec City in September 2000.

Perhaps this is enough to demonstrate that this volume owes many more intellectual and practical debts that can possibly be recognised in a brief list of acknowledgements. This author (at least) is as much a receiver, interpreter and retransmitter of collectively generated ideas and experiences as an isolated individual thinker. Some influences can be explicitly identified and consciously acknowledged, but the more important may well be tacit and indirect. Some may be straight borrowings from elsewhere, some are transmutations, but authors can also be heavily influenced by what they resist and even reject. Atomistic models of proprietorship hardly capture this reality.

My closing—and fundamental—acknowledgements are to my family and my college, both of which—in their quite different ways—have provided me with the support without which my efforts at dialogue, reflection, and synthesis would have been far more of a struggle.

Nuffield College   Laurence Whitehead
Oxford
April 10th 2000

Contents

Contents

Introduction

> Events, past and present . . . are the true, the only reliable teachers of political scientists . . . Once such an event [as the spontaneous uprising in Hungary] has happened, every policy, theory and forecast of future potentialities needs re-examination.
>
> (Hannah Arendt)

In 1956 Hannah Arendt was reacting to the experience of the Hungarian uprising which signalled the bankruptcy of Soviet political theory. But the underlying truth is more general, and still applies even in the post-Soviet world. As this book goes to press the news in coming in of a massive terrorist attack on New York and Washington, DC. This is a very different script from the dramas of democratization discussed in Chapter 2, but it may well prove a further confirmation of Arendt's thesis. This volume is concerned with theories of democratization, and the two-way interaction between theory and experience in this field. Here, too, events have repeatedly challenged the prevailing orthodoxies, and may continue to do so. Indeed, it was certain shocking and violent events of the early 1970s that first attracted the new field of comparative democratization studies. The turning-point was an act of great symbolic violence—the strafing of the Presidential Palace (the Moneda) in Santiago in September 1973. The ensuing collapse of Chile's venerable democracy marked something approaching the low point in the fortunes of this system of government, at least for my generation. Barely six months later a peaceful revolution in Lisbon launched Portugal onto a tortuous but ultimately highly successful transition from police state to modern democracy. Greece, Spain, and Peru followed shortly thereafter, and the comparative analysis of processes of democratization followed soon after.

At first this seemed like a marginal phenomenon, and a minor and limited area of scholarship. However, over the past twenty years the reality of democratization has been diffused across the globe penetrating into the most remote and improbable of locations. Who in the mid-1970s would even have dreamt of the democratization of Albania, of Cambodia, of South Africa, or of East Timor? Trailing behind this reality there has sprung up a mini-industry of analysts, advisory agencies, comparativists, consultants, and every associated variety of commentary and scholarship required to calibrate, to classify, and to contain the resulting shocks and surprises. By the end of the twentieth century it might have been expected that the so-called 'third wave' of democratization would have crested and subsided, and that scholarly analyses of the associated phenomena would have caught up. This volume is constructed around the alternative hypothesis that the global upsurge of democracy has not yet exhausted its capacity to surprise, and that the emerging scholarship remains vulnerable to the further unfolding of its object of study.

Advances towards democracy in countries like Georgia, Indonesia, and Paraguay test assumptions of linear causation and conceptual closure to near breaking point. At times such democratizations can seem as erratic, unpredictable, and prone to metamorphosis as the life trajectory of the butterfly. What the analyst may eventually pin down for comparative inspection may be no more than the dried tissue of the insect after all the life and movement has been drained from it. Other democratization processes may seem to exhibit far more regularity and stability, but even so a single generation could be too short a period to permit a definitive judgement. Apparent stability may sometimes turn out to be no more than metastability (i.e. only in the face of small disturbances). The global economy and the international balance of power have provided untypically favourable conditions for democratization over the past twenty years, and it remains to be tested how well these new regimes would resist in the event of a return to more 'normal' and therefore more turbulent settings. In view of these considerations this study differs from much of the contemporary literature on democratization in that, where possible, it incorporates a long historical perspective, and draws on comparisons that, for example, sometimes go back as far as the early history of the USA.

As the variety of democratizations has multiplied, so has the scholarly and analytical literature proliferated. Empirically minded social scientists have vied with normative political theorists and constitutionalists, with practitioners of comparative historical analysis, with area studies specialists, and with single country experts to cover all this new terrain. This volume does not attempt to survey all the different approaches to democratization studies that have been proposed or attempted. Instead it pursues one particular theoretical standpoint, compares that with challenges posed to all analysis by the still unfolding experiences of contemporary democratizations, and reflects on some methodological issues that arise from this endeavour.

The theoretical starting-point, elaborated in Chapter 1, is that 'democracy' is best understood not as a predetermined end-state, but as a long-term and somewhat open-ended outcome, not just as a feasible equilibrium but as a socially desirable and imaginary future. This constructedness means that there can be no single 'cook book' recipe for democracy applicable to all times and places. It must be the court of democratic opinion (rather than a stipulative definition) which arbitrates disputes over precisely what should count in each setting. This refers not to the passing opinions of an arbitrary local majority, but rather a reflective opinion shaped by regional and global as well as domestic influences. From this stand-point it follows that democratization—the process of moving towards this not entirely fixed future state—must be analysed as a complex dynamic and long-term affair. It will also be 'open-ended' in the sense that it always remains open to further reconsideration and revision in the light of experience. Chapter 2 builds on this per-spective by offering a reconsideration of the opening (or 'transition') phase of democratization, invoking the metaphor of a dramatic or theatrical performance. This heuristic device directs attention to the socializing or re-educating effect that a democratization may produce on its audience (on the citizens of the prospective new democracy). Chapter 3 follows up on this approach by re-examining theories of 'civil society' and by exploring the possible interconnec-tions between the emergence of civil society and processes of democ-ratization. Both theory and experience are considered under this heading, and the chapter underscores the unhelpfulness of linear schemes of causal connection in this regard. Chapter 4 shifts from societal variables to questions of institutional design, and reviews various aspects of 'accountability' that are often considered crucial for democratization. Again both theory and experience are invoked, and again any confidence in tight causal connections is brought into question.

Since the current 'wave' of democratizations has coincided with the failure of the Soviet socialist experiment and the strengthening of internationalized market processes, it is hardly surprising that the classical problem of how to accommodate huge concentrations of private economic power within a democratic framework has become so salient. In many new democracies the issues connected with what may loosely be labelled 'political corruption' have come to dominate public attention. They may have the potential to distort or even derail some processes of democratization, and they certainly affect the structure of civil society and the workings of systems of 'accountability'. Chapter 5 considers political corruption in general, and the financing of political processes in particular. Chapter 6 pursues a related but perhaps narrower and more technical line of enquiry, namely the 'delicate balance' that needs to be struck between the requirements of solid monetary authority, on the one hand, and the need for democratic consent and control over key aspects of economic structure and policy, on the other. Again theoretical considerations require attention, but tempered by consideration of our experience of how central banks in 'really existing' new democracies actually behave. Chapter 7 deals with another apparently rather narrow topic which is nevertheless at the centre of public concerns in many new democracies: the delivery of 'citizen security'. Here, even more than before, the divorce between theory and official discourse, on the one hand, and lived experience, on the other, can be extremely wide and can have the most far-reaching implications for the way any given democratization process may unfold (or go into reverse). The topic of citizen security turns out to be far from narrow, and indeed this chapter reconnects with earlier discussions concerning the nature of civil society problems of institutional design, and the potentially corrosive power of private wealth.

Chapters 8 and 9 deal with different methods of handling the complexity and variety of democratization experiences in particular countries and regions. They are partly about comparative method, but are mostly concerned with substantive illustrations of how democratization processes may be compared. Three types of comparison receive attention: comparisons across large regions, and paired comparisons in Chapter 8; and an illustrative single country analysis of Chile treated as an exemplary or paradigmatic case, in Chapter 9.

The concluding chapter takes stock of the entire discussion, in particular spelling out the rationale for the theoretical perspective adopted in this volume. It makes a case for 'useful knowledge', practical reason, and an 'interpretative' approach to the understanding of democratization processes. But it acknowledges that these are all controversial claims in contemporary social science. The perspective adopted in this book involves commitment to some non-mainstream positions on comparison, interpretation, and explanation, and where necessary the implications of these positions have been drawn to the reader's attention. The focus of this volume is not on social science in general, but rather on the specific problems of theory and method that arise if we are to generate useful (and ideally cumulative) knowledge about democratization. This particular object of study has a series of characteristics that make it analytically quite intractable—low predictability in most fields; proliferation and diversity of cases; long causal chains with scope for multiple pathways and complex feedback mechanisms; a shared vocabulary, but with multiple shades of meaning and little terminological closure; some elements of teleology and normative social construction that invite permanent contestation. Where such characteristics prevail many social scientists may hesitate to tread, especially if it seems possible that future developments will continue to destabilize their findings. However, the aim of this volume is to persuade the reader that, even so, useful comparative work *can* be undertaken in this field, and also that it *should* be. The object of study is too prominent, and too worthwhile, to be set aside. It concerns what James Rule calls 'first order' questions—'the kinds of questions that draw people to study social life in the first place, and that are consistently raised anew in the minds of non-specialists seeking reasoned bases for action in the face of endemic social tensions'. It concerns what he calls 'things that we need to know about the social world' (interpreting 'we' as inclusively as possible). And it may help to generate 'theory for coping'[1] ideas which may be in short supply in many new democracies, and not only there.

---

[1] James B. Rule, *Theory and Progress in Social Science* (Cambridge: Cambridge University Press, 1997), 46, 242, 203.

1

On 'Democracy' and 'Democratization'

> A democracy exists only insofar as its ideals and values bring it
> into being.
>
> (Giovanni Sartori)

Is the Russian Federation under Vladimir Putin correctly classified as a 'democracy'? Is Indonesia engaged in a process of 'democratization' following thirty-two years of authoritarian rule under General Suharto? Was Colombia for forty years one of the best established democracies in Latin America, and what is it now? For that matter, is the European Union either a democratic entity or a means for the promotion of democracy within its area? Was the USA democratic before the abolition of slavery, or did it democratize thereafter? If the second, how do Jim Crow laws fit into a process of democratization, and is that process now complete? Was the presidential election of 2000 consistent with America's image as the world's oldest and most secure political democracy? All round the world new political experiences continually test, bombard, and interrogate established labels and ways of theorizing about political reality.

This book is a meditation on such experiences, and their implications for our repertoire of general concepts and theories concerning democracy and democratization. The key conclusions are that we need a 'floating but anchored' conception of democracy, and that democratization is best understood as a long-term process of social construction. The obvious place to begin is therefore with some discussion of these two key terms as they bear on contemporary experience, together with the linkages between them. This is the (mainly theoretical) task of this chapter.

The first part of this chapter was originally published as 'The Vexed Question of the Meaning of "Democracy"', *Journal of Political Ideologies*, 2/2 (1997), and has benefited from helpful suggestions from Jerry Cohen, Michael Freeden, Andy Hurrell, and Mark Philp, although I was unable to do justice to them all.

This chapter prepares the way for subsequent more detailed consideration to such questions as how to organize our analysis of the interactional complexities of a democratic transition (Chapter 2); what variants of 'civil society' can be expected to support processes of democratization, and where friction may arise between these two overlapping but partially competing abstractions (Chapter 3); and how theories of institutional design relate to lived experiences of democratic construction. As this discussion proceeds, theory will be increasingly subjected to reality checks in the light of experience. Thus the kind of questions posed in the first paragraph of this chapter will be addressed incrementally rather than head on. By the end of the book, while direct answers will not necessarily have been provided to each question, we should be in a better position to tackle problems of this kind (notably in Chapter 10). First, then, we shall consider democracy and democratization in the light of their 'really existing' manifestations.

On Democracy

To begin with a topic that has already been examined from every conceivable angle for over twenty-five centuries[1] might seem unpromising, but it is also inescapable. In what follows the reader will find the following central arguments developed: (i) if theory is to be examined in the light of contemporary experience, it is necessary to work with a moderately 'constructivist' approach to the meaning of 'democracy'; (ii) put differently, context matters when attempting to pin down the applicability of this term in very wide range of historical, cultural, and social contexts where it is currently being employed; (iii) since democracy is both a descriptive label and a desirable value, and since the precise outer boundaries of the concept are inherently debatable, there is bound to be disagreement over particular applications of the term; (iv) indeed a good case can be made that it is something deeper than the reflexive nature of our political cognition itself that renders democracy an 'essentially contested' concept; (v) however, this is far from conceding that anything goes. On the contrary there can be both a core of meaning that is 'anchored' and a margin of contestation that is 'floating'; (vi) in contemporary conditions there is a dominant conception of democracy which differs from earlier views, and which may itself mutate; (vii) whatever the prevalent hegemonic conception of democracy it is always provisional and subject to further challenge and development in the light of collective deliberation; (viii) this

---

[1] See e.g. the sweeping survey in John Dunn (ed.), *Democracy: The Unfinished Journey: 508 B.C to A.D. 1993* (Oxford: OUP, 1992).

deliberative filter also serves to stabilize understanding of the term, it provides much of the 'anchoring'.

Let us now consider a few illustrations of the issues that contemporary experience poses for our thinking about democracy. For example, does the term 'democracy' carry just the same connotations after the end of the cold war as it used to in a bi-polar world? Is the core meaning of the word really identical in Chinese, or in Arabic, to its meaning in English, or in Greek? Does it make no basic difference to their understanding of the term that different people may occupy radically different positions in a political hierarchy (e.g. no difference to the understanding of Afrikaners and so-called 'Bantus' under apartheid; no difference to the understanding of males and females, or true believers and sceptics, in an Islamic theocracy?). How can the value-laden overtones of the word be kept from destabilizing our usage, in a period when power and resources flow to those who can get themselves classified as democrats and when those doing the classification are often not dispassionate observers, but actively interested parties? Can we disregard historical change, and assume some underlying continuity of meaning for the term extending through the city-states of antiquity to the nation-states of modernity into the electronically integrated world that may soon be upon us?

This list of questions highlights the difficulties arising from the claim that the term 'democracy' has a clear core meaning that is universally applicable and that is essentially objective. Yet this is not a claim that can be abandoned lightly. Certainly those who aspire to the construction of a rigorous 'theory' of democratization will require a standardized unambiguous and empirically testable definition of what they would call the 'dependent variable'. In addition, there is a much wider range of analysts who, without embracing such strict criteria of objectivity, are nevertheless bound to hold out for a relatively stable and uniform definition of the term. For in the absence of an agreed core of meaning and some shared assumptions about the evidence that would be needed to justify use of this term, how can there be reasoned dialogue about the international scope and significance of democratic aspirations? Even those who regard 'democracy' as an inherently normative label may have good reason to favour clear and impartial procedures for evaluating the status of claimants to the title. And even those who regard a 'minimalist' or 'procedural' definition as incomplete or culturally biased must consider what may be lost if this consensual language is replaced not by universal commitment to a more ambitious definition but by an inability to agree on a standard meaning, with the resulting licence for subjectivity and arbitrariness.

Although most analysts will therefore be understandably reluctant to surrender the idea of a specific verifiable and generally applicable meaning attaching to the word 'democracy', these difficulties do not just attach to one particularly abstract and desirable labelling exercise. Indeed the problems exemplified by our question about 'democracy' arise far more generally in the field of social theory and description. 'Democracy' and its negation, 'authoritarian rule', are both terms loaded with evaluative and context-dependent connotations that impede consensus on a single timeless and objective definition. (If the suspension of habeas corpus by unilateral presidential instruction is a paradigmatic example of authoritarian rule, where does that leave Abraham Lincoln in 1861? Confederates gave one answer to that, federalists another, and contemporary analysts can hardly provide an answer of their own except by looking beyond the bare fact to some broader judgement of political context.[2]) Not just regime types but the very notions of 'political regimes', and of 'politics' in general, are subject to similar problems of definition. Not just political concepts but social categories in general ('class', 'community', 'consensus') can be viewed as socially constructed and so may be socially contested, with the result that their core meanings may generate controversy as well.

Since our concern is with how contemporary experience may challenge or destabilize pre-existing theory, this chapter does not attempt to provide a timeless and universal type of conceptual analysis. It is more about 'really existing' democracies ('polyarchies' in Robert Dahl's terminology[3]) rather than about one or more idealized variants of a 'possible' democracy (a 'model' of democracy like the eight summarized by David Held).[4] Elucidating the meaning of a democratic concept or ideal is undoubtedly a worthy enterprise. But tracing the obstacles to a generalized consensus concerning the

---

[2] Mark E. Neely, jnr., has provided a fascinating demonstration of the extent to which the 'bare fact' of the suspension was successfully divorced from its broader political symbolism, not only in the mind of President Lincoln, but also in the collective American consciousness. 'For the most part . . . the debate over habeas corpus was conducted . . . at a broad politically symbolic level rather than at a jurisprudentially profound and precise one. That is true of both sides in the debate, and it is true of much of the debate over the issue conducted in history books written since the war.' *The Fate of Liberty: Abraham Lincoln and Civil Liberties* (New York: OUP, 1991), 224.

[3] Robert Dahl, *Polyarchy: Participation and Democracy and Opposition* (New Haven, Conn.: Yale University Press, 1971). Compare Robert Dahl, *Democracy and its Critics* (New Haven, Conn.: Yale University Press, 1989).

[4] David Held, *Models of Democracy* (2nd ed. Cambridge: Polity Press, 1996).

essential elements of 'democracy' as the dominant institutional practice of the post-cold war world is an equally necessary and worthwhile undertaking.

To demonstrate this I will first review the standard 'minimum', or 'procedural' definition (usually said to have originated with Joseph Schumpeter) and then show why it is both insufficient, and too demanding, at the same time. I will show that it is insufficient, because it excludes the inescapably teleological component of democracy which is what gives it emotional force. And it is too demanding because 'really existing' democracies cannot be expected consistently to conform to the minimum standard that it stipulates.

One succinct overview of current orthodoxies on the meaning of democracy has been provided by Philippe C. Schmitter and Terry Lynn Karl. They distinguish between concepts, procedures, and operative principles. At the *conceptual* level the most distinctive feature of democracy is said to be the existence of a broad category of 'citizens', who can hold rulers accountable for their actions in the public realm through the competition and cooperation of elected representatives. Democratic *procedures* are said to be indispensable for the persistence of democracy, although on their own they are not sufficient conditions for its existence. Schmitter and Karl recapitulate the seven 'procedural minimum' conditions for democracy suggested by Robert Dahl, and add two more of their own which reflect the wider range of democratic experiments attempted since he first wrote. These conditions are:

1. Control of government decisions about policy is constitutionally vested in public officials.

2. Elected officials are chosen in frequent and fairly conducted elections in which coercion is comparatively uncommon.

3. Practically all adults have the right to vote in the election of officials.

4. Practically all adults have the right to run for elective offices in the government.

5. Citizens have a right to express themselves without the danger of severe punishment on political matters broadly defined.

6. Citizens have a right to seek out alternative sources of information. Moreover, alternative sources of information exist and are protected by law.

7. Citizens also have the right to form relatively independent associations or organizations, including independent political parties and interest groups.

8. Popularly elected officials must be able to exercise their constitutional power without being subjected to over-riding (albeit informal) opposition from unelected officials.

9. The polity must be self-governing; it must be able to act independently of constraints imposed by some other overarching political system.[5]

Finally with regard to *operative principles*, Schmitter and Karl argue that these express the way in which democratic regimes actually function. They amplify 'by the consent of the people' to a more cumbersome and conditional formula 'by the contingent consent of politicians acting under conditions of bounded uncertainty'.[6]

This is a valiant and up-to-date effort to pin down the dominant political science understanding of what democracy presently *is*. But it is at once too precise and too incomplete to sweep away the difficulties raised in the first paragraph of this section. It is too precise, among other things, because it implies that there were no democracies before universal adult suffrage. (Switzerland, for example, only became a democracy in 1971, when women finally gained the vote.) It also leads to other questionable conclusions, such as that the United States did not fulfil its procedural minimum requests for democracy prior to 1965 (the Voting Rights Act); and that the United Kingdom's democratic status remained in doubt to the end of the twentieth century (given the residual legislative over-ride power of the unelected House of Lords, the absence of a freedom of information act, and the quasi-legislative role increasingly arrogated by the European Court). The ninth procedural minimum is the most exacting of all. Even on a narrow definition of what constitutes an external constraint (i.e. a relative inability to resist external coercion or unwanted imposition) it brings into question the possibilities of democratic government in a widening range of small and dependent nations (e.g. most Caribbean and Central American ostensible democracies, the Baltic Republics, etc.). On a broader view of the way in which virtually all modern states are increasingly constrained by a dense mesh of legal, institutional, economic, and social interdependencies, it may be wondered whether unfettered self-government is still an option available to even the strongest of territorially bounded polities. Overall then, widely accepted 'minimum' conditions seem on a literal reading so exacting

[5] Philippe C. Schmitter and Terry Lynn Karl, 'What Democracy is . . . and is Not', in Larry Diamond and Marc F. Plattner (eds), *The Global Resurgence of Democracy* (Baltimore: John Hopkins University Press, 1993), 45.

[6] Ibid., 46.

that many real existing democracies probably fail to qualify on one test or another.

At the same time, however, this inventory of 'what democracy is' can also be faulted for its low ambition and its omissions. The stress is overwhelmingly on *procedures* of public decision-making and accountability, to the disregard of *outcomes*[7] and the near exclusion of *broader social values*. Provided the procedural requirements are met, these other considerations are handled by reference to the diversity of *types* of democracy (Scandinavian social democracy may represent one subcategory and Japanese money politics another, but they are both democracies in the essential minimum respects). But on this reasoning, provided the procedural requirements are observed, we would be obliged to classify political systems as democratic without regard for the social inequities they accommodated or the policy injustices they perpetrated. For this procedural minimum tends to crowd out the space for any variety of substantial or legal rights. Yet we should not overlook Schmitter and Karl's initial assumption of the existence of a broad category of 'citizens' (or in Dahl's version the centrality of 'participation'). Reintroducing this dimension reopens the floodgates to all kinds of 'substantive' considerations. Particiaption, for example, always embraces questions both of procedure and of outcome. The interplay between the two can best be highlighted by viewing democracy as an 'error correction' mechanism: a procedure that constrains the authors of damaging policies to attend to feedback from those opposed to the resulting outcomes.

If outcomes are excluded the minimum definition offers incomplete protection of basic personal freedoms (as I show in greater detail in Chapter 7, which concerns citizen security). Thus, for example, women could be democratically veiled and denied driving licences, or even access to education. Street children, immigrants, 'Indians' and gypsies could be democratically disadvantaged. Destitute 'citizens' could be rehoused in cardboard boxes (where they would be less likely to register for the vote), and health care

---

[7] Outcomes are much emphasized in David Beetham (ed.), *Defining and Measuring Democracy* (London: Sage, 1994). But even the Beetham volume, with its emphasis on standardized indicators, contains various recognitions of the inescapable role of judgement in the labelling process. For example, Beetham writes: 'In my view it is those involved in the democratic struggles in such countries who are best placed to judge the appropriate criteria against which their political systems should be assessed' (p. 41). Likewise the chapters by Biryukov and Sergevev on Russian culture and Western democracy, and by Parekh on multiculturalism, tolerance, and democracy.

could be redeployed to cosmetic surgery while the old and the sick
were left to the mercy of the market place. These are of course, not
just theoretical possibilities but palpably real implications of
endorsing a procedurally minimal account of what political democracy can, and cannot, be expected to contain. Given these implications there is bound to be a contest over whether the positive
connotations associated with the word 'democracy' can be appropri-
ated by those willing to confer on it such a restrictive social content.

Performance-based conceptions of democracy are indeed superficially attractive, because they offer objective validation to what
might otherwise be dismissed as rhetorical claims, and because
they strengthen the link between 'democracy' and broader notions
of the good society, thus explaining why democracy is (or should be)
strongly desired. But insisting on standardized outcomes regardless of context or resources is in fact both historically and culturally
insensitive. It may strengthen the legitimacy of democracy for those
groups, or whole societies, who are within near reach of the specified performance standards. But it is likely to generate disaffection
among those for whom these particular outcomes are unattainable.
Large groups in most new democracies may have to content themselves with very low levels of substantive public policy performance
for generations to come (inadequate access to health and education
services, little or no official protection of their personal security,
weak or absent rule of law, etc.). From the standpoint of this volume,
moreover, the main problem with insistently *substantive* conceptions of democracy is that by definitional fiat they tend to render
undemocratic all outcomes other than the one specified, and that
even applies to alternatives chosen in accordance with the full *procedural* requirements for a democratic decision. For example, for a
substantive viewpoint it is difficult to accord the status of 'democracy' to any society in which most women are confined to the
domestic sphere, or most unskilled workers lack the autonomy
needed to explore and promote their own interests. Yet in procedural terms it is perfectly possible to envisage a democratic decision
to reinforce such restrictions.

But is there not some inconsistency in faulting any definition as
simultaneously too demanding and too restrictive? We could reply
that this definition is too demanding in procedural matters and too
restrictive on questions of substantive content, thus implying that
all we need is a rejigged definition. But in truth the issue is deeper
than that, as can be shown by a brief review of recent theoretical
work on the morphology of our central political concepts. Any
definition of a political concept can be *both* too restrictive *and*

too inclusive at the same time, if that concept is 'essentially contestable'[8]—that is, if more than one alternative and overlapping meaning can be sustained with equal validity, by rival political communities or alternative schools of interpretation ('ideologies').

A summary overview of contemporary democratic experiences indicates the contestability, fluidity, and context-dependence that frequently attaches to the meaning of the term. Such experiences suggest that:

1. This is not a concept with a timeless single meaning that is intrinsically derivable either from logical analysis or from empirical reference. Its meaning seems to vary across a substantial range, depending upon historical and cultural conditions and customary usages, which are malleable.

2. However, there are definite limits to the range of permissible variations in meaning, and these limits give the concept its substantive edge. Characterizing these limits is nevertheless tricky, since there is neither an indispensable stand-alone core element (the 'minimum' definition) nor an immutable outer boundary of meaning.

Democracy may mean the rule of the people, as its etymological meaning indicates (taking into account the burdens of translation from the Greek), but there is no logically entailed definition of either 'rule' or 'people', or any *logical* reason why this arbitrary word—combination, which signals the apparently ineliminable component of democracy, should not be altered or made unrecognisable to earlier users over time. Indeed the deft implicit insertion of liberal into many current accepted uses of democracy suggests a struggle—unsuccessful to date—over granting ineliminable-component status to a new, tacitly implied notion.[9]

3. This reference to 'struggle' highlights the fact that democracy is such a desirable label that control over its meaning necessarily becomes an object of political contestation. This 'essential contesta-

---

[8] This term originated with W. B. Gallie, 'Essentially Contested Concepts', *Proceedings of the Aristotelian Society*, 56 (1955–6), 167–98, where it was illustrated with reference to democracy. Those who find fault with 'essential contestability' on philosophical grounds may follow Glen Newey in recasting the same claims about democracy as a *political* dispute. This recasting draws attention to the power requirements of contestation, and comes at no analytical cost. See his 'Philosophy, Politics and Contestability', *Journal of Political Ideologies*, 6/3 (Oct. 2001).

[9] Michael Freeden, 'Political Concepts and Ideological Morphology', *Journal of Political Philosophy*, 2/2 (1994), 147. See also Michael Freeden, *Ideologies and Political Theory: A Conceptual Approach* (Oxford: OUP, 1996). For a lucid statement of the view that liberalism and democracy antagonists see Norberto Bobbio, *Liberalismo e democracia* (São Paulo: Editoria Brasiliense, 1988).

bility' is a distinctive feature of our key political concepts, both because of the good or bad consequences for particular interests that will flow from adopting one meaning rather than another, and because although the concept has real substance, its meaning is not fixed by some extra-political authority (logic, incontestable evidence) to which ultimate appeal can be made.

4. The outer boundaries of the concept are also to a significant (although again not unlimited) extent malleable and negotiable, because in any particular historical or cultural context they will depend heavily on the status of overlapping adjacent concepts (it is vital to stress here that political concepts are not mutually exclusive from each other, but rather overlap and display blurred boundaries). Thus, the value of democracy can be strongly promoted in a context that also highly emphasizes the value of equality. Or, it can be equally strongly promoted in a context that strongly stresses the sanctity of property. Depending upon which of these adjacent values permeates the cultural landscape, both the centre of gravity and the outer limits of the concept of 'democracy' will be shifted in a corresponding direction. For example, in the Western political tradition liberty has become conventionally affiliated with democratic self-government. In isolation each of these concepts is rather 'thin', but in close association with each other the meanings of both can be filled out in a particular manner. Liberty is thereby construed in a particular manner (emphasizing self-determination) and democracy is also invested with specific connotations that are not inherent to the term as such (limited popular government).

With the benefit of this understanding of the morphology of central political concepts, we can now return to the question posed in the first paragraph of this section on 'democracy'. Language is one very definite and very explicit aspect of culture, the vehicle through which each society's understanding of politics is articulated. It is more than likely therefore that the resonances of the term 'democracy' may be significantly altered in the course of translation, say from English into Chinese, or from Greek into Arabic. But translation is only one particularly manifest example of how cultural context may affect conceptual understanding. Within the English language, for example, British and American understandings of such key terms as 'rights', 'rule of law', and 'authority' can be subtly differentiated,[10] and have evolved very significantly over the past three centuries of

---

[10] Thus e.g. the right to own firearms is a constitutive element of the US conception of democratic citizenship, but is entirely absent in the British conception and is little emphasized in most other Anglo-Saxon democracies.

liberal constitutionalism. Therefore even in mainstream English 'democracy' is a term whose meaning can be filled out in various alternative ways according to the temporal and spatial context. It may change still further when taken up in South Africa or Sri Lanka or Hong Kong. In post-apartheid South Africa, for example, the 'procedural minimal' definition could authorize the wholesale dispossession of the white elite, so they can be expected to insist on a more substantive conception which respects established rights and entrenched minority guarantees. The newly enfranchised black majority can also be expected to insist that 'real' democracy must affect policy outcomes, and redress inherent exclusions. Similarly, any concept of democracy relevant to Sri Lanka would have to fill out the relationship between central authority and provincial or other subnational levels of representation. In Hong Kong it is impossible to avoid the issue of what kind of democracy can be secured in the absence of sovereignty. These three examples each demonstrate in the clearest terms that 'context matters' for our understanding of political concepts, even within a single language family, and during an era of global liberal ascendancy that some have labelled the 'end of history'. Although we find some range of variation among English speakers, the stress tends to be on US-influenced usages of key terms. This highlights the possessive individualist adjoining values and results in the de-emphasis of concepts such as 'the state' 'the community', and 'the nation', which resonate more strongly in, for example, much European discourse about democracy. Note that these illustrations refer not just to variations in the *quality* or local content of democracy but invite reconsideration of our overall conception of its substance. If, say, Israel and Switzerland can both be classified as examples of democracy then clearly we are applying the same designation to some very substantially contrasting political regimes. What is involved here is not just shades of difference of degree, but starker differences of kind. Note also that, although these 'hard cases' invite such reconsideration, they do not necessarily promise renewed closure. On the contrary they could just open up the 'essential contestability' of our democratic discourse.

In addition to these reflections on the morphology of our political concepts we may also need to bring in some considerations from cognitive psychology. A case can be made that there is something distinctively deliberative (one might even claim proto-democratic) about the ways in which we apprehend and contest rival conceptions of the term 'democracy'. In order to grasp this idea it is necessary to redirect our attention from an implied social consensus regulating the *meaning* of our central political concepts to related processes of personal *cognition* and socialization. If, following Schmitter and Karl, we regard 'citizenship' as a defining ingredient of democracy then the cognitive skills essential for the exercise of citizenship are themselves an indispensable component of the concept. That is to say, democracy requires or assumes the existence of autonomous agents, each forming their own judgements in the light of collective discussion and debate. Each agent will by definition have his or her own separate consciousness, but in order to act as citizens all agents must form some shared understandings about the nature of politics and the procedures of political dialogue.[11] Hence the concept of democracy entails some relatively specific properties of individual consciousness, and some pooled beliefs about the values of deliberation. If so, the democracy has either an elective affinity, or perhaps even a necessary connection, with a particular type of cognition ('reflexive thinking') and a particular social orientation (an 'ethos of responsibility'). This is not to claim that every individual citizen must invariably think reflexively or act responsibly[12] (that is the error of classical republicanism). But for democracy to exist there must be *some* available community of reflexive and responsible citizens, and that pool must *not be too exclusive*. In other words, the citizens at large must have at least some potential to participate with some minimum degree of cognitive competence, from time to time, or at least in the event of real emergencies.

If some degree of generalized cognitive competence is an essential minimum prerequisite for political democracy, then the deliberative essentials of that competence ought to be built into any account of the meaning of the concept of 'democracy'. Deliberation *may* give rise to a consensus on meaning (although it may also clarify the irrevocable nature of differences over meaning). But even if it does produce a consensus it will be an agreement of a distinctively provisional and conditional kind. Agreement will only be so deep and only last for so long as the separate consciousnesses involved remain persuaded. In political life in general, and with regard to

[11] Compare Stuart Hampshire, *Justice as Conflict* (Princeton: Princeton University Press, 2000).

[12] Collective political cognition and democratic deliberation operate at a substantially more sophisticated level than the average consciousness of the individual participant might suggest, because such processes are weighted towards the involvement of the most active. But even at the median level of consciousness citizens conduct an internal dialogue between what is publicly asserted (at their level of interest) and what is privately accepted. Thus at some basic level not only an activist fringe but the population at large interrogate, and subjectively verify or contest, whatever political discourse they receive from the public sphere.

key political concepts in particular, there is never any definite 'cut off point' beyond which the matter is settled beyond all further reconsideration. On the contrary, even when the social consensus over a particular policy or a particular political discourse seems at its most overwhelming, the separate consciousnesses of individual citizens continue to engage in critical deliberation, rechecking, interrogating, and reinterpreting what seems to have been agreed. Stuart Hampshire calls this 'conflict in the soul' and contrasts it with 'conflict in the city'. This is an inherent feature of political deliberation and therefore an indispensable characteristic of democratic debate. Thus democracy precludes conceptual closure concerning its own identity, and hence democratization must be understood as an open-ended process. Democracy is 'essentially contestable' not just because our values may differ, or because our political concepts may lack ultimate logical or empirical validation, but also because our political cognition is inherently critical and reflexive.

The following (slightly but not entirely hypothetical) example may clarify the point. Suppose that some historical process (such as the victory of the West in the cold war) throws up an unprecedentedly strong and universal consensus on a single set of democratic values, anchored in a precisely specified definition of what democracy is, and is not. In that event, overt value conflicts and conceptual disagreements over the meaning of the term would by definition cease. Does it then follow that the consensual meaning of the term would thereafter become incontestable? It does not, since—again by definition—every citizen would retain an autonomous capacity for political cognition and evaluation, and democratic debate persuasion, and socialization would not cease. Therefore each individual citizen would continue to compare the hegemonic consensus about the meaning and value of democracy with a personal judgement (both analytical and emotional) about the authority, coherence, and merits of the prevailing political order as seen from his or her specific perspective. Such individual reflections and judgements are inescapable components of any account of democratic political cognition, but of course this should create no presumption that the individuals in question must be isolated, asocial, or narrowly rational in their deliberations. Group and community debate, socialization pressures, and emotional as well as calculating forms of reflexivity are all be to expected. In due course there are bound to appear *some* citizens who will articulate minimally cogent objections to the consensus view. However minoritarian their views, they are by assumption entitled to debate with the polity at large. The rest of the citizenry, however ostensibly convinced they might be by the hegemonic discourse, retain independent cognitive capacities and therefore remain potentially open to persuasion or reconsideration of their opinions. For this democratic reason and this reason alone, in political affairs not even the strongest value consensus and the most robust conceptual edifice can ever become wholly immune to doubt and renegotiation. In actual practice, of course, as the post-cold war period has quickly demonstrated, conflicts over values and differing interpretations of the facts never disappear, even in the wake of the most stunning victories. As illustrated by a recent event—the September 2001 terrorist attack on New York—the collective consensus on democracy may veer abruptly from a discourse stressing its association with freedom to a quite different emphasis on its linkage to security.[13] If history pauses, it soon starts up again and never ends. Indeed the current explosive expansion of information technology may well be extending and deepening the possibilities both for individual reflection and for social deliberation, thereby widening the scope for collective scrutiny of currently hegemonic conceptions of democracy.[14] *Any* definition of 'democracy' will remain in this sense 'essentially contestable', precisely because *all* worthwhile conceptions of democracy must incorporate a cognitive capacity to challenge reigning orthodoxies.

This last sentence contains an apparent paradox, the resolution of which is critical if we are to counter the changes of relativism and subjectivism. On the one hand we have denied the existence of a fixed or core meaning to the term 'democracy' that can be detached from a given temporal and spatial (or cultural) context, and we have stressed the provisional and debatable characteristics of all definitions. But on the other hand, we have also invoked certain ineliminable components of the concept, such as accountable procedures, citizenship, and reflexive deliberation. So, is the meaning of democracy essentially anchored in some way, or does it basically depend on taste and fashion?

The metaphor of an anchor is helpful in this context, for it indicates how even in the physical world an entity can be constrained

---

[13] Indeed, even before 11 September 2001 security already took precedence over freedom as the litmus test for democratic performance in various countries and regions. Compare Ch. 9 (on Chile), or consider Israel. See also Anita Inder Singh, *Democracy, Ethnic Diversity, and Security in Post-Communist Europe* (London: Praeger, 2001).

[14] See Philippa Norris (ed.), *Critical Citizens: Global Support for Democratic Government* (Oxford: OUP, 1999).

without being fixed. This is the only possible response to the charge of 'relativism'. Democracy has some indispensable components, without which the concept would be vacuous, but these indispensable elements are skeletal and can in any case be arranged in various possible configurations. At best they only generate a 'thin' account of democracy that may be universally applicable but at the cost of much imprecision and ambiguity. The richness of the concept derives from its contextual elaborations, which are variable and may tug in opposed directions. Returning to the metaphor of a boat at anchor, democracy will look different depending upon whether it has been stranded on a mud bank or towed out towards deep water by the pull of a powerful current.[15]

But of course 'democracy' is a far more abstract and intangible idea than 'boat', and it is also heavily charged with value connotations. As Sartori said in 1962, democracy is a 'deontological' concept: 'What democracy *is* cannot be separated from what democracy *should* be. A democracy exists only insofar as its ideals and values bring it into being . . . in a democracy the tension between fact and value reaches the highest point, since no other ideal is further from the reality in which it has to operate.'[16] Since it is an appraisive as much as a descriptive concept we need to consider not just semantic, epistemological, or ontological relativism, but also the more awkward charge of *moral* relativism.[17] Once we retreat from universalism and objec-

---

[15] It will look different, will behave differently, and demand a different regime for its crew, yet it will still be a boat and not a buoy because its indispensable components remain those of a boat. The Arabs may call it a dhow and design it in one fashion, whereas the Chinese may call it a junk and the native Americans may call it a kayak and each may construct it with a quite different fluvial context in mind. This is the least troubling aspect of the issue of relativism, for abstract categories can invariably be broken down into more differential and context-dependent subcategories.

[16] Sartori's initial position deserves to be quoted in full: 'A democratic system is established as a result of deontological pressures. What democracy *is* cannot be separated from what democracy *should* be. A democracy exists only insofar as its ideals and values bring it into being. No doubt, any political system is sustained by imperatives and value goals. But perhaps a democracy needs them more than any other. For in a democracy the tension between fact and value reaches the highest point, since no other ideal is farther from the reality in which it has to operate. And this is why we need the name democracy.' Giovanni Sartori, *Democratic Theory* (Detroit: Wayne State University Press, 1962), 4. Sartori's earliest explanation shows why Dahl's descriptive neologism 'polyarchy' cannot substitute for the more prescriptive 'democracy'. A quarter century later he expanded his account of the deontological dimension of democracy in his *Theory of Democracy Revisited* (Chatham, NJ: Chatham House Publishers, 1987), part 1, ch. 4.

[17] These various dimensions are concisely unpacked in Rom Harré and Michael Krausz, *Varieties of Relativism* (Oxford: Blackwell, 1995).

tivism in our standards of definition of key political concepts, how can we defend ourselves against purely arbitrary and self-interested attributions of meaning that would debase our language (and therefore our capacity for deliberative dialogue) and destroy our moral compasses? The historically undeniable fact that both political and economic monopolists have tended to dress themselves in the garb of democratic respectability while promoting rival objectives is no excuse for us to endorse their misuses of language. But if neither an appeal to logic nor to empirical evidence will suffice to arbitrate between 'contested' versions of the meaning of democracy, then what have we left but a scramble between rival subjectivities, in which those with the sharpest elbows can often be expected to prevail over those with more exquisite democratic sensibilities?

The charge of moral relativism directs attention to a real danger and therefore serves a constructive purpose. It can, however, be countered once we recall the distinction between (i) acknowledging the inevitability of conflict and (ii) concluding from it that anything goes. The concept of democracy may be 'essentially' contestable, but the grounds on which it can be validly contested are nevertheless quite restricted. There may be no single timeless stipulative definition that can be imposed from without regardless of local conventions and understandings, but there is a broad stream of meaning within which democratic discourse is mutually intelligible. Attempts to appropriate the term for meanings outside that stream have to be resisted not least because they would destroy the possibilities of reflexive dialogue on which any democracy must rest. Since there is no external fiat that can stipulate the precise status of each claimant to the designation of 'democracy', the main court that can adjudicate between valid and abusive challenges will have to be the court of democratic opinion, a court whose proceedings will, of course, be structured by the advocacy of opinion leaders and experts, perhaps—but not necessarily—enlightened, as in any court. But this is not the formal adjudication of a public debate in which a majority votes one way or the other. On the contrary the adjudication has to be performed in the consciousness of individual citizens, and for that reason as Hampshire has underlined it will always be provisional and open to reconsideration.

The key principle is that the citizens of a political community always have three possible ways to respond to a claim about the meaning of democracy. They can (*a*) accept that it is worthy of consideration ('valid'); or they can (*b*) identify it as unworthy ('invalid'). These two alternatives are sufficient to exclude the possibility that 'anything goes', and to erect a strong barrier against the wilder consequences that have been associated with moral relativism. The third alternative (c) is more complex, but in the last analysis should be reassuring to those who think our political concepts need to be both definite and open-ended. This third response can be that the proposed meaning of democracy is unfamiliar, and unproven, but not so absurd as to be clearly invalid. In this case the challengers can only win around the court of citizen opinion and secure acceptance for their interpretation as a permissible contestant in the public discourse if they can overcome the doubt and resistance initially elicited by their contentions. To persuade the community to take an unfamiliar interpretation of democracy seriously it will be necessary to parade a variety of credentials—clear logic, good evidence, familiarity with the culture, and a reputation for sound judgement may all be needed to pierce the defensive barrier of conventional thinking. Sometimes abusive claims may succeed, and on other occasions potentially 'valid' interpretations may fail to pass the test. There can be no guarantee *either* that only morally sound interpretations of democracy will be validated or that all morally sound interpretations will get even a provisional hearing.[18] But the critical point for our purposes is that this deliberative filter constitutes a major socially grounded protection against the destruction of meaning and value that would otherwise accompany the contestability of concepts.[19] It is a protection which *includes* appeals to logic and evidence, but which also expresses 'common sense' and cultural context. Flyvbjerg (resuscitating Aristotle) would call this phronesis (practical knowledge) and would rate it at least as highly as theoretical or technical knowledge as a way of arriving at truths about society. Though

---

[18] When most citizens process cognitive claims they may well be more interested in the practical implications for themselves of accepting a particular meaning (the 'use value' of the definition) rather than the search for definitional accuracy for its own sake (its 'truth value'). Even if its truth value helps a definition pass the 'might be valid' test, it could well be that 'use value' will prevail over 'truth value' when determining which of two contested meanings gains more general assent.

[19] Flyvbjerg makes the case for *phronesis* (the production of knowledge in which the particular and the situationally dependent are emphasised over the universal and over rules) and links it in particular to social science: Bert Flyvbjerg, *Making Social Science Matter* (Cambridge: CUP, 2001). This parallels arguments I made, drawing mostly from Mill on judgement, in an overview of 'Democratization Studies', in Robert E. Goodin and H-D Klingemann (eds.), *A New Handbook of Political Science* (Oxford: OUP, 1996), 360–3.

not an ultimate or monotone protection it provides a well-grounded, broad-based, and even a proto-democratic defence against the excesses of relativism.[20]

However, this defence rests upon the operation of a deliberative filter, and the filter is assumed to work well because it is embedded in a social community. So, at the global level there is still a major difficulty to be resolved, before the excesses of relativism can be contained. How are conflicts over the meaning of democracy to be adjudicated in the international arena, at least without simply endorsing post-cold war American intellectual hegemony? One possibility (implied by Huntington's 'clash of civilizations')[21] is to acknowledge the existence of more than one cultural bloc in the world, each with its own independent deliberative filter.

Thus, for example, the Islamic world would promote its alternative conception of government by the people, distinct from, or even in opposition to, the Western liberal conception of democracy. But this assumes a degree of separation and non-communication between rival blocs, and indeed a radical estrangement from the Other, that in no way corresponds to what should have been learnt from the ending of the cold war. Worse still, it implies a refusal to deliberate except with those safely corralled within one's own camp. It therefore promotes an inward-looking and unreflective version of democracy, even in the liberal West. A second possibility is to seek

[20] The notion of citizen deliberation as a means of adjudication between contested claims of democracy might seem open to the charge *either* of circularity *or* of unanchored relativism. But both criticisms would be misplaced, as can be shown by reference to such contemporary hard cases as Cuba and Iran. If the citizens of Cuba, relatively isolated from their neighbours, were to deliberate and conclude that their one-party communist form of government was democratic, would we be required to allow that adjudication to over-ride more conventional external judgements and definitions? Theoretically, this might be required, in my view, but *only* if the citizens of Cuba really were free to deliberate (e.g. they would need open access to competing viewpoints and their personal conclusions would decide the outcome) and even then they would only have arrived at a *provisional* verdict. Therefore, the resulting 'communist democracy' would remain permanently dependent upon the revocable endorsement of its citizens. In due course—given the assumed access to competing viewpoints—both Cuba and its neighbours would arrive at a single verdict on whether or not this variant of democracy was admissible. This is because over time either Cuban opinion would be swayed by exposure to external scepticism, or external resistance would be weakened by Cuban persuasiveness. In this context, it helps that democracy is an unattained ideal as much as a descriptive label.
[21] Samuel P. Huntington, *The Clash of Civilizations and the Remaking of World Order* (New York: Simon & Schuster, 1996).

adjudication at the international level. This might be advanced through the strengthening and democratization of regional and global political institutions.[22]

As at the national level, institutional provisions are unlikely to generate much normative coherence if they are not embedded in some broader social framework of support and guidance. At the international level the most promising area to search for such a collective basis for a deliberative filter would be the emerging network of specialists, lobbyists, activists, and practitioners (an 'epistemic community') that has been gradually reinforcing the commitment to relatively precise and operational notions about the enforcement of human rights, and about the linkage between some specific conceptions of human rights and of democratic rights. This incipient 'international civil society' dedicated to the promotion of universal rights and standards might in due course prove robust enough to act as a counterweight to the distortions of power politics and the dissensus over values, but for now it is clearly a fragile basis for the generation of coherent norms that could then be authoritatively implemented by international institutions (which are themselves also quite vulnerable to power politics).

It is an interesting mental experiment to imagine the conception of democracy that would best reflect the distribution of beliefs and interests that one would find in a representative global constitutional assembly. Like the whites in South Africa, one could envisage that the Anglo-Saxon theorists of democracy would develop a heightened interest in the protection of minority rights in such a setting. But as a practical matter any such extension of cosmopolitan governance would have to proceed at no more than a snail's pace, and on terms rigorously dictated by the minority of 'haves'. Whatever other concessions the Western powers might theoretically be induced to make, the last redoubt they would surrender would be the right of outsiders to adjudicate in favour of any external judgement about the West's democracy. The third alternative would be to shift attention away from the power-based question of 'who adjudicates?' towards the society-driven issue of 'who deliberates (and about what)?'. Here one could argue that shared problems (of environmental management, of economic and technological interdependency, of political security) are rapidly generating common or overlapping interests. Deliberation arises not because of reasoning from first principles, or due to the creation of artificial

---

[22] See David Held, *Democracy and the Global Order: From the Modern State to Cosmopolitan Governance* (Cambridge: Polity Press, 1995).

institutions, but because it becomes necessary in order to tackle social needs. Convergence over values, interests, or the meaning of the key concepts needed for a shared discourse may come later as practical cooperation becomes institutionalized. Viewed from this standpoint the presently existing divergences between different culturally based understandings of democracy can potentially be superseded through interactive cooperation. If a unified conception eventually emerges this will be a new variant, produced by deliberative experience, rather than as the imposition of one hegemony or one majoritarian opinion, over the alternatives.

In short, a good defence against unbridled relativism over the meaning of 'democracy' can be constructed through the invocation of practical knowledge and the processing of inevitable disagreements through a deliberative filter of collective reflection. These procedures can eliminate indefensible claims, and can stabilize the core meaning of the concept. But, since conflict in the soul and conflict in the city can never be wholly eliminated from reflection about social concepts and since historical change and cultural diversity remain unending, these procedures will never generate a completely timeless and universal consensus definition. On this 'interpretavist' view our conception of democracy can be anchored, but not immobilized.

Where does this analysis leave the initial 'procedural minimum' definition of democracy outlined by Schmitter and Karl? We have seen that no unitary definition can be incontestable or universally applicable without regard to context. We have also noted that in some detailed respects concerning procedures this particular definition is too precise, and that in one major respect (concerning the substantive content of democracy) it adopts a position of extreme non-commitment. In the 'real world' procedures are invariably more hybrid than this definition demands, and there can be no such radical divorce between process and outcome as it presumes. All these points may be granted, and yet some variant of this definition can still be urged as the strongest contestant for our allegiance in the immediate post-cold war world. Indeed, it could be argued, this definition remains essentially contestable, but those advocating a lower procedural threshold will have to cope with the sorry record of many democratic experiments which neglected some of these requirements, and those advocating a more substantive definition will equally have to overcome the change of utopianism, a charge which has become far more lethal in the wake of the Soviet collapse. Yet, it is also a problem that this procedural minimum definition seems so ill suited for historical applications and so closely associated with a single rather restricted tradition of political thought and practice (US constitutionalism). That may limit its acceptability in other cultural contexts (e.g. in parts of Asia and the Islamic world), and may give it a relatively short shelf life, if America's current position of global leadership proves ephemeral.

Even within the USA the gap between the minimum prescribed procedural norms and actual political practices was shown to be disconcertingly wide in the presidential elections of November 2000, notably in Florida.[23] 'Really existing' democracies often fall far short of Dahl's 'polyarchy', let alone of the more idealized conceptions celebrated in democratic theory. Nevertheless, since this section has argued that *all* definitions of democracy are context-laden and time-constrained, this one may be no worse than any alternative. Indeed Schmitter and Karl could argue that it remains relatively better, in that at least for the time being US political leadership *is* established, and the definition (particularly in its extended nine-point form) makes a serious attempt to generalize from a wide range of contemporary political experiences.

So, although we cannot accept that in some ultimate sense this procedural minimal definition captures all that democracy *is* (let alone *can be*), we may conclude that contingently and for the present period it provides a rather coherent and broad-based exposition of the predominant view. It therefore provides the baseline for the contemporary debates about democratization which occupy the rest of this volume. As we shall see, the meaning of 'democracy' is likely to remain contested, and even to some extent unstable, as current processes of democratization unfold.

On 'Democratization'

If democracy itself is to be viewed as *both* a contextually variable *and* a 'deontological' concept, then 'democratization' cannot be defined by some fixed and timeless objective criterion. For example, the simple 'two turnover test' says that a democratization begins with the exit of an authoritarian regime and ends after competitive elections have given rise to two successive peaceful transfers of government between contending parties. But by this test neither Italy nor Japan had completed their democratizations for forty years after the installation of their current democratic constitutions, nor is it foreseeable when South Africa will reach that point. Equally,

---

[23] See Martin Merzer, *The Miami Herald Report: Democracy Held Hostage* (New York: St Martin's Press, 2001).

Colombia, Sri Lanka, or Venezuela had qualified by the 1960s, notwithstanding the palpable evidence that thereafter many major tasks of democratic construction remained to be tackled. Hence this definition of democratization is simultaneously too permissive for some cases and too exacting for others, just as our foregoing analysis would lead us to expect. The more sophisticated alternative has been to argue that democratization is complete when all significant political actors accept (with good grace or ill) that the electoral process has become 'the only game in town' for reallocating public office. By this criterion it is again questionable when or whether democratization has been completed in, say, Italy[24] or Spain. (Are the Basque separatists a 'significant political actor'? This is a matter of careful and contestable evaluation and judgement, not of self-evident objective truth.) By the same criterion we would have to conclude that democratization had been completed in, say, India, Uruguay, or Venezuela in the 1960s—although in all these cases the subsequent course of political development revealed the severe practical incompleteness and normative inadequacy of these accomplishments. Again the definition imposes closure on processes that are in practice still open-ended, value-laden and transgressive.

In contrast to such litmus test conceptions of democratization the theoretical perspective of this volume is 'interpretavist'. It can be stated, concisely, as follows. Democratization is best understood as a complex, long-term, dynamic, and open-ended process. It consists of progress towards a more rule-based, more consensual and more participatory type of politics. Like 'democracy' it necessarily involves a combination of fact and value, and so contains internal tensions. The objective of this section is to clarify what this theoretical perspective involves by indicating (i) how it differs from the predominant alternative; (ii) how it connects to the account of democracy that precedes it; and (iii) (in outline) where it belongs in the permanent debate about how to conduct social analysis in general, and comparative politics in particular. Later chapters develop this perspective and apply to a succession of subthemes and accompanying experiences, while the final chapter reviews this key claim in the light of the contemporary evidence.

First, there is an alternative theoretical perspective that commands considerable academic support, and that deserves respect. If we could all agree on a straightforward, objectively measurable, and

---

[24] It is a matter of fine judgement whether the Communist Party, the heirs to fascism, or indeed strong currents within the Christian Democratic Party ever fully embraced this doctrine, and the Northern League (which rose to prominence in the 1990s) explicitly did not.

unambiguous definition of democracy, then democratization need not be either a particularly complex, an excessively protracted, or an erratic process, and once it is over the outcome could be stable, predictable, and uniform. Such a democratization might be envisioned as a clear, quick, rational construction, ending in closure (or modelled as the adoption of standardized rules of the political game known in advance to generate a stable equilibrium). Closure or 'consolidation' is supposedly attained through durable compliance with the rules and procedures stipulated in Dahl's account of polyarchy (although we have seen that in practice this is far from straightforward). According to this perspective, before there was political monopoly, now there is political competition, and the transition from one state to the other can be brought about rapidly, unambiguously, and permanently, provided the prescribed institutional changes are implemented correctly. While a consolidated democracy may implicitly be viewed as a desirable outcome, this approach highlights a certain range of objective facts, and marginalizes their value connotations. This seems like a clear, satisfying, and parsimonious framework of analysis (made particularly explicit in the various high-quality studies devoted to aspects of what is usually labelled the 'consolidation' of democracy[25]), and it is no doubt particularly illuminating about a certain sub-set of cases (the southern European democratizations, and Spain in particular, correspond pretty well with this formula). But from the perspective of this volume the key deficiency of this approach is that most contemporary democratizations violate one or more of its basic assumptions.

No doubt these formulations state the alternative theoretical perspective too crudely, but the object here is not to set up a straw man only to clarify standpoint of this volume. Here, by contrast, there is an emphasis on the *complexity* of most contemporary processes of democratization, meaning that, as they unfold from pre-existing non-democratic conditions, they carry a great deal of historical baggage with them. The typical unfolding of a democratization process also involves many false starts, misjudgements, detours, and unintended consequences. There is usually a wide disjunction between how participants and informed observers anticipate *ex ante* that the process will develop, and how it is seen to have transpired *ex post*. In a complex process this will usually include great imprecision

---

[25] J. Linz and A. Stepan, *Problems of Democratic Transition and Consolidation* (Baltimore: Johns Hopkins University Press, 1996). R. Günther, N. Diamandourous, and H.-J. Pühle (eds.), *The Politics of Democratic Consolidation: Southern Europe in Comparative Perspective* (Baltimore: Johns Hopkins University Press, 1995), etc.

about such key questions as how long it will take; who will win or lose; and what, with hindsight, will constitute the most distinctive features of the eventual outcome.[26] (The democratization of the Soviet Union since Gorbachev provides an extreme illustration of the kind of complex process envisioned here, but Argentina, Nigeria, or Venezuela would serve as well.) The *long-term* and *dynamic* aspects of such processes are of course closely connected with their complexity. Of course there is a spectrum of experiences here, and it is possible to emphasize those that advanced fairly rapidly and without too many deviations towards a predetermined outcome. Even the strongest examples (Spain, Slovenia, etc.) can be analysed from the theoretical perspective of this volume, whereas arguably it may strain the evidence of most cases far more to evaluate them by the yardstick of a hypothetically rapid and complete consolidation of democracy. The tension between democratic aspirations and the new regime's desire for closure point to a fact/value instability that would be hidden by the language of consolidation. A long-term and dynamic perspective opens the way to a fuller exploration of the *quality* of the emerging democracy, and to the potential feedback between quality and viability. But perhaps the most clear-cut theoretical dichotomy concerns the last of the four terms under consideration here. According to the perspective of this volume, even in the long term the outcome of most processes of democratization is relatively *open-ended*, whereas the alternative perspective rests on expectations of a rather rapid and decisive closure of options concerning the political regime. The relative open-endedness of the process under review here is in part a reflection of the understanding of democracy expounded in the first section of this chapter, and it also expresses a broader standpoint about what we should expect from social analysis in general, and from comparative politics in particular.

As with the earlier account of democracy as both anchored and floating, there is a difficult balance to be struck when characterizing democratization processes as both long-term and relatively open-ended. Any process must involve a lapse of time during which

---

[26] There is an evident contrast between this perspective, and the standpoint adopted by Adam Przeworski, *Democracy and the Market* (Cambridge: CUP, 1991). This influential early volume acknowledged the diversity of starting-points, but anticipated subsequent convergence, thereby de-emphasizing complexities and open-endedness. My standpoint is closer to that of Philippe C. Schmitter and Javier Santiso, 'Three Temporal Dimensions to the Consolidation of Democracy', *International Political Science Review*, 19/1 (Jan. 1998). They differentiate between time, timing, and tempo, including 'coping with uncertain moments, simultaneous sequences, and compressed rhythms' (p. 84).

a determinate change is under way.[27] When the change is completed and the time has therefore expired, the process ends. We can allow that some changes require a large amount of time, and that more than one outcome is possible by the time the process is finally completed. But the more extended the lapse of time and the more diverse the eventual outcomes, the more elusive the concept of a 'democratization process' is liable to become. So how can we characterize such episodes to give them the rigour and precision necessary for a comparative discussion, without artificially truncating or misclassifying their results?

A partial reply can be derived from the *second* clarification, which links this perspective on democratization to the preceding account of the meaning of democracy. If 'democracy' is viewed as a contested and to some extent unstable concept, anchored through the invocation of practical knowledge and a deliberative filter of collective deliberation, then democratization can only come about through a lengthy process of social construction that is bound to be relatively open-ended. However, although the resulting processes of democratization may be lengthy, erratic, and contested, they should generate quite enough evidence to confirm their existence. Our theoretical perspective points to the specific and observable activities that should be taking place as each process unfolds. For example, we would expect to encounter public debate over how the democracy is to be constituted and what is to count as a satisfactory format for a democratic regime. In its absence, we can dismiss the claim that a democratization process is under way. However, even in the presence of such a debate, it could be that the democratization was losing momentum or being stifled. But since we recognize that the process may be erratic and subject to reversals, our account of democracy would counsel against jumping to hasty conclusions that the process has failed. Even in adverse circumstances, the persistence of organized efforts to put democratization back on track would normally deserve to be given the benefit of the doubt. By this test we should scan the globe for incipient processes of democratization even in apparently unpromising settings. The long historical perspective and non-linear outlook adopted here enlarges our universe of potential democratizations. Equally, even when by the standards of the 'consolidation' literature democratization seemed most complete, our perspective would keep us alert to continuing public debates that could indicate further developments in the process.

[27] A. Schedler and J. Santiso, 'Democracy and Time: An Invitation', *International Political Science Review*, 19/1 (1998).

The open-endedness of the eventual outcome can also be accommodated—at least in principle—by our suggestions concerning the 'floating but anchored' features of our conception of democracy. This allows a variety of possible outcomes to count as the end of the process while also limiting the range of possibilities to those involving the satisfaction of some quite specific and demanding conditions. At this level of theoretical abstraction, however, it is not possible to provide a sharp-edged definition that cuts off all debate about whether or not a given democratization process has been satisfactorily concluded. A more contextualized discussion of particular cases is required in order to generate clarity on the issues involved here. The eventual classification of specific processes will depend more on practical reason (Aristotle's phronesis or Mill's informed judgement) than on any stipulative definition.[28]

A *third* clarification concerns the relationship between this perspective on democratization and the conduct of social analysis in general, and comparative politics in particular. In this case our subject matter is democracy. If it had been chess we could have defined precisely what must qualify for that designation and what aberrant variants are excluded. But this chapter has made the case that the meaning of democracy is not so easily pinned down. It contains some necessary practices, but it also expresses ideals and values that are at least partially subjective and variable across time and space. Standard definitions of democracy can at one and the same time be too precise and too incomplete. The concept has to be anchored to be usable, and yet it may also float at anchor. It may have some ineliminable components, but it also has a contextually variable outer boundardy. Whatever reservations the reader may have about all this, let us for the sake of argument make the assumption that this is indeed the nature of our subject-matter. If so, how can we proceed either to theorize about it, or to check our theories against experiences of its construction? If the outcome we are seeking to explain—democracy—is somewhat variable and even unstable in content, then the process or processes through which it comes about—democratization—will necessarily be relatively

---

[28] Compare David Collier and Robert Adcock's conclusion that 'generic claims that the concept of democracy should inherently be treated as dichotomous or graded are incomplete. The burden of demonstration should instead rest on more specific arguments linked to the goals of research. We thus take the pragmatic position that how scholars understand and operationalize a concept can and should depend in part on what they are going to do with it.' David Collier and Robert Adcock, 'Democracy and Dichotomies: A Pragmatic Approach to Choices about Concepts', *Annual Review of Political Science*, 2 (1999), 537.

open-ended, and may well be protracted, complex, and erratic. That could simply be the nature of the subject-matter we are seeking to understand. If so, how can the analysis proceed? There are those who would shy away from even attempting to analyse such processes because of their lack of rigour and precision. There are others who would demand more precision than the subject-matter allows. The third possibility, the approach attempted in this volume, is to accept the subject-matter as it presents itself, and to theorize about it within the limits that that permits (hence the reference to 'theory and experience'). The case for this approach is that the subject matter is of such practical importance that it requires reflective scholarly attention, but that the advance of understanding in this field will not be served by spurious precision or the determination to detect law-like regularities when no more than provisional and qualified conclusions can be established.

On this view democratization is a process of movement towards an outcome that is neither fully stable nor entirely predetermined. But is there any scholarly procedure for studying such processes? There is certainly a philosophical literature concerned with the unfolding of potentialities. There is also a scientific literature (for example concerning the development of life forms).[29] While these two scholarly traditions could offer some reassurance they are both very distant from the kind of social enquiry under consideration here. But consider contemporary analysis of the unfolding of the European Union. This is often couched within a teleological framework, in which movement is assumed to be towards an 'ever closer union'. The nature of the final outcome may be less than fully specified, the sequence of developments may not be entirely predictable, and the time frame may be indeterminate. Nevertheless social analysts believe they can achieve clarity and advance understanding by examining such a process. If so, then a similar approach to the comparative study of democratization should be equally warranted. Or recall that many economic liberals believe that the construction of market economies is the dominant theme of the post-cold war world. Here too, precise outcomes, predictable sequences, and specific time frames may be undetermined. That does not prevent a

---

[29] For an instructive survey see Ullica Segerstråle, *Defenders of the Truth: The Sociobiology Debate* (Oxford: OUP, 2000). Stephen Jay Gould's position has an obvious resonance here: 'What happens makes sense but life's history could have cascaded down millions of other equally sensible alternative paths, none (or preciously few) of which would have led to the evolution of self-conscious intelligence.' 'Fulfilling the Spandrels of World and Mind', in J. Selzer (ed.), *Understanding Scientific Prose* (Madison: University of Wisconsin Press, 1993), 332.

flourishing scholarly literature concerning both the theory of marketization (or the spread of global capitalism, if that language is preferred) and the feedback between theory and experience. If *these* topics can be illuminated by scholarly enquiry, notwithstanding all the imprecisions of terminology and the complexity of the causal chains involved, then so too can the comparative politics of democratization. Even if the European Union falls apart, or marketization goes into reverse, this kind of value-oriented and teleologically structured social analysis will continue to inform our understanding of the possible worlds between which we navigate. In the same way democratization will deserve scholarly attention (at least from those committed to practical reason) whether or not the enthusiasm of today's democratizers proves well-founded.

If a contemporary process is correctly identified as long-term and open-ended, then clearly the analyst cannot know with certainty what will be the eventual outcome. It may therefore be objected that what we have classified as 'processes of democratization' will turn out to be something quite different. But it is the process and not the outcome that defines our object of study. It is usually possible to establish with reasonable confidence that there has been an *intention* to democratize (e.g. as signalled by the terms of a foundational pact, or the drama of a theatrical transition). Moreover, such intentions are normally followed by rather clear and visible measures of implementation (the return to barracks, the convening of elections, the design of new institutions). Even in countries such as Algeria or Myanmar, where the sincerity of the original intentions may be doubted and the follow-up measures were promptly abandoned and reversed, we can still refer to an ongoing process of democratization if we can establish that the collective imagination has been gripped by the vision of a future regime change of this type. In some cases it may be difficult to establish with confidence just how powerfully this picture of a desirable future has in fact influenced behaviour, and in principle it is evidently possible that more than one imagined future may occupy popular consciousness at the same time (e.g. there may not be clarity about whether Algeria's thwarted process of democratization was that alone, or also and equally an aborted process of Islamicization). Conceived in this manner, long-term processes of democratization may not yield to the kind of binary classification and objectification that is to be found in many international tabulations (e.g. Table 1 presents the Freedom House rankings for 2001). But for all that our object of study may take this form, and if so it will be necessary to compile the available composition evidence in a manner which attends to this in-built fuzziness.

What such areas of study indicate is that there are at least *some* important areas of social enquiry where it is both possible and necessary to study processes of change which do not necessarily end in predetermined outcomes of equilibria or consolidation, and which may not proceed in predictable and necessary sequences. There may be multiple paths eventually leading to similar outcomes (consider the alternative routes to democracy followed by Britain, France, and Germany respectively over the past two centuries). So we may need to explain 'equi-finality' despite path divergence. Equally, highly similar processes may debouch into contrasting outcomes (think of the decolonization of Barbados and Grenada respectively). Stage theories and assumptions of linear progress may help to organize and interpret such material, but they should be regarded as no more than heuristic devices, not necessary or assured sequences. Cyclical theories of democratization (as first formulated by Polybius in book 6 of *The Rise of the Roman Empire*) have the same heuristic value as linear theories.[30] Although such processes may not be amenable to law-like prediction, they may still be understandable if analysed and compared using assumptions appropriate to the subject-matter and checked by experience. Among the assumptions most likely to prove appropriate when analysing democracy and democratization it would seem reasonable to highlight the importance of persuasion, deliberation, the generation of consent, and the promotion of civility and accountability. At any rate these are all topics that will be developed more fully in later chapters. Chapter 4, for example, tackles the effects of constitutional design, bearing in mind that constitutional rules serve to separate decision-making procedures from policy outcomes. Such attempts at separation provides one promising strategy for the analysis of open-ended processes.

In conclusion, this volume explores a theoretical perspective on democratization that can be accommodated within the practices of social analysis in general, and comparative politics in particular, even though it does not occupy the current mainstream of these disciplines. The argument is that this 'interpretavist' perspective is appropriate to the subject-matter under investigation. Indeed it may be superior to alternative approaches, to the extent that it avoids spurious rigour and untenable claims of causal necessity. Instead it draws attention to the normative, transformative, and

[30] This argument is developed more fully in my chapter on 'The Viability of Democracy', in John Crabtree and Laurence Whitehead (eds.), *Towards Democratic Viability: The Bolivian Experience* (Basingstoke: Palgrave, 2001), 16–18.

persuasive components of democratization and to its reflexive and self-directing characteristics. Indeed it might be thought that any analysis which omits or downplays these aspects of the process is radically incomplete and likely to prove misleading.

Chapter 2 builds on the initial approach outlined here, focusing more precisely on democratic transitions. It explores their dynamics by looking at their capacity to resocialize the public into democratic norms. This focus can be achieved by invoking the metaphor of democratization as a theatrical performance.

The Drama of Democratic Transitions

Founding elections are, therefore, moments of great drama.
(O'Donnell and Schmitter)

Introduction

This chapter proposes an interpretative framework for the comparative analysis of democratic transitions. It argues that the complex dynamics, shifting agendas, and multiple interactions that characterize all such processes can be integrated and brought into focus by the construction of an analogy with theatre and drama. Every democratic transition obeys the logic of a public dramatic performance. This is not the only possible analogy. Multiple chess games have been proposed as another interpretative framework, for example. Alternative metaphors include 'elite pacts', 'crafting institutional design', and even the flow of ocean waves. All these images have been proposed as ways of ordering the confusing and contingent multiplicity of events and initiatives that seem to concatenate without much apparent structure during the compressed interval between the disintegration of an authoritarian system of rule and the emergence of a democratic alternative. The comparative study of democratic transitions focuses on this limited period of chronological time, during which an apparently almost unlimited range of experiments may be attempted by an indeterminate variety of often hitherto unknown or marginal political actors.

At least in retrospect, some democratic transitions can be viewed as relatively orderly processes kept within predictable limits through the tacit or explicit collaboration of the major power contenders, whose identities and resources were apparent from the outset. But even such 'negotiated' transitions carry a charge of dramatic tension while they are in process. Like a high wire act in the circus, it may all be carefully rehearsed and predictably successful, but the audience is riveted by the possibilities of mishap, and the star performers only succeed because they are alert to consequences of carelessness.

One possible research strategy in such conditions is to try to observe and evaluate all of these fragmentary and atomized processes, in the expectation that a picture of the whole transition can be constructed by somehow adding together all these component parts. But this method requires absorbing an impossible amount of detail, most of which can be seen with hindsight to have been irrelevant. Even where the analyst successfully identifies in advance the most strategic actors and the most promising strategies, the high level of contingency and unpredictability which characterizes most democratic transitions means that the partial insights thus gained are incapable of accounting for the total process. This is why holistic metaphors, analogies, and models have been invoked, usually *post hoc*, to provide structure and perspective to processes that seem almost impossible to read while they are under way, even though they may become retrospectively quite intelligible.

Metaphors, analogies, and models are all powerful cognitive strategies for ordering our analysis of complex processes. They are overlapping, but distinct, methods of simplification.[1] Each has its own strengths and limitations. This chapter focuses on one specific *analogy* (or sustained and systematically elaborated metaphor), a theatrical analogy. It proceeds on the assumption that a metaphor is a condensed analogy, and that the first step in making sense of any socially explanatory metaphor is to unpack the implicit analogy it condenses. Whereas *models* are deductive systems derived from explicitly stated assumptions, *metaphors* achieve their cognitive effects more surreptitiously. This is not, however, an argument for dispensing with all metaphors and analogies, and working solely with models, for that would narrow the range of cognitive strategies available to us to the point where many fundamental social processes would be put beyond the reach of holistic interpretation. Democratic transitions, and longer term processes of democratization, figure among the complex dynamic processes that cannot be adequately apprehended solely through formal modelling. Indeed, it may be the case that much of social reality lies outside the scope of strict modelling procedures, and that alternative strategies of cognition are indispensable for interpreting the world. In general

---

[1] This paragraph draws heavily on the work of Arjo Klamer, Thomas C. Leonard, and James Bernard Murphy, in Philip Mirowski (ed.), *Natural Images in Economic Thought* (Cambridge: CUP, 1994), chs. 2 and 19. The glossary on pp. 45–8 provides the framework of distinctions followed here.

terms, we interpret the social world around us by methods that include imagination, empathy, and intuition as well as logic and reason. By extension, our understanding of political realities requires the development of explanations that are not solely causal, but also more broadly interpretative. In this case, explanations that incorporate appropriately selected metaphors enable us to employ the insights derived from one known field by projecting them onto another, in a manner of 'creative illumination rather than correct assertion'.[2] However that may be in general, the literature on comparative democratization abounds with metaphors, analogies, tacit knowledge, and leaps of reasoning that owe more to induction than to logico-deductive procedures. Instead of despairing at this allegedly 'unscientific' state of affairs, this book proposes to make the best use of the available theorizing by exploring and comparing the various procedures, and considering how well they illuminate experience.

In this chapter one heuristic metaphor is considered. Before proceeding we need to distinguish between three types of metaphor. A *constitutive* metaphor seeks to frame the thinking about its principal subject to the point of constituting that field of cognition. Thus, for example, 'rational expectations', can be viewed as a constitutive metaphor in that it represents human subjectivity (including its interpretive and emotional as well as its calculating components) as if only simple utility maximization determined all choices of action.[3] Constitutive metaphors may generate or inspire both formal models (e.g. game theory) and confirmatory heuristic metaphors (such as the 'multiple chess game' application in democratization studies). But so long as the assumptions underlying a constitutive metaphor remain implicit it can lie dormant or unquestioned, sheltering behind these derivations. Constitutive metaphors can only be interrogated if their implicit assumptions are made explicit, and if their condensed analogies are unpacked and subjected to comparative scrutiny.

---

[2] A phrase I owe to Michael Freeden, who believes that explanation is always ephemeral and can at best reflect current understandings and who assesses the acceptability of an explanation mainly by the attractiveness of its interpretative web (personal communication).

[3] Perhaps the most successful and pervasive of all constitutive metaphors in social theory is that of 'natural selection'. Darwin was not at all surreptitious about this. 'In the literal sense of the word, no doubt, selection is a false term; but who ever objected to chemists speaking of the 'elective affinity' of the various elements . . . Who objects to an author speaking of the attraction of gravity as ruling the movements of the planets? Everyone knows what is meant and implied by such metaphorical expressions; and they are almost necessary for brevity.' (From paragraph two of chapter 4 of *The Origin of Species*).

This chapter explores a *heuristic* metaphor that does not spring from or serve to confirm the constitutive metaphor of rational expectations, but that covers similar ground on the basis of an alternative analogy. A heuristic metaphor is any strategy of simplification that motivates enquiry into the principal subject by juxtaposing attributes or relationships of the subsidiary subject. Clearly this definition leaves scope for some heuristic metaphors with poor explanatory power. The aim of this chapter is to show that the analogy between a democratic transition and a public drama is as productive a cognitive strategy as the available alternative simplifications.

Theatrical dramas, like chess games, and also like many democratic transitions, begin at a clearly defined point, condense a great deal of complex and often unexpected narrative into a limited chronological space, and then achieve a moment of resolution which is supposed to crystallize the significance of what went before. The drama ends, the game is won or lost, the democratic institutions are launched into operation. So at least we have some kind of an analogy. But do we have an interpretative framework worthy of the effort? Before we can address this issue some clarification of terms is required.

Since all reasoning by analogy is treacherous, it is not claimed that this perspective trumps alternative approaches, and can be relied upon to do the whole job of explanation. But the chapter does aim to show that it can offer a productive supplement/alternative to the other currently available perspectives. The next section pursues the analogy. The following section broadens out the discussion to consider the dramatic component in all forms of government, and the question of the historical linkage between theatre and the emergence of classical democracy in the ancient world. The concluding section sets out a provisional balance sheet of the advantages to be derived from using this technique, together with some observations about its limitations and potential pitfalls. Although the whole chapter focuses on democratic transitions, the moral and interpretative influences of a good democratic production should live on in the minds of the spectators long after the final curtain, and similar effects can be observed on the political stage. Consequently, the interpretative framework developed in this chapter is also involved later in the book, when considering democratization as a broader and more long-term process.

What Interpretative Performance Standard should we Require from a New Metaphor?

Democratization as Drama

Several of the established metaphors and analogies in the area of democratization studies have been quite suggestive. But each contains its specific assumptions and built-in biases. For example, if democratization is viewed as essentially a question of elite pacting, then where do we find the elements of public persuasion and responsiveness required to construct broader citizen understanding and support for the agreement reached? If democratization is mostly about 'crafting institutions', then how do we accommodate the associated requirements of rhetoric, skill, and judgement that we expect from a successful wordsmith and craftsman? If democratization can be viewed as the unfolding of a complex, multi-level, game of chess, then how do the chess-masters (or authors of the game) monitor and orchestrate the movements of all the many players on the board?[4] If democratization reflects a shift in the long-run balance of class power, than how is that change in background conditions are converted into the strategies and interactions of more fully individualized decision-makers and their followers? Can the actions of these political players be simply read off from, say, their

---

[4] In 1866, George Eliot published the following commentary on the 'principal--agent' problem, written in terms that seem especially well adapted to recent discussions in the democratization literature: 'Fancy what a game of chess would be if all the chessmen had passions and interests, more or less small and cunning: if you were not only uncertain about your adversary's men but a little uncertain also about your own; if your knight could shuffle himself on to a new square by the sly; if your bishop, in disgust at your castling, could wheedle your pawns out of their places; and if your pawns hating you because they are pawns, could make away form their appointed posts that you might get checkmate on a sudden. You might be the longest-headed of deductive reasoners, yet you might be beaten by your own pawns. You would be especially likely to be beaten, if you depended arrogantly upon your mathematical imagination, and regarded your passionate pieces with contempt. Yet this imaginary chess is easy compared with the game a man has to play against his fellow-man with other fellow-men for his instruments. He thinks himself sagacious, perhaps, because he trusts no bond except that of self-interest; but the only self-interest he can safely rely on is what seems to be such to the mind he would use or govern. Can he ever be sure of knowing this?'

Chapter 29 of *Felix Holt, the Radical* (Harmondsworth: Penguin, 1972), 383. In the manuscript version she first wrote 'Cambridgeians' but changed this to 'deductive reasoners'.

class background, or don't we also need to consider their more personal beliefs and motivations?

As we have seen, even the rational choice perspective can be classified as a metaphor, or condensed strategy of simplification by analogy, perhaps more general and more powerful than those reviewed so far, but also an interpretative framework that highlights certain kinds of connections, and screens out others. The key inspiration is surely the model of economic man in classical and neo-classical economics. This metaphor can be refined and adjusted—bringing in broader conceptions of rationality, looser accounts of calculation and self-interest, etc., in order to encompass a wider range of political and social phenomena. But it remains open to the same principles of criticism as the other metaphors just discussed. We should not just assume that it travels from its original specialized social setting or interpretative field to all other domains—that hypothesis needs to be checked against evidence and theory that is grounded in phenomena under study. Although our central concern is with contemporary democratic transitions, this chapter also invokes earlier 'foundational moments' in the long history of Western democracy, and assumes that these episodes shape and constrain the course of democratization viewed as a longer term process. If the social process that concerns us is democratization we can ask what aspects are highlighted, and what aspects are likely to be concealed, by the use of each particular interpretative framework, and how does each compare with alternative perspectives or analogies? For example, if democracy is both a system of rules of the game *and* a normative ideal, can the rational choice perspective accommodate the impulses to action that arise from enthusiasm for the ideal, as opposed to calculated self-interest regarding the writing of the rules? Can it accommodate processes of persuasion and justification which lead those with the capacity for violence to relinquish their most direct instruments of self-assertion, and to redefine their objectives to make them attractive to their former enemies or victims?

This section makes the case for the theatrical metaphor, addressing its handling of normative conflict; of the role of leadership; of the issue of persuasiveness (including its relationship to violence); of the connection between narrative tension and its resolution; of the elapse of dramatic time; of the explanation of motives and of character development; and of the connection between public performance and private persona. All these feature as recurrent issues in the comparative analysis of democratic transitions, and indeed, they all have considerable bearing on character and durability of post-transition processes of socialization into acceptance (or otherwise) of the new democratic regime.

First, then, any regime transition dramatizes an underlying normative conflict. Incremental changes can be achieved through stealth, and without attracting too much attention, but systemic changes to entire national systems have to be publicized and forcefully advocated. This is essential in order to overcome all the resistance, inertia, and scepticism that would otherwise stymie them. So the partial failings and scattered deficiencies of the *ancien régime* have to be integrated into a holistic indictment. Many of those who normally remain on the sidelines of public affairs may be persuaded that on this occasion the principles at stake are so all-encompassing that they too should become involved. If such new sources of participation are to be mobilized not only must the past be dramatically indicted, but also some persuasive image of a better alternative must be brought into focus, and must be promoted in a way that captures the popular imagination. Moreover, in order to engage the action participation of many normally rather passive spectators, some more or less convincing narrative must be proposed to illuminate the path from the stigmatized past towards the desired future. To launch a democratic transition is thus an inherently normative and collective enterprise. In this respect, at least, it closely resembles the staging of a vivid drama.

Now consider the role of leadership in this enterprise. This is often viewed as an embarrassing residual category—an awkward piece of ad hoccery. What can social science say about such uniquely personal attributes, it is often objected. But there *are* some more or less useful social science generalizations about political leadership, which is, after all, a recurrent and systematic reality, not just a unique one-off distraction. In any case, from the viewpoint of those seeking to generate adequate explanations of democratic transitions, if social science does indeed have nothing to say about the emergence, quality, and role of political leadership in such processes, then usable explanations will have to be sought elsewhere.

The Western dramatic tradition has been centrally concerned with exploring and explaining the attributes and pitfalls of various kinds of political leadership since ancient times. Anyone following the public career of Nelson Mandela, Aung San Suu Kyi, Václav Havel, or the many lesser luminaries of contemporary democratizations would recognize the recurrent themes of struggle, isolation, steadfastness, and symbolic embodiment that are the standard fare of such dramas. But we should not just single out the heroic strain in democratic leadership, of course. There are also late converts, accidental leaders, and figures who attract expectations they are entirely unsuited to fulfil. Given the strong elements of contingency that characterize most democratic transitions, it is of very real significance to the dynamics of the process whether one type of leader prevails or another. The unexpected death of President Elect Tancredo Neves in 1985 seriously destabilized the Brazilian transition to democracy; the personality defects of Abdalá Bucaram greatly aggravated instability in Ecuador; and the leadership failings of Joseph Estrada and Abdurrahan Wahid have been accused of inflicting similar harm in the Philippines and Indonesia respectively. Comparative politics needs to include orderly discussion and evaluation of this dimension of democratization. And, as in any good political drama, the leading opponents of democracy also need to be clearly characterized, both in order to clarify the normative principles at stake, and in order to explain the outcomes.

The most essential aspect of political leadership is the capacity to persuade—and perhaps inspire—others. This is not just a question of appealing to their direct self-interest, or threatening them with coercion. It involves a capacity for rhetoric, an ear for the musicality of language, an ability to judge the mood of an audience, to conjure up images of possible futures, and to divert attention from intractable obstacles. In short, leadership requires mastery of a range of performance arts (nowadays the television sound-bite comes in too). And this is particularly true of the relatively open and unstructured performances that are often required in the course of democratic transitions. (Remember Yeltsin climbing on the tank in front of the threatened Duma, in August 1991.) Weberian 'charisma' is worth invoking here, provided we keep in mind that this refers not so much to some unusual quality within the leader as to the beliefs that he elicits and that are projected on to him. Understood in this way, 'charismatic leadership' approximates in form to the performance of a convincing dramatic actor.

In principle, one might expect that any theorist who focuses on the role of agency and choice, rather than on structural constraints and determinants, would recognize the central place of leadership skills and persuasive arts in the resulting theory of action. Yet curiously, the rational choice perspective denies itself access to the very properties of social and political action that are most needed to create consent and to inspire innovation. Its impoverished account of actor motivations tends to reduce leadership to a mere brokerage function, if that. But, in democratic transitions, above all when the political choices under discussion concern such overarching macro issues as the type of regime, and the rules of the game, agents need to be guided, reassured, and persuaded by convincing and authoritative leaders. A satisfactory account of democratization can hardly dispense with an analysis of how such leaders arise, and the methods they use to shape the choices of others. The notion of democratization as drama directs our attention to this essential aspect of the process.

Of course, the manner in which such issues are presented and elucidated is different in a drama from the straightforward exposition one might associate with, say, an academic lecture. In the theatre the analytical and imaginative attention of the audience is engaged through an unfolding narrative. Typically there are unexpected twists in the plot, which grip the attention of the audience and elicit their emotional identification. The narrative tension underlines the normative conflict, and feeds the viewers' appetite for a satisfying resolution. The tension, unpredictability, and drama of a democratic transition works on its participants in much the same way. There is no certainty of a happy end, the process of transition is studded with surprises, the entry of new and untested characters, fears of deviation, or even tragic plot reversal. A purely rationalistic account of motivation fails to capture the ways in which participants in a political transformation become caught up in the action, at least temporarily galvanized by the hopes and fears it arouses into greater involvement than any 'free rider' could understand. The theatrical metaphor helps fill this gap in our account of motivation, both through the interactions portrayed on the stage, and through the identification elicited in the auditorium.

One key reason why a dramatic performance can seem so gripping is that it condenses an extended and symbolically charged narrative into the time frame of a single continuous viewing. By contrast, all real-life social processes take much longer, and are punctuated by more distractions. Even the shortest of democratic transitions take weeks or months, and most drag on for years or even longer. Even so, there is an acceleration of pace—a sense of a beginning, an unfolding, and potentially also of an ending—which makes a process of transition more self-contained, and more dramatic (more like a theatrical performance) than routine politics. Indeed, as the crumbling of the old regime accelerates there usually comes a rather compressed period of time in which a great deal seems to happen very rapidly. Old certainties dissolve, new voices make themselves heard—often stridently. The unexpected or even the unthinkable becomes daily fare. Such episodes can never last for very long. The tension and uncertainty would be unendurable, and most participants have other aspects of their lives they must also attend to. Nevertheless, transitions generally include compressed episodes of political drama which can be fruitfully analysed by analogy with the rhythms of a theatrical performance. The tempo or rhythm of events shapes their impact.[5] (Chapter 9 evaluates Chile's democratization experience from this theoretical perspective.)

Conversely, it is extremely difficult to dispense with such a cathartic stage in the unfolding of a transition. Some democratic leaders believe they have such a clear understanding of the endpoint they have agreed to reach that they would like to proceed directly from the demise of the authoritarian regime to the unveiling of a consolidated democracy without undergoing the dramatic tension and distracting uncertainties of the intervening transition period. For example, this was long the ambition of the Mexican PRI, until its defeat in the election of 2000, and also of the KMT in Taiwan (two cases that are treated as a 'paired comparison' in Chapter 8). What the drama metaphor would suggest, however, is that, in the absence of this cathartic period of collective reflection (which needs to progress through its logical stages in order to achieve narrative coherence), the habits and assumptions characterizing the authoritarian regime cannot be expressively repudiated. Consequently, the way cannot be cleared from the termination of an old set of rules of the game to the desired end-point—the collectively acknowledged (and even sanctified) installation of a democratic alternative. Just as the audience needs the performance in order to absorb the drama, so also the citizens need a visible transition in order to internalize changed rules of political action.

Finally, it is of more than semantic interest that, just as a rational choice analysis would focus on explaining the observed behaviour of social actors, so also a theatrical framework of interpretation would direct attention to understanding the public performances of stage actors. Drama involves the presentation of action and choice in a framework that makes it intelligible and significant. Sometimes characters publicly explain their motives; at other times we are invited to deduce them from the structure of the situation and the development of the performance. Motives can be mixed, their implications for action can be indeterminate. In a convincing drama we observe characters trying to decide between competing rationales for action, living with the unforeseen consequences of their previous actions, adjusting to the anticipated or unanticipated

---

[5] See Javier Santiso, 'Théorie des choix rationnels et temporalités des transitions démocratiques', *L'Année sociologique*, 47/2 (1997).

reactions of other characters on the stage, even undergoing character development as the narrative progresses. In a democratic transition similar conflicts, adjustments, and efforts at overcoming past identities can also be observed. For example, since 1990 it has been possible to observe the reshaping of military doctrine and practice in both Eastern Europe and in Latin America, so that the armed forces can repackage themselves as servants of constitutional government and protectors of human rights. All the tensions and ambiguities of a good drama make their appearance in the course of this elaborate public performance.

It is worth noting at this point that any private opinions and personal struggles of conscience that may be experienced by the actors in a democratization drama need not enter into our analysis, whether we adopt a rational choice framework or a theatrical perspective. In both cases what counts is the public's interpretation of the observed behaviour, and the publicly stated reasons that may accompany it. We can believe or disbelieve those reasons as we choose. The actor can always be assessed through his (or her) performance *for others*. Ultimate inner motivations are probably inaccessible, and in any case not required.

But although there are some semantic and even structural similarities between the social actor invoked by the rational choice perspective, and the dramatic actor of the theatrical metaphor, we should not overlook the differences. On the political stage a rational calculating actor would almost certainly be judged a *bad* actress, since she would lack all sense of narrative form or dramatic tempo, she would display no psychological depth of characterization, she would be unable to stir the empathy of her audience, or to react convincingly to the performances of the other players. Her portrayal of how one character attempts to swing the choices of the rest is unlikely to carry much conviction, since she could only invoke a reductionist model of motivation that would be likely to alienate and offend those she hoped to influence or control. Like the geometer, Velásquez, in *The Manuscript Found in Saragossa*, she would be unable to dance because there are 'no dance steps which are produced by a point of origin whose sequence is governed by a consistent rule'.[6]

---

[6] Jan Potocki's *The Manuscript Found in Saragossa* (Harmondsworth: Penguin, 1995, English tr.), 229. In fact Velásquez seems the perfect embodiment of the 'rational fool' almost two centuries before Amartya Sen rediscovered him. His father taught him how to describe human action and emotion by geometrical figures, but he kept falling over because the action of walking did not always obey logical rules. He was alarmed by the telling of stories that 'begin in a simple way and you think you can already predict the end. But things turn out quite differently. The first story

A theatrical performance, like a democratization initiative, requires team-work and the efficient coordination of a large number of secondary participants. While the attention of the audience may be fixed on the star performer, her accomplishments depend upon the reliable support of an entire cast and support team. But this can be granted without surrendering the stage to the rational actor hypothesis.

Ernest Gellner probably struck the right balance between the overestimation of instrumental rationality and its denial, with his image of man as the 'gaffe-avoiding animal', which is another way of referring to the competent performer required to play the supporting roles, so that the great actors can declaim their soliloquies.

A great part of our life is spent not so much (as those social sciences which are inspired by the ends–means model would suggest) in the pursuit of aims, but in the avoidance of gaffes. . . . For much of their life, men are not maximizing anything or striving for some concretely isolable end, but are simply eager to be included in, or to remain within, continuing play. The role is its own reward, not a means towards some further end-state. . . . The role is a fulfillment and not an instrument.[7]

But, he added, it would still be disastrously wrong to ignore material, non-conceptual, non-conventional constraints. Even a theatrical performance requires discipline, coordination, the mastery of collective action problems, and the management of a succession of intractable resource constraints. So it is also with any democratizing initiative. The visible political leader, no matter how untried, will need to coordinate a support staff, who can help her to sustain her performance and to avoid career-destroying gaffes.

That completes this brief survey of the strong points of the theatrical metaphor as an interpretative device for structuring the comparative analysis of democratic transitions. There is also a need to consider the way longer term processes of democratization and institutionalization may be affected by the quality of the dramatic performance staged during the transition period. For example, it could be argued that the Peruvian transition of the late 1970s failed to create the conditions for subsequent cumulative progress towards democratic consolidation because only old and discredited actors

engenders the second, from which a third is born, and so on, like periodic fractions resulting from certain divisions which can be indefinitely prolonged. In mathematics there are several ways of bringing certain progressions to a conclusion, whereas in this case an inextricable confusion is the only result'. (p. 334).

[7] Ernest Gellner, *Relativism and the Social Sciences* (Cambridge: CUP, 1985), 72–3.

returned to the stage, and they continued to perform for a restricted urban and Europeanized elite audience without extending their range to attract a substantially rural and indigenous mass electorate. By contrast, the Spanish transition may have produced better results in part because the King and the Communists and the *carabineros* between them put on such an edifying and instructive performance that the whole of Spanish society was re-educated by it.

The parallel between a dramatic performance and a democratic transition is no casual or arbitrary analogy. To situate it accurately we need to stand back a little and reflect on the broader relationships linking drama, government, and the origins of democracy. The next section of this chapter attempts that task. Then the conclusion attempts to draw up a provisional balance sheet between the advantages and limitations of the 'drama' perspective, including some consideration of the possible pitfalls and of the relationship between this kind of work and other strategies of explanation.

Drama, Government, and the Origins of Democracy

All forms of government involve flows of communication between rulers and their subjects. The direction of flow may be highly unequal, with some rulers broadcasting but hardly receiving, while at the other extreme subjects may bombard their leaders with messages and appeals that elicit barely any coherent response. Whatever these variations, there is no way to govern, administer, dictate, arbitrate, adjudicate, guide, interrogate, or represent a political community, except through influencing the understanding of the individuals who compose it. This holds true for governments based on coercion as much as for those based on persuasion or representative deliberation. And in order to hold the attention of subjects or citizenry with diverse interests and an unequal capacity for deliberation, all rulers must engage in some dramatic or theatrical manner of presentation. This is required not merely to focus attention, but also to highlight and standardize the issues that must be presented to public consciousness. Except in very small-scale face-to-face communities it is not possible to circumvent this requirement by individual debate or negotiation with each citizen or subject taken separately. They must at a minimum be grouped into audiences, each of which may be addressed in a distinctive manner, according to their distinctive priorities and grasp of the questions at stake. To some extent all rulers address multiple audiences at different levels of sophistication, but even if communication between government and the governed is fragmented in this way, the separate audiences are all engaged in what must inevitably be somewhat theatrical two-way flows of public communication. Moreover, where audiences are fragmented there will always be a more abstract public opinion or collective consciousness, extending beyond each specific audience, and inducing governments to adjust, reconcile, or harmonize their individual or segregated performances in order to generate a community-wide minimum of shared understanding.

All forms of government therefore involve a dimension of theatricality.[8] There is always some kind of *official stage* (ranging from the very pompous and remote, to the falsely intimate, like a fireside chat) from which those in authority speak to those whose public affairs they wish to regulate. There is always in addition some form of *official script* (a decree, a speech for the record, a debate, a consultation, or even a *fatwah*) to which the political community can be directed, if not always for enlightenment then at least for verification and interpretation. This is perfectly compatible with the possibility that in many forms of government it is the unofficial aside, the insider's reinterpretation, or the unstated background assumption that drives the course of public affairs far more than any officially authorized declamations. After all, any theatrical performance of merit will involve an interplay between the declared purposes of the characters and the implicitly indicated or suggested sources of their conduct. Moreover the unfolding narrative will always be angled *to arouse and persuade*, and not merely to recite or chronicle. Government is never an entirely disinterested or backward-looking process of merely ordering the record of the past (however important that may be as check on misgovernment, or as a baseline for future choices). It always involves the selection, ordering, and presentation of information with an eye to the influence that it will exert over the understanding and expectations of the public to whom it is addressed. Indeed a government that neglected to arouse

---

[8] In extreme cases theatricality may expand to occupy the central place in political life, displacing governance and administration. This is how Clifford Geertz characterizes 19th-century. Balinese politics, overwhelmingly preoccupied with the symbolism of hierarchy: 'It was a theatre state in which the kings and princes were the impresarios, the priests the directors, and the peasants the supporting cast, stage crew, and audience . . . mass ritual was not a device to shore up the state, but rather the state, even at its final gasp, was a device for the enactment of mass ritual. Power served pomp, not pomp power'. Clifford Geertz, *Negara: The Theatre State in Nineteenth Century Bali* (Princeton: Princeton University Press, 1980), 13. Compare L. Pye and M. Pye, *Asian Power and Politics: The Cultural Dimensions of Authority* (Cambridge, Mass: Balknap Press, 1985), and David I. Kertzer, *Ritual, Politics, and Power* (New Haven, Conn.: Yale University press, 1989).

and persuade its subjects or its public would in due course lose their attention and therefore their compliance. Thus, effective government requires the at least intermittent production of stirring narratives or morally charged symbolic incidents which re-engage the attention of the public before it falters, and which moves citizen opinion in directions compatible with government policies. This brings in the inherently two-way nature of such political communication flows. For, as in any theatre, the *audience is never unconditionally controlled* from the stage. However hypnotic the performance, some will be more entranced than others, and for all the suspension of disbelief is time-limited. In any case only a minority of theatrical performances, and a still lesser proportion of governmental dramas, are particularly hyponotic. Thus, performers must always be alert to the fearful possibility of audience disenchantment, knowing how readily it can lead to disbelief, and even to open disapproval. No matter how infrequently our political or theatrical actors are exposed to the sanction of the slow hand-clap, the possibility is always present and every performance must in part be tailored to its avoidance. This explains why there are *some* miscues which governments take inordinate trouble to avoid (never admit you launched an unprovoked attack, never confess that you simply wasted the money through negligence, etc.). Actors may be able to charm, distract, or bamboozle their audiences, but they can never afford simply to disregard them. Nor can governments ever afford to cease anticipating the reactions of their subjects.

Cynical and over-saturated modern audiences may find it impossible to reconstruct the harmony, trust, and enchantment with which many earlier theatregoers may have greeted many premodern stage performances. Secularization introduces an additional barrier here, in that a good deal of traditional theatre was imbued with strands of religiosity. Monarchical and aristocratic forms of rule were often similarly insulated from critical feedback by long established attitudes of deference to constituted authority. But even in a hypothetically deferential and superstitious past the same principles of theatricality invariably applied, albeit perhaps with more cushions of security than in the twentieth century. Tocqueville suggested that one of the first indicators of the decline of aristocratic pre-eminence in society at large was likely to be seen in the rise of demotic themes as objects of attraction at the theatre.[9]

_____

[9] Alex de Tocqueville *Democracy in America*, part 2, ch. 19. 'If you will judge beforehand of the literature of a people that is lapsing into democracy, study its dramatic production . . . In democratic communities . . . drama becomes more striking,

A century later, the theatrical innovations of Brecht and Pirandello may well have prefigured the erosion of the mass identities which some had supposed would structure all modern politics. Indeed, in the current neo-liberal era, it is difficult to avoid identifying the one-liner, the sound-bite, and the advertising jingle, as the predominant dramatic form that corresponds to contemporary political fragmentation. But even if we endorsed such schematic and reductionist equations between particular forms of theatricality and the corresponding systems of political organization, the point would still hold that in all these diverse settings the art of government proves to be highly theatrical. Not only politics, but also drama, can take many forms. An epoch of heroic politics may be mirrored in Shakespearian tragedy, whereas in an era of cynicism disbelief in such values as public service may be better reflected through nihilistic satire. But both tragedy and satire involve the use of a stage and a script to arouse and persuade an audience which possesses the autonomy to respond with approval or reproof as it sees fit. Any audience with such autonomy can be expected to experience most performances differentially. But the differences and instabilities of the typical audience response will nevertheless be structured by shared absorption in a collectively understood drama. In this sense, disagreement and deliberation over the meaning of a theatrical performance mirrors the pluralism within shared assumptions that we associate with a fully constituted citizens' democracy.

Some forms of modern politics may involve more audience participation than in the classical theatre. Metaphorically, as well as literally, actors may be planted in the third row, spectators may be swept into the footlights for a quick turn, and rival performers may compete against each other for the allegiance of the auditorium. Special effects may overshadow the efforts of mere human performers to arouse and amaze. But we should not confuse the blurring of the audience/actor distinction with its abolition. Nor should we conclude from the multiplicity of theatrical forms now available that the underlying dramatic forms can be abandoned. Unless some linking narrative, or unifying interpretation, informs the structure of the work, communication between the performers and their viewers will break down and everyone will go their own way. Similarly, in the political realm, modern government may

more vulgar, and more true.' (New York: Vintage edn.; 1945, 1st publ. 1838), 84. Is it possible to reconcile this insight from Tocqueville with the thesis associating the origins of democracy with Protestantism? As he notes in the same chapter, the Puritans who founded the American republics professed an especial abhorrence for the stage. Presumably their collective dramas were enacted in the church.

deploy more diverse and fragmented methods of communication than in the past (from the tabloid slogan to the computerized 'personal' letter), and its political interlocutors may be more diverse and ambiguous in status than in earlier times. More sophisticated methods of 'feedback' (surveys of public opinion, minutely disaggregated analysis of voting behaviour, etc.) may substantially displace the traditional instruments of oratory and crowd management. But all these innovations make government a more elaborate and specialized performance: they in no way dispense with its underlying dramatic structure.

Thus far, the discussion in this section has dealt with the features of theatricality shared by all forms of government, but of course these are much more central and pronounced in some contexts than in others. Our principal concern is with democracy and democratization, and it is here that communicative flows between officialdom and citizenry presumptively move to centre stage. But before following the spotlights we need to recall that, even during the most riveting of democratic performances, government is never just concerned with the winning over of public opinions. Backstage or in the shadows there are always others organizing the props, closing the accounts, recruiting the actors, scouting for new scripts. If government always incorporates an element of theatre, so it also invariably includes a substantial dose of administration, and recurrent efforts to marshal and organize public resources. Governments necessarily communicate with their subjects not just through discourse, but also—following Foucault's terminology—through 'discipline'. In general, outright coercion is an inefficient instrument of government, and even the coerced will respond better if supplied with some kind of rationale to which they may seek to adjust. Thus reliance on governmental sources of discipline can hardly dispense with the need to produce and transmit an official discourse. But equally, not even the most persuasive and captivating of government communicators can entirely dispense with the accompanying requirements for a minimum of organization and social discipline. In practice, processes of political communication will always be structured to accommodate or support these necessary accompaniments of order. Theatre can only proceed if the audience understands how to take its place, and when to attend to the activities of the performers. Democratic politics is only possible after the citizenry has been self-consciously constituted as such, and some procedural understanding has been established concerning the scope and limits of public deliberation.

Let us now return to the stage as it appears in the course of the drama of 'democratization'. Here, for at least a brief interlude, the

constraints of administration, organization, discipline and 'govern-
mentality' are draped in darkness. The construction of a political
democracy appears to be eye-catching performance art. Even the
turgid prose of the professional political scientist reflects something
of this with its emphasis on 'political actors', 'crafting', and the
thrills and spills of some potential 'rupture'.

A brief digression into the classical world should serve to demonstrate that the association between democracy and drama is more
than a purely arbitrary analogy. In the Western historical tradition
the two were intimately connected. This is not just a curious fact
about fifth-century Athens, but a deeply embedded aspect of
European language and thought which therefore recurs in successive guises at foundational moments in more modern times. The
link arose from the need to educate citizens for membership of a
political community. Under aristocratic rule, political education
could be confined to a privileged few and transmitted through personal contact. But under democratic rule some more collective form
of communication and socialization was required. Greek drama
(both tragedy and comedy[10]) became a crucial vehicle of public
instruction in democratic Athens. According to Werner Jaeger, 'the
writer of tragedies was an important political figure . . . tragedy
shook the complacent certainty of humdrum daily life by incompa-
rably daring and lofty imaginative language'.[11] Similarly, in the
realm of comedy, Jaeger claims that

standards of spiritual health . . . were brought to judgement in the theatre
before the whole Athenian people. This was a transference of the idea of
responsibility which is inseparable from liberty and which was realised in the
democracy by the institution of *euthyné* . . . [it was] the essence of Athenian
democracy that limitation was not by officials, but by public opinion.'[12]

Thus Greek theatre may have set the parameters for democratic
participation, but of course it was concerned only indirectly with
specific policy decisions. Thus oratory, eloquence, and rhetoric
emerged as vital attributes of political leadership under direct
democracy. Theatrical techniques of dramatization were deployed
to persuasive effect by those who could only act (i.e. deploy power)

[10] See David Konstan, *Greek Comedy and Ideology* (New York: Oxford University
Press, 1995).
[11] Werner Jaeger, *Paideia: The Ideals of Greek Culture*, i (Oxford: Blackwell,
1954), 248.
[12] Ibid. 364–5. 'in legal language the punishment which makes a man return to
the line he has transgressed is called euthyné, straightening—there, the sophist
believes, the educational function of law is made manifest' (p. 311).

so long as they could also secure public assent. Martha Nussbaum offers an exposition of public rationality in classical Greece that encapsulates the linkage between drama and democracy, and that articulates an Aristotelian outlook of striking relevance for students of contemporary democratizations. The following five features of this outlook resonate through most of the chapters in this volume:

a) deliberative procedures appropriate for contradictory, incommensurable, plural values not measurable by any unitary quantitative standard;
b) the priority of the particular in rule-based judgements;
c) the rationality of emotions and imagination;
d) the value of claims generated by literary excursions of sympathy, pity and fear;
e) the role of leadership and citizenship in a society of cultivated perceivers'[13]

The most famous instance of democratic oratory, reinvoked countless times across subsequent centuries, was of course the funeral oration of Pericles in 431/430 BC:

Our system of government does not copy the institutions of our neighbours. It is more the case of our being a model to others, than of imitating anyone else. Our constitution is called a democracy because power is in the hands not of a minority, but of a whole people. When it is a question of settling private disputes, everyone is equal before the law; when it is a question of putting one person before another in positions of public responsibility, what counts is not membership of a particular class, but the actual ability which the man possesses. No one, so long as he has it in him to be of service to the state, is kept in political obscurity because of poverty. And, just as our political life is free and open, so our day-to-day life in our relations with each other . . . We are free and tolerant in our private lives; but in public affairs we keep to the law. This is because it commands our deep respect.[14]

As an objective analysis of the structure of Athenian politics this speech leaves much to be desired, of course, but as the classical exemplar of how to persuade citizens to participate in, and feel loyalty towards, a system of collective deliberation it has proved immortal. As critics have frequently observed, however, this oratory

---

[13] This synthesis of Martha Nussbaum's 50-page argument is taken from Hayward R. Ailker, *Rediscoveries and Reformulations: Humanistic Methodologies for International Studies* (Cambridge: CUP, 1996), which includes various other demonstrations of the insights that modern social science can derive from rediscovering classical authors.

[14] Thucydides, *History of the Peloponnesian War*, tr. by Rex Warner (Harmondsworth: Penguin, 1972), 145.

was used to sustain an imperial war as much as to vindicate democratic participation, and more generally the methods of rhetoric and theatrical dramatization can be used for diverse political ends, as readily to suppress democracy as to extol it. Nevertheless, the arts of political persuasion are indispensable to democratic systems, and are central to processes of democratization, and these classical precedents confirm the common genesis of popular rule and of political theatre.

Finally, as Quentin Skinner has recently reminded us, we must note that in the classical tradition the link between oratory and popular government can also be expressed negatively. This was hinted at ironically by Tacitus in AD 101, when he concluded his dialogue on oratory by indicating that the scope for this art had recently diminished, since 'what is the use of making numerous speeches before the populace, given that public issues are no longer considered by the uneducated multitude but rather by a single individual who is supremely wise'.[15]

The theatricality of direct democracy in classical Athens demonstrates that our analogy between politics and drama is far from arbitary. But modern representative democracy often seems far removed from that forebear with which it happens to share a common name. So does this digression have any bearing on contemporary constitutional democracies? Without wishing to overstress the association, one might consider the US Declaration of Independence ('to secure these rights, governments are instituted among men deriving their just powers from the consent of the governed') or the Gettysburg Address ('a new birth of freedom—and the government of the people, by the people, for the people, shall not perish from the earth'). With reference to the Declaration of Independence, it is worth quoting John Adams, nursing a grievance over his defeat by Thomas Jefferson in the US presidential election of 1800, who expressed the 'realist' view of the business of politics, and attempted to dismiss his rival's rhetorical excesses and emancipating visions, as follows: 'Was there ever a Coup de Theatre that had so great an effect as Jefferson's penmanship of the Declaration of Independence?' Although it was Adams himself who had invited the young Jefferson to draft the declaration, he subsequently told him that its significance had been vastly overrated: 'dress and ornament rather than Body, Soul and substance', merely 'a theatrical side

---

[15] Quoted in Quentin Skinner, *Reason and Rhetoric in the Philosophy of Hobbes* (Cambridge: CUP, 1996), 70. The contrast is with Cicero's earlier stress on the value of developing one's rhetorical skills, and applying them to public affairs which applied to the republican period.

show'. And yet he had to concede that 'Jefferson ran away with the stage effect . . . and all the glory of it'.[16] More than that, it might be thought, Jefferson's performance skills captured the imagination of generations to come, and so helped to establish the new US democracy on the firm foundation of shared beliefs and discourse. With reference to the Gettysburg Address, the nearest equivalent to a Periclean funeral oration known to US democracy, Gary Wills supplies the relevant background. Referring to the official oration at Gettysburg by Edward Everett (which preceded President Lincoln's immortal address) Wills writes:

Like the Attic orators—and dramatists—he knew the power of symbols to create a people's political identity . . . It does not overstate Everett's ambition, in this crowning effort of his oratory, to say that he hoped to accomplish something like the impact of Greek drama as well as of the Greek Epitaphios. As Aeschylus had used the gods to explain Athenian ideals to the Athenians, he would use Greek ideals to explain America to Americans.[17]

In practice Lincoln's much sparer use of language achieved an effect that Everett could only dream of. But does such rhetoric have any 'real' political consequences? Joseph Ellis suggests that America benefited from a 'remarkable explosion of leadership at the very start of the American Republic', in part because the founding fathers operated under 'the self-conscious sense that the future was watching', and this 'elevated the standards and expectations for all concerned. At least in a small way, we are complicitous in their achievement because we were the ultimate audience for their performance.'[18]

Finally, here is an extract from the constitutional convention of 1824 which drafted the first liberal constitution of an independent Mexico:

A Congress is the theatre in which the deputies perform with the populace serving as interested spectators. On this stage it becomes easy to see who is fit to be a congressman, and who is only out to serve his own interests or those of some corporate body. In this way the people gain access to irrefutable evidence concerning the virtues or defects of their representatives, and on this solid basis they can decide to re-elect or not.[19]

[16] Joseph T. Ellis, *American Sphinx: The Character of Thomas Jefferson* (Vintage, 1998), 291/-2, quoting two letters from John Adams to Benjamin Rush (1805 and 1811) and one to Jefferson (1813).

[17] *Lincoln at Gettysburg: The Words that Remade America* (New York: Simon & Schuster, 1992), 51–2.

[18] Ellis, *American Sphinx*, 300–1.

[19] Assembly member Rejón, arguing in favour of the system of direct election to congress that was in fact adopted. Quoted in Juan A. Mateos, *Historia Parlamentaria*

A Critique and a Tentative Balance Sheet

This concluding section deals with two alternative lines of criticism of the case for the theatrical analogy, which are placed in the broader context of discussions about which theory and method, or combination of *theories* and *methods*, offers most promise of advancing the comparative analysis of democratization processes. The first line of criticism is aimed at disqualifying the approach just outlined, whereas the second grants it some space but warns of the pitfalls and reserves judgement until the results are in.

We shall first bluntly state the case for disqualification. The theatrical analogy may sound an intriguing metaphor, but it is not and cannot be made a strictly 'scientific' theory. It contains so much subjectivity that it may not even be a very reliable method of hypothesis formulation. It lacks a cut and dried separation between the reality to be explained and the external causes that are supposed to do the explaining, and it does not seem very interested in value neutrality. What kind of objective evidence or independent verification procedures could we adopt to test the claims made? Could they be replicated by any analyst, or do they depend upon the judgement or tacit knowledge of particular practitioners? The approach seems to license long chains of causation with indeterminate outcomes, rationalized *post hoc* by arbitrary shifts in the level of analysis (from personal leadership to supposed collective norms, etc.). So it breaks most of the methodological taboos it would need to observe if it were to qualify as science. And it also fails to qualify as good history, since it aspires to identify recurrent patterns and underlying processes observable in different contexts, rather than simply to explain as clearly and thoroughly as possible unique events or episodes. From a historian's point of view, it contains too much subjectivity, too many a priori assumptions, before one has examined the specific evidence, perhaps also a dependence on unsubstantiated counter-factual speculation. So 'it isn't good history, it isn't good science'—at best it is just an inductive or phenomenological redescription.

This disqualification rests on an unstated and unproven assumption. The assumption is that—provided all such errors and deviations from social scientific orthodoxy are eschewed—the remaining techniques and methods will deliver all that is worth knowing about

de los Congresos Mexicanos de 1821 a 1857 (Mexico City, 1882), 370–1, as transcribed by José Antonio Aguilar Rivera, *En Pos de la Quimera: Reflexiones sobre el Experimento Constitucional Atlántico* (Mexico City, 2000), 160; my trans.

democratization and democratic transitions. When the programme has reached fruition, and has demonstrated how well it can compare and explain actual processes of democratic transition, it will set a performance standard by which alternative approaches should be judged. If it fulfils its promise, then the alternatives will be unable to match its level of explanatory power and should no longer attract much academic attention (although even in this case a dominant paradigm may be enriched by borrowings from the insights of less successful rivals). But so long as its only claim to exclusivity rests on its own account of its internal elegance and lucidity, analytical progress demands that pluralism should prevail. Challenges relying on alternative or complementary theories and methods should be welcomed, since the best of them will set the performance standard that then has to be beaten by all future contenders. This chapter has rested on the alternative judgement that, at present, the explanatory power of the existing accounts of democratic transition remains quite modest. There is scope for considerable improvements, both in theoretical rigour and in empirical coverage. On this basis it is intellectually legitimate to explore whether a theatrical metaphor can provide added value as an interpretative framework.

So this line of argument rules out of consideration a perspective that at least deserves some kind of hearing. If the only licensed strategies of enquiry are the most scrupulously 'scientific' searches for regularity, and the most professionally historical reconstructions of unique events, then we may have to wait a very long time before there is anything substantive we are qualified to say about contemporary processes of democratization. Moreover, if we embrace such strict methodological purism, the performance standards required of the eventual explanations, if and when they do arrive, are likely to be low, since there is so little competition, and so much implicit or provisional knowledge has been ruled out of court. In the mean time, politicians will act, publics will believe, and pundits will pontificate, as if they were in possession of useful knowledge about democratization processes, but their claims will not be subjected to academic scrutiny or critical scholarly revision, because we refuse to speak on their terms.

So how can these various disqualifying criticisms be countered? First, it must be accepted that the theatrical analogy attempts to provide a phenomenological redescription of the various processes under study. The social phenomena in question exist, they are recurrent, they seem to present some common features, they are politically and socially important, and of course, they are very complex dynamic processes. So they call out for explanation and analysis. If we use the comparative method to tackle such sprawling and multi-form realities, this almost inescapably requires resort to a substantial degree of induction. That is to say, our assessment of what is to be compared and where to start the analysis must be to a considerable extent guided by our initial observations of the main features presented by the cases in question. If so, phenomenological redescription is not itself a disqualified procedure. Induction and deduction have to proceed in tandem if we are to construct not just elegant but also relevant models to account for such processes.

This is where resort to metaphors and analogies comes in. Having provisionally scanned the main features of our complex phenomena we need to construct some analytical or interpretative framework which will help us to identify which variables or areas of possible causal connection deserve further and closer investigation.

Here we begin to move from the terrain of outright disqualification to the more congenial terrain of balance sheets, comparing the strengths and weaknesses of alternative approaches. Clearly the theatrical metaphor is not a fully specified theory and can never be expected to generate law-like regularities. Even so, it could merit a significant place in the sun, if it spawned productive hypotheses that could later be assessed by more conventional methods of either historical or comparative enquiry. Moreover, if it is true that even the more rigorous theoretical constructs are metaphors with their own built-in assumptions and blindspots, the theoretical metaphor could serve as an important reality check or corrective to theories that, although they are more elegant, also tend towards reductionism, and the disregard of relevant data.

Hopefully, at this point the theatrical analogy is no longer completely disqualified as an instrument in our armoury of democratization studies. As we have seen when reviewing the history of drama and its inter-relation to the history of democracy, this particular metaphor is not arbitrary and ungrounded. At least it has a more democratic genealogy than theories derived from Hobbes and his justification of absolutism. With regard to the charge of *ad hoc* or *post hoc* shifts in the level of analysis, such shifts may be required by the complexity, indeterminacy, and hybridity of the processes under consideration. The main test of a good explanation in the democratization field should be that it beats the competition in the specific instance for which it has been compiled. As we shall argue throughout this book, that is not a very demanding performance standard to meet. Most claims to have identified law-like regularities in the democratization area are quickly followed by unpredicted experiences that either modify or even repeal the law in question.

This theatrical metaphor has more going for it if it is viewed as an interpretative framework for deepening our understanding of a specific democratization process than if it is regarded as a stepping stone towards the confirmation of a covering law. By its nature, a dramatic presentation directs attention to a unique situation, even if it also hints at the universal implications of the narrative. A good drama relates social context to the actions of the players. It therefore provides 'thick' or context-laden explanations of behaviour. A convincing account of democratization in a specific country requires good knowledge of the context (including the relevant history, the cultural idiom, the named collective symbols or reference points). If you abstract from all that you are likely to end up with an empty theorem about cause and effect which carries little conviction with the population in question, however solid it may seem to a disembodied social scientist, if fails to connect meaningfully with their understanding of their own predicament. The theatrical analogy overcomes that limitation of other methods. If provides a defence against the imposition of 'prefabricated' categories that have not been made locally intelligible. If in country X democratization is understood in terms of a procedural minimum definition, or as an expression of the rise of the working class, or of the triumph of capitalism, or whatever, this must be because of some striking public performance that created awareness of that meaning.

Most of the democratization literature has suffered from the distortion of focusing on the national political arena to the relative neglect both of extra-national and subnational processes that are often of equivalent importance. The metaphor of the single stage risks reinforcing that distortion. The literature on 'elite pacts' and 'crafting institutions' has been criticized for its 'voluntarism'—that is, for making the assumption of some unified directing will, in control of the whole process. The analogy with drama risks reinforcing that questionable assumption since, of course, all players have authors and directors, however much they work to create the illusion of spontaneity. Many democratic transitions are indeed characterized by improvisation and unscripted intrusions onto the public stage—they are genuinely Pirandellian—and our metaphors need to accommodate that fact.[20] Similarly, the metaphor implies a

[20] Public dramatic performances can, of course, take many forms—not just historical drama, but farce and psychological tragedy; not just theatre, but circus and soap opera. So my metaphor is very stretchable but at least such stretching can be made explicit.

single unified and homogenous audience, permanently following a single plot line. The reality, of course, is that most citizenries-in-formation are heterogeneous, dispersed, easily distracted, and attend only selectively to parts of the ongoing political narrative. Another potential distortion arises from the fact that a dramatic performance focuses attention on one particular process by literally screening out other often closely related activities. Thus the analogy risks implying that the design of new political 'rules of the game' proceeds as shown to the public, and in isolation from other germane developments which are handled offstage. Furthermore, most theatre operates within a long-standing set of shared traditions and expectations. Although there may be new twists in the plot, the format is comfortingly familiar, and the experience of theatre-going normally reaffirms a collective sense of identity and even serenity. Democratic transitions, by contrast, are often more alarming, disruptive, divisive, and unpredictable than this. Finally then, when the curtain goes down everyone knows that the performance is over, and the audience disperses to their separate private existences. The end-point of a democratic transition is much less clearly demonstrated, and different groups reduce their political engagement at different stages in the process.[21]

In conclusion, it is worth exploring the metaphor of democratization as a dramatic public performance, as one method among many to advance comparative analysis of such processes. This metaphor is not intended to trump the alternatives, but it may usefully complement them and even serve as a reality check when other perspectives claim too much for themselves. For example, the theatrical image invokes the public nature of all regime change, and emphasizes the interaction between the performers and their audience, the language of 'elite pact' highlights the complex bargaining that goes on between key actors before they even present their results to a wider public. There is certainly an important difference of emphasis here, and some experiences of democratic transition are closer to the smoke-filled room account than to the amphitheatre. However,

---

[21] To compare democratic transitions by reference to a theatrical metaphor implies that the analyst is standing outside both the performance and the audience. She is, if you like, a theatre critic. But the prime test of the play is whether it engrosses its audience. In the same way the prime test of a transition is whether it persuades its citizenry. An external analyst may claim that all the requisites for democratization are present, but if the society involved is not persuaded the process will not be real. Likewise, a theatre critic may praise a performance, but that is no use unless the audience responds. Naturally one would expect some convergence between social science and citizen perceptions of democratization, but just as audiences do not necessarily see eye to eye with critics this cannot be taken for granted.

drama comes in many forms, and it would not be difficult to incorporate most of the contents of a conspiratorial conclave into an audience-gripping public performance. In fact, a pact to democratize that was not communicated to a wider public would hardly serve its purpose, and once it has been communicated the public will demand 'insider' accounts of what really transpired. Consequently, the theatrical metaphor can usefully be run in parallel with that of the secret bargain, and need not be displaced by it.

Rather than viewing these metaphors as a substitute for good history, or for more narrowly 'scientific' strategies of comparative explanation, they can be pursued in a manner that reinforces more traditional accounts, and facilitates the formulation of comparative hypotheses. In this way the self-conscious use of appropriate metaphors can contribute to the cumulative growth of knowledge. In comparison to other more well-established perspectives, the method certainly has some weaknesses, but it also displays specific strengths and helps to identify some of the blindspots of alternative approaches.

This has been an argument in favour of methodological pluralism. It assumes that the appropriate test for each method is whether it can match or supplement the explanatory performance standard of others.[22] At least in the field of democratization studies there is general recognition that the standard attained so far is not that high. Theory has often lagged behind experience. There is, therefore, room for more and better work within the established explanatory paradigms.[23] There is also scope for casting the net wider, particularly if the objective is—as it needs to be—to explain the many often specific configurations arising across the growing universe of contemporary democratizations. There is also a pragmatic argument for pluralism in the analysis of democratic transitions, and although it would not

[22] For a lucid discussion of game theory, and its strengths and limitations when used to model processes of liberalization and transition, see Gerardo L. Munck, *Game Theory and Comparative Politics: Theoretical and Methodological Perspectives* (Cambridge: CUP, forthcoming). As in this chapter Munck first makes the best case he can for the utility of his chosen method and then frankly acknowledges the limitations, which are considerable. His third step is to seek a way forward by integrating various types of game theory with historical institutionalism, a challenging task. On this basis it does not seem self-evident that game theoretical techniques have yet trumped alternative strategies of explanation. There thus remaining scope for a plurality of approaches, including this theatrical metaphor.

[23] For encouraging indications that methodological pluralism may be staging a come-back, and that established research paradigms can be reinvestigated, see James Mahoney and Dietrich Rueschemeyer (eds.), *Comparative-Historical Analysis* (Cambridge: Cambridge University Press, 2002).

carry full analytical weight standing alone, it is worth adding here because it clarifies what is meant by 'performance standards' in this type of activity, and why they matter. Why is it important to analyse processes of democratization? Well, of course, all significant social processes are worthy of analysis by social scientists. But in addition to pure intellectual curiosity, there is a more pressing and practical motive for seeking clarification when the process concerned is democratization. In literally scores of countries over the past decade, decision-makers, academics, and citizens in general have found themselves wrestling with the challenges and uncertainties of creating new, more stable, accountable, and open political regimes. In the absence of comparative or theoretical guidelines they would have no choice by to operate by rule of thumb, perhaps drawing on selective episodes from their own national experiences, or perhaps reasoning in a purely deductive, or purely moralistic, manner. If they made mistakes, or unconsciously repeated errors committed elsewhere, the costs for themselves and for the political well-being of their societies could be extremely high. So they quickly developed an intense appetite for nuggets of transitology. For example, all Latin American democratizers carried around with them some half-digested ideas about the relevance to themselves of Spain's peaceful democratization. Often their initial understanding of the Spanish case was deficient, and the ability to adjust it to their own circumstances was lacking. In this setting, systematic and careful comparative discussions could be of considerable practical value, as well as being of theoretical interest. The performance standard required would inevitably fall far short of the demands set by strict academic disciplinarians. But there was a premium on speed, on relevance, and on the delivery of middle range and approximate conclusions that could then be recalibrated to a specific national conjuncture. By *this* pragmatic performance standard (as compared to the ignorance and improvisation that would have followed without any transitology), early academic work on comparative democratizations was unusually productive and worthwhile.[24] Of course, it was somewhat *ad hoc* and metaphorical in character, and it contained an unstable mixture of analysis and prescription ('thoughtful wishing' was the catch-phrase). But it was available and adaptable when it was needed (which is unlikely to be the case for the fruits of a hard-nosed 'scientific' research programme), and it is corrigible in the light of

[24] The simple observation that democratization was unlikely to be achieved through mass rebellion from below and instead would require some re-accommodation between authoritarian and democratic elites was intuitive in most countries, but opened new vistas once explained.

ongoing experience. Indeed, it even contains some scope for quasi-experimental observation.[25] The predictive power of most transition 'theory' (middle-range generalization) was certainly quite modest, but that faithfully reflected the large part played by contingency in each specific process of democratization.

The following chapters examine a series of key facets of democratization viewed as a long-term process. Each presents some theory, and then interrogates it in the light of relevant experience. In terms of our theatrical metaphor these discussions involve a shift in focus away from the short period when an unfamiliar script is first performed before an uninitiated audience. For example, the next chapter on 'civil society' questions the composition of that audience and indicates that some may own their own private boxes and may even enjoy every privilege of backstage access (we could say they possess 'high social capital'). At the other extreme may be those who find themselves crowded onto the top row at the back of the stalls, perhaps barely able to see or hear, and possibly even unfamiliar with the standard conventions of the theatre. Where such is the case, the latest production is unlikely to grip the two imaginations to the same extent or in the same way. Over the longer term their respective attitudes to the theatre could be expected to diverge. Metaphorically speaking, this would be one way of structuring the study of the imperfect fit between an unevenly constituted civil society and a purportedly universal system of democratic citizenship. In the same way it would be possible to introduce the discussion of successive topics using the same metaphor (e.g. accountability can be investigated in terms of the interaction between official discourse and audience feedback). To indicate such possibilities is not to overstretch the use of one particular metaphor, but merely to show that the image of a public dramatic performance is quite as capable of extension beyond its core domain as are the alternative available devices for organizing the analysis of these complex dynamic processes (e.g. elite pacts, game theories, rational actor models).

---

[25] At the end of 1981, Guillermo O'Donnell and I, among others, concluded from the Greek and Portuguese cases that external military defeat could precipitate a democratic transition. Unfortunately, we said, this is an exceptional route which is unlikely to be repeated. But then General Galtieri, who had not heard our discussions, provided a confirmation.

On Civil Society

> The civility that makes democratic politics possible can only be
> learned in the associational networks; the roughly equal and
> widely dispersed capabilities that sustain the networks have to
> be fostered by the democratic state.
>
> (Michael Walzer)

If democratization is viewed as a long-term, complex, and partially
open-ended process then our theatrical metaphor needs to be sup-
plemented by a more extensive explanatory account. Before a democratic transition can begin there must be a political community
receptive to democratic aspirations. After the regime change has
taken place, the same community must respond to the new possibilities for political participation. The stability and overall direction
of the process will depend on this larger social context. Several
alternative strategies have been attempted to characterize the societal variables that may encourage democratization (or not). Causal
connections have been sought between democratization and such
elements as 'modernization', per capita income levels, the expansion of commercial society, the rise of a 'middle class', the emergence
of organized labour, and more culturally specific variables such as
Protestantism, ethnic homogeneity, and so on. However, if democratization is viewed as a partially normative process of social construction and persuasion, then such tight patterns of causal
determination are improbable or, if found, are unlikely to remain
stable. This chapter therefore considers an alternative type of
explanation that directs attention to discursive and interpretative
processes that are more compatible with the view of democratization developed in Chapter 1.

Theorists of 'civil society' attempt to explain processes of democratization by reference to societal context, often touching on many
of the same variables adopted by other research strategies, but their
accounts are more normative and less determinist. This chapter
first outlines the genealogy of such theories, and then settles for a

stipulative definition, since otherwise the term remains opaque. This highlights the issue of 'civility', and therefore directs attention to the scope for 'incivility' within a democratic framework. After reviewing the resulting potential for tension between 'civil society' and 'democratic citizenship', it outlines some relevant experiences from new democracies. It concludes that the civil society debate helps to situate processes of democratization in their long-term societal context, but it also confirms the gap separating normative theory from 'really existing' democratic experiences.

In Chapter 2, the analogy between a democratic transition and a theatrical performance focused attention on the strategic interactions of the key political players. This is a powerful device for structuring the analysis of complex dynamic processes involved during the initiation of a new democratic regime. However, as many and varied contributions to the theory of democratization have pointed out since the publication in 1986 of *Transitions from Authoritarian Rule*, strategic interactions are only one component of the story. The societal foundations of democracy, the social and cultural orientations of the population as a whole, also have to be taken into account. For some critics of 'transitology', the strategies and performance skills of elite actors explain very little of the long-term variance in regime types, and still less of the 'quality' of democratic outcomes where they have occurred. Before the curtain first rose on Act 1 of our political drama, it may be that the crucial determinants of democratization had already been set in place through, for example, the establishment of dense associative networks capable of constraining the discretionary power of the authoritarian state. Where such 'civil society' customs and practices proved capable of resisting anti-democratic governments, it might only be a matter of time before liberalization and subsequent democratization took their (almost inevitable) course. The Solidarnosc movement in 1980s Poland, with its firm patriotic and religious as well as its more strictly political foundations, is often taken as the archetypal example of this type of social precursor to political change; similar interpretations were also developed elsewhere, notably in the chapter on Spain in the *Transitions* volume.

Such discussion of the social foundations of democratization could equally well imply that where no well-structured civil society had come about the mere initiation of a democratic transition would be unlikely to lead to the desired outcome. Even when the right political actors appeared on cue in Act 1 and followed the script, the effect of the performance would be lost if the audience failed to react in the required manner. According to this line of argument, in the

absence of a robust 'civil society'—or, alternatively, a healthy accumulation of 'social capital' or an established ethos of social 'trust'—
the strategic interactions of key political actors would produce a
superficial and transient effect. The theatre of democratic politics
would thus stand empty after a short run—or perhaps the audience's demand for free-style wrestling would triumph over thespian
attempts to mount an edifying spectacle. The *opera bouffe* politics of
post-transition Paraguay provide an illustration that could easily
be generalized.

Theories of Civil Society

The constitutive metaphors of 'civil society' and, to a lesser extent
'social capital', provide condensed analogies that may help structure and simplify our thinking about the complex and untidy long-
term changes involved in democratization. Instead of focusing on
political actors and their strategic interactions, we shift our gaze to
large-scale and broadly based features of entire political communities. The 'civil society' metaphor may be used at international and
subnational levels, but for the most part it is used to refer to
national societies. 'Social capital' provides a parallel metaphor,
although the term is frequently used by those of an individualistic
outlook to cover terrain already claimed by the theorists of 'civil
society'. I therefore concentrate here on civil society, referring to
social capital theory when it has something of interest to add.

The decision to view these two perspectives as constitutive
metaphors requires some justification. The theatrical metaphor may
illuminate democratic 'transitions', but the imagery of 'civil society'
and 'social capital' are not so obvious. The metaphor of 'civil society'
is perhaps more concealed than 'social capital'. Even if 'capital' is a
rather elusive and abstract social construct, most users of the term
will be aware of its technical connotations in economics and finance.
Capital goods (usually machines) are used to make other goods;
hence accumulation of a 'stock of capital' enhances one's productiv-
ity. Similarly, in finance, 'capital' is assets that are held to generate
dividends or income; the greater one's capital the more financial
resources one can deploy. So when a political unit is attributed high
'social capital', the term suggests the accumulation of some stock of
durable resources that can enhance its social effectiveness. Of
course, there is no literal stockpile of funds or productive resources,
and it is unclear how social capital can be preserved until needed, or
deployed to produce otherwise unattainable benefits. Theorists of

social capital tend to gloss over such difficulties in seeking to turn this condensed analogy into something more objective, given, and (they hope) measurable. Still, the metaphor has yet to succeed in concealing its origins as an artificial and arguably over-extended analogy.

Theorists of 'civil society' have had more success in erasing its highly specific origins, converting it into a free-standing category of thought that comes to mind when westerners make comparative statements about the density of associative life in different political communities. Given the Latin roots of both halves of the term, as well as the complex connotations of both 'civility' and 'society', it is not surprising that non-Western discourses tend to lack an equivalent concept. Some familiarity with the Roman law tradition may indeed be required to set the concept in motion. Beyond that restricted culture zone, it has become customary to speak of 'non-governmental organizations' and to treat NGOs as the recognizable equivalents of 'civil society' in all corners of the modern world. However, NGOs tend to lack the surrounding ethos, the sense of authenticity, and the spirit of autonomy celebrated by theorists of civil society. They cannot be relied upon either to stand together or to constrain the excesses of authoritarian power, as civil society enthusiasts would wish. Nor do NGOs necessarily have the well-structured community support that civil society would claim to possess. If civil society is to play the role of *primum mobile* in the long-run processes of democratization, it must be more than a cluster of NGOs. To identify such additional qualities, we need to investigate the genealogy of the term in Western social thought. Such investigation uncovers concealed assumptions, including the negative analogy which differentiates it from an imaginary state of nature. By condensing and concealing that analogy it has become a constitutive metaphor.

In the standard theoretical literature, civil society is a collection of associations—for Michael Walzer 'the space of uncovered human association'[1]—whose members are free to enter or leave, to engage with or remain passive, as they please. This excludes such primary associations as the household or (in traditional societies) the church, whose membership is predetermined. It also excludes hierarchical institutions, such as conscripted armies and state bureaucracies, which impose vertical discipline on their members. Between these extremes, there may be an independent sphere of voluntary association where interactions are governed by some

[1] Michael Walzer, 'The Idea of Civil Society', *Dissent* (spring 1991), 293.

minimum principles of autonomy and mutual respect ('civility'). In order for such principles of civility to be secure, there must be some self-limitation by both the state and the primary associations, under which they must either agree or be obliged to limit their claims on community members' loyalties, thereby providing them with a sphere of autonomous action. This is where the Roman law tradition contributed to the possibility of civil society. Clearly, mere subjection to a particular legal jurisdiction is insufficient to generate either 'civility' in outlook or 'civil society' as an associational form.

Not all societies endorse the principles of civility and self-limitation, and even when acknowledged in theory the boundaries and degree of associative freedom will vary over time. A 'strong' civil society would be one in which the boundaries are set wide, the principles of civility are generally accepted, and the beneficiaries of associative freedom are active in promoting and defending their sphere of autonomous action. Where a strong civil society thus defined is established, democratization should be easier and more durable; where it is absent or weak, democratization would be precarious. Yet the definition leaves some important issues unresolved. Different kinds of voluntary (or at least non-coerced) associations are possible. Does it make no difference whether these are associations for economic advantage or for the public good; whether they are evenly distributed or highly concentrated in certain locations and among well-placed minority groups; whether they include political parties; whether we include the media, labour unions, associations of ex-combatants? In this account, there is 'no hope of theoretical simplicity'.[2]

Even if agreement is possible on a clear definition of the boundaries of civil society across nations and over time, the result will be static and descriptive. How can such an 'empty box' descriptive category shape such a dynamic long-term political process as democratization? Such a linkage would need to provide not just a description but an explanation of how the norms of 'civility' can become compelling enough to reproduce themselves over generations and to over-ride the loyalty demands of states and primary ascriptive groups.

In Western social thought, the traditional way of generating this explanation is by invoking the hypothesis of a 'state of nature'. The

[2] Ibid. 293. Katherine Fierlbeck is more severe. Civil society is 'impossible to locate or define with any clarity or consistency; it lacks a thorough and insightful account of power relations; it does not distinguish between its normative and analytical functions' ('Fetishizing Civil Society', Canadian Political Science Association, June 1996).

contrast between a hypothetical state of nature on the one hand, and the logic of association in autonomous communities on the other, can be used to generate a simplified explanation for the existence of a complex associative life in a wide array of specific communities. This generative power is achieved by abstracting from all history, culture, and context. No matter what their actual community may be, members can imagine a state of nature bereft of hierarchy and tradition. This hypothetical alternative to any really existing experience would be a frightening social void. Such a contrast serves to underline the indispensability of social structure and political order. It can be invoked to explain and justify civil society through a negation. If the 'state of nature' is unlivable, then all who grasp this truth will have to accept some degree of self-limitation and extend a degree of choice and freedom to others in order to achieve a minimum of civility and autonomy for all. Such reasoning has served to turn the opaque category of civil society into a constitutive metaphor powerful enough to reshape theorizing about the social foundations of democratization.

Nevertheless, a serious genealogical investigation of the notion of 'civil society' would only begin at the state of nature. Since the seventeenth century, this theoretical construct has evolved, migrated, been submerged, and re-emerged in diverse guises. The Anglo-Saxon tradition associated it with contract theory and individualism. The Scottish Enlightenment linked it to the rise of commercial society. In the German tradition, it was historicized and raised to a higher level of abstraction by Hegel and Marx. In post-communist Eastern Europe, it became identified with Western liberties and the rejection of 'totalitarianism'.[3] This capacious theoretical/descriptive device has thus been deployed in diverse settings at different times with widely varying connotations and shades of meaning. Such variations have been mirrored in experience. The civil society that inspired Hobbes or Locke was very different from that which motivated Hegel's theorizing or Tocqueville's reflections. For Hobbes, civil society is the response to the perils of the state of nature, and for Hegel it reflects the growth of commerce as a sphere supposedly independent of politics. In Tocqueville, it fills the void left by the absence of an aristocracy. Such characterizations of civil society, each abstracted from a very distinct and specific social reality, posited the inclusion (or exclusion) of different corporate and

[3] Charles Turner, Clive Tempest, and Grazyna Skapska all shed light on the ephemeral specificity of the 'civil society' debate in post-communist Eastern Europe. See their chapter in Robert Fine and Shirin Rai (eds.), *Civil Society: Democratic Perspectives* (London: Frank Cass, 1997).

collective entities. For Hegel, religion pertained to the higher realm of state action, while for Tocqueville it was the voluntary expression of local self-organization. For Marx the association of workers into unions was a fundamental reality, while for Tocqueville it was the local newspaper which brought scattered American settlers into closer association with each other. Such differences in emphasis and conception reflect both contrasting sociological reference points and varying theoretical positions concerning the base of state organization and the source of collective action.

Suffice to say that we are still without a single, unified, and consensual meaning for the term. Today's writers on 'civil society' leave it uncertain whether trade unions occupy a central or a marginal role in their conceptions, or whether the media are to be viewed as internal or external. It is unclear whether the neutral rule of law is an essential precondition and support, or a utopian ideal that civil society activists should use to critique existing strictures of political manipulation. They fail to agree on whether political democracy sprouts from, coexists with, or threatens to pollute the dense associative principles of civil society. What the Poles have in mind when they analyse civil society is only loosely comparable to what the Mexicans or the South Africans take the term to mean. Some such variations in meaning may be closely aligned with the assumptions of democratization theory, but others are not.

Tocqueville was perhaps the first major theorist to present civil society as an indispensable counterpart to a stable and vital democracy, rather than an alternative to it. However, the voluntary associations at the core of his notion of 'civil society' were quite distinct from the social entities envisaged by either Hegel or Marx, who took the term to involve the pursuit of material self-interest. It was the containment of such materialism within the confines of benevolent voluntary institutions (which could be viewed as extensions of the family or as practical applications of religious faith) that inspired Tocqueville. Contrary to some recent neo-Tocquevillean literature, the original was neither pre-political (the institutions of local government figure prominently in his account of American democracy) nor sentimental (his strictures against social and intellectual conformity in small-town New England contrast with fashionable contemporary nostalgia). What underpinned America's democratic political institutions for Tocqueville was the profusion of voluntary public associations which enabled isolated individuals to cooperate for collective purposes despite the absence of an aristocracy and the remoteness of the federal state. In this conception of civil society ('associations that are formed in civil life without reference to political objects'[4]), commercial, educational, and religious activities are all included. Indeed, in addition to the division of labour, he refers to 'associations of a thousand other kinds, religious, moral, serious, futile, general or restricted, enormous or diminutive (. . .) to give entertainments, to found seminaries, to build inns, to construct churches, to diffuse books, to send missionaries to the antipodes'. He even adds (in a way foreshadowing Foucault), 'in this manner they found hospitals, prisons, and schools'. This therefore provides a context for Putnam's angst about the decline of bowling as a recreational activity, which he took to reflect a deep crisis in contemporary American democracy.[5] Tocqueville's conception, for the first time, viewed civil society and democracy as inherently linked, whereas for previous authors they were seen as disconnected and, indeed, potentially antagonistic. However, his aim was to explain American democracy, not to produce universal theory.

The idea that some forms of associationalism may underpin political progress while others do not has a long pedigree, including Ibn Khaldun in fourteenth-century North Africa. Domingo Sarmiento provided the classical Latin American formulation with his dichotomy between civilization and barbarism:

before 1810, two distinct, rival, and incompatible forms of society, two differing kinds of civilisation existed in the Argentine Republic: one being Spanish, European, and cultivated, the other barbarous, American and almost wholly of native growth . . . I have described the artificial associations formed in idleness, and the sources of fame among the gauchos—bravery, daring, violence, and opposition to regular law, to the civil law, that is, of the city. . . . The revolution of 1810 carried everywhere commotion and the sound of arms. Public life, previously wanting in this Arabico-Roman society, made its appearance in all the taverns, and the revolutionary movement finally brought about provincial, warlike associations, called montoneras, legitimate offspring of the tavern and the field . . . [who] applied the knife of the gaucho to the culture of Buenos Aires, and destroyed the work of centuries—of civilisation, law, and liberty.[6]

[4] Alexis de Tocqueville, *Democracy in America* (New York: Vintage, 1945; 1st publ. 1838), ii, ook 2, ch. 5, para. 2.

[5] Robert D. Putnam, *Bowling Alone: The Collapse and Revival of American Community* (New York: Simon & Schuster, 2000).

[6] Abstracted from ch. 3 in Domingo F. Sarmiento, *Facundo, or Civilisation and Barbarism* (Harmondsworth: Penguin, 1998, 1st publ. 1845), 54–9. Sarmiento's diatribe is a polemical restatement of an idea with a very ancient pedigree. Among the best theorists on the fragile political equilibrium between urban commercial sophistication and the martial solidarities of pastoral communities is the Abu Zaid Ibn Khaldun *Mugaddima*, tr. F. Rosenthal, London, Routledge & Kegan Paul, 1958—from a 14th-cent. Arabic text. Where Ibn Khaldun improves on Sarmiento is in his

Similar polarities have resurfaced in the public discourse emerging from the terrorist attacks on New York and Washington in September 2001. However hard it may be to imagine, the perpetrators of such acts may also be the products of a dense associative life, not agents of any state policy but the uncoerced expression of some society's voluntary endeavours.

A Working Definition

If mafias, *montoneras*, and terrorists are not to be included in our conception of civil society we will need to stipulate some general definition which—without being too culture-bound—highlights the importance of civility. This chapter will therefore appropriate a recent formulation proposed by Philippe Schmitter. This has the merit of being distilled from a wide variety of contemporary social realities and does not generalize too obviously from an ethnocentric core. It is structured by Schmitter's underlying preoccupation with the requirements for the consolidation of modern democratic regimes, both old and neo-democracies. His definition reads as follows:

a set or system of self-organised intermediary groups that:

a) are relatively independent of both public authorities and private units of production and reproduction, i.e. of firms and families.
b) are capable of deliberating about and taking collective actions in defence/promotion of their interests or passions;
c) but do not seek to replace either state agents or private (re)producers or to accept responsibility for governing the polity as a whole;
d) but do agree to act within pre-established rules of a 'civil' or legal nature.

He adds that 'civil society, therefore, is not a simple but a compound property. It rests on four conditions or norms: 1) dual autonomy; 2) collective action; 3) non-usurpation; 4) "civility"'.[7] Like most

recognition of the interdependence between the two contrasting associational forms, and in their potential for stable coexistence. But both authors differentiate between opposing principles of social solidarity, acknowledging that the rural (or traditional) can be as dense and politically effective as the urban. Whereas Sarmiento equates civilization with only one end of this continuum (and Putnam takes a similar line about democracy), the best classical authorities took a more holistic view, and were less inclined to champion one form of associationalism to the exclusion of all alternatives.

[7] 'On Civil Society and the Consolidation of Democracy: Ten Propositions' (mimeo, Stanford Dept. of Political Science, July 1995). Note that this definition includes trade unions but excludes private firms. Where does it leave privately owned communications media, or established churches?

definitions, this can be read in a variety of ways, but seems to exclude mafia and *montonera*-type organizations (under both 3 and 4) and indeed more generally the 'segmentary' types of organization that so troubled Gellner because he thought them oppressive of individualism.[8]

At the risk of definitional overload, we need to flesh out Schmitter's fourth norm and add to the term 'civility'. Collingwood's definition introduces a more intimate dimension of civility, based on inter-personal behaviour:

Behaving 'civilly' to a man means respecting his feelings, abstaining from shocking him, annoying him, frightening him, or (briefly) arousing in him any passion or desire which might diminish his self-respect; that is threaten his consciousness of freedom by making him feel that his power of choice is in danger of breaking down and the passion or desire likely to take charge.[9]

This may be regarded as an essential aspect of civility not covered by minimal conformity to pre-agreed rules. Otherwise, obeying the letter but not the spirit of an agreement would have to be regarded as 'civil' behaviour, as would obeying uncivil agreements.

Civility and Incivility

Following this working definition, it is unlikely that we will find forms of voluntary (or at least uncoerced) associative organizations distributed evenly across the geographical and social terrain covered by the modern territorial state. Uneven development is a virtually inescapable characteristic both of Hegel's corporations and of Tocqueville's newspaper-coordinated local associations. This is also true if we regard church-sponsored collectivities as a crucial compon-ent of civil society. Like labour unions and other forms of community organization, they are more densely concentrated in some areas and social strata than others. Equally, if we follow Parsons in stressing the centrality of educational institutions (especially universities), unevenness is again evident. Schmitter's definition carries the same

[8] Ernest Gellner, *Conditions of Liberty: Civil Society and its Rivals* (London: Allen Lane, 1994), 8–10.

[9] R. G. Collingwood, *The New Leviathan: On Man, Society, Civilization and Barbarism* (Oxford: OUP, 1992), paras. 35–41 (p. 292). Does the norm of civility also apply to the treatment of outgroups, those not covered by pre-established rules, or not socialized into this conception of self-respect? Collingwood went to press at the darkest period of the Second World War (Jan. 1942) and seems a little ambivalent over this crucial issue.

implication, in that the four conditions he specifies are more reliably fulfilled in some locations than others—especially 'civility', but also dual autonomy. Although some of these patterns of distribution may be offsetting (strong working-class associations where higher educational coverage is weak, etc.), others are cumulative. By whatever definition, civil society is probably 'denser' in Hampstead than in Brixton, in Santa Monica than in East Los Angeles. Whatever the precise components of civil society, some sections of the citizenry will be over-supplied with 'dense associative life', others under-provided. This is probably true even of Habermas's 'lifeworld of communicative interaction', though it is hard to be certain.[10]

Neither market nor state can be relied upon to even out this uneven social geography: the market obeys consumer sovereignty, and is skewed towards high income earners; in the state, the sovereign assembly is also typically skewed towards the polity's most articulate and best organized groups. Theorists of associationalism wish to preserve its voluntary and participatory features and therefore resist centrally imposed standardization, regarding state regulation as a threat to liberty.[11] What countervailing mechanism can they point towards to even out inequalities in civil society? Unless such inequalities are contained, 'civil society' will be out of sync with democratic citizenship. Modern liberal constitutionalism extends the scope of citizenship (formal political rights) to virtually all adults. Historically, today's almost universal and inclusionary conception of citizenship rights was only brought about through pressure and agitation by and on behalf of those who were initially excluded or marginalized. The result is that nowadays the overwhelming majority of representative polities are strongly tilted towards universality, and the exceptions to this rule are gravely disadvantaged. Such exceptions (the incarcerated, the certifiably insane, the incompetent, refugees, and asylum-seekers) are narrowly defined and carefully delimited. There is a strong presumption against the withdrawal of citizenship rights, both in long-established democracies (polyarchies) and the new and more fragile constitutional regimes (neo-democracies).

[10] In his account of what he calls the 'structural transformation of the public sphere', Habermas views civil society as the arena in which pluralistic public opinion makes itself felt as an independent source of power. But of course some voices express themselves more loudly than others in the arena of public opinion, and not all the opinions expressed in an unconstrained public arena will be equally 'civil'. Jürgen Habermas, *Strukturwandel der Öffentlichkeit* (Frankfurt: Suhrkamp, 1993).

[11] For a vigorous recent presentation of this case see Paul Hirst, *Associative Democracy: New Forms of Economic and Social Governance* (Cambridge: Polity Press, 1994).

While modern citizenship may assume the guise of universality, the same cannot necessarily be said for civil society, particularly if 'civility' is understood more as a behavioural characteristic than subjection to the rules of civil law. Where this is the case, a substantial gap will remain between the universalistic conceptions of modern political society and the more restrictive and exacting notion of civil society. The interstices between these two social forms may engender multiple variants of 'incivility'. The quality and stability of both contemporary neo-democracies and long-standing 'polyarchies' alike are likely to be affected by the solidity and structure of civil society. In Michael Walzer's formulation, 'Only a democratic state can create a democratic civil society; only a democratic civil society can sustain a democratic state. The civility that makes democratic politics possible can only be learned in the associational networks; the roughly equal and widely dispersed capabilities that sustain the networks have to be fostered by the democratic state.'[12]

The weakness of civil society and the dangers 'incivility' are evident in many neo-democracies. In both post-authoritarian and post-communist settings, efforts at democratization are frequently overshadowed by antisocial forms of individualism and group organization that substitute for, or even seek to subvert, the sort of civil associationalism favoured by theorists of 'civil society'. The term 'mafia' is an internationally recognizable shorthand for such incivility. Were this just a matter of criminality, it would be of limited significance to students of politics, however difficult for the police to handle. It is of greater interest when democratization requires the extension of political and citizenship rights to large sectors of the population who have little experience of democratic politics and are susceptible to co-optation and control by mafia networks. It is also a key concern where uncivil forms of association either survive the disintegration of the *ancien régime* or arise out of political struggles between groups 'disloyal' to the newly established and fragile constitutional order. Clan, ethnic, linguistic, religious, and regional divisions frequently reinforce such group conflicts, which can be further exacerbated by the uncertainties arising from democratization. Intolerant and uncivil forms of associationalism are particularly prevalent where claims to privilege and property are politically contestable; where servants of the old regime still seek impunity for past misdeeds: where there is fear of revenge; and where the justice system seems unable impartially to uphold the rule of law. Such characteristics are found in many neo-democracies.

---

[12] Walzer, 'Idea of Civil Society', 302.

Political democracy typically occurs in territorially bounded communities where 'civil society' and accumulations of 'social capital' are unevenly distributed. To make such a democracy work requires coordination—and, indeed, the broader harmonization of relations—between sectors or regions with generous 'social capital' endowments and strong 'civil societies' and others without these advantages. An authoritative national state is therefore normally a requisite of a functioning democracy. Those groups and regions with the best endowments can, in principle, play a central role in bolstering an effective democratic regime. However, concentrations of trust, norms, and networks that facilitate coordinated action can be directed against a national democracy if this is seen as too responsive to the demands of those with low social capital. The white minority in South Africa or the pro-Pinochet middle classes in Chile both enjoyed plentiful social capital, which they used to defend their interests against the perils of democracy. No doubt some of the perils they identified were real and posed threats to effective governmental performance, but those with abundant social capital and the densest associative life can also use it to defend their privileges and to marginalize the less well-endowed majority.

In most neo-democracies the main advantages of civil society thus tend to be highly concentrated among a minority of the population, and these are not infrequently derived from privileges conferred by a pre-democratic power structure. In so far as the 'rule of law' constitutes an essential component of civil society, 'really existing' democracies frequently fall far short in the area of publicly provided and impartial justice, a point developed in Chapter 7.

Civil Society versus Democratic Citizenship

Civil society also develops unevenly over time on a logic distinct from that of state formation. The resulting patterns of associative life and social communication will typically be highly structured, with both insiders, traditionally favoured sectors and marginal or excluded sectors. New democracies will only tend to work well if they can restrain such exclusionary tendencies and induce those with the most 'social capital' to adopt a broader and longer term view of their civic engagement with national society as a whole. The politics of democratization is largely about that, and about the reciprocal process of inducing those at the margins of civil society to exercise both patience and self-restraint and to shun incivility.

Whereas civil society develops in an incremental and organic, but uneven and perhaps reversible way, modern political regimes are often constituted abruptly and at short notice. Examples include the 'new states' created in Europe after 1918, in Asia after 1945, in Africa after 1960, and the neo-democracies created in the wake of the Soviet collapse of 1989/91. In nearly all, formal political equality among all citizens was a principle established at a specific moment, and the newly created citizenry acquired a full panoply of democratic political rights. Yet such sudden creation of new inclusionary political societies may well not coincide with the pre-existing maps of associative life. The obvious question that therefore arises in the new democracies is how the associative and communicative practices of 'civil society' are to be squared with the aspirational or juridical fictions of 'political society'. If there is more than one historical route to the establishment of a civil society, it would seem to follow that there could be more than one way in which civil society can relate to the construction of a democratic political regime.

Evidently, civil society could experience slow growth, eventually creating the conditions for political democracy. This is the Whig interpretation of British history, and it also applies to one dominant view of the democratization of Spain. But the reverse sequence could be the case, where a formal political regime would be implanted and only subsequently would civil society—perhaps nurtured by a protective liberal state—gradually mature. This would be a standard Western model for theorizing democratization in many post-communist states, but it could also apply to 'protectorate' experiences like Puerto Rico and Hawaii. Other combinations are also theoretically possible: a civil society which attains a high level of development, but without ever producing a democratic political regime (Hong Kong); a civil society which develops on the basis that its freedoms and rights can only be secure if non-members are excluded from full political participation (be they Palestinians, Southern blacks, or Turkish Cypriots). Where new political frontiers are incongruent with older maps of associative life, it is just as likely that peripheral or cross-border civil societies will be weakened as that core civil societies will be reinforced.

Viewed in this broadly comparative manner, there seems no strong reason—either theoretical or empirical—for presuming the existence of only one strongly determinant relationship between civil society and political democracy. According to Ken Newton, 'The relationship between social trust and social capital (or civil society), on the one hand, and political trust and political capital, on the other, is not simple or straightforward.' He goes on to say that 'A relationship exists, as social capital and civil society theory predicts, but not at the individual level, and only in a complicated and indirect manner at the system level.'[13] But if the two are so readily separable, and in principle incongruent, then Walzer's theory of a mutually supportive interdependence will be difficult to realize in practice.

In those social locations where civil society is weak or absent, the reverse of Schmitter's four conditions apply, namely: (1) encroachments on dual autonomy, which (2) subvert the capacity for deliberation, encouraging (3) usurpation, and (4) incivility. This abstract formulation embraces a great variety of more specific possibilities, since threats to civil society can come from many sources (and often by several at the same time), and can be driven by political, socioeconomic, or even by technological processes. Consider this quick listing of some of the most celebrated historical examples: the Nazi party's subversion of civil society in Weimar Germany, the SED in post-1945 East Germany, the mafia in republican Sicily, Catholic clerical conformism in, say, rural Eire, Islamic fundamentalism in the *bidonvilles* of the Mahgreb, state-imposed conformity in Singapore, and some would add media-manipulated docility in Eisenhower's America, amoral familism in the Philippines, or caste-based exclusivism in some parts of South Asia. This should not be read as lumping all these diverse phenomena into an undifferentiated amalgam of 'threats to Western liberty'. Nor should one lightly endorse all the specific historical and social judgements of responsibility that it implies. In a grounded analysis of any specific case, we should expect to find multiple causation and some degree of structural determination, rather than just the will of a single illiberal agency. It is usually too easy to identify a single decontextualized 'other' as a problem (although Osama bin Laden seems bent on proving the exception). In the instances listed above, about half were examples of encroachments from above (the state) and half from below (illiberal society). In general one should expect some interaction between the two.

There is also a range of unintentional, non-political, or 'structural' threats to civil society which, while tediously familiar, require listing: unemployment, which is hardly conducive to civility or collective deliberation; criminality, which erodes dual autonomy and

---

[13] Kenneth Newton, 'Trust Social Capital, Civil Society, and Democracy', *International Political Science Review*, 22/2 (2001), 211. The relationship he identifies at the system level is 'mediated by the effectiveness of social and political institutions'—a huge intervening variable.

encourages usurpation (as discussed further in the next chapter); monopolistic systems of local social control, which regardless of political intent block off deliberation, foster intolerance, and obscure the legitimacy of alternative viewpoints; the atomizing effects of market supremacy; and so forth. Again, this is not to amalgamate all these structures into an undifferentiated threat, nor to imply that they are either separately or jointly determinant. On the contrary, the purpose is to demonstrate their heterogeneity and fragmentation, since this implies that civil society will come under pressure from multiple sources and that in any modern polity it is likely to coexist with substantial and persistant sources of incivility.

What requires emphasis here is that in a modern democracy these pockets or strata of incivility possess political rights and are just as entitled to their share of representation in the making of public policy. Depending on their size and capacity for political articulation, they will help steer the course of democratic government. They may indeed shape the rules and affect the resource allocation that underpins the more clearly 'civil' part of society. If we regard 'autonomous deliberation' as a key ingredient of a robust civil society, political democracy may well empower political forces that have no interest in fostering such practices. It may instead view them as either wasteful or even threatening. Similarly, there can be no guarantee that electoral majorities will always favour the preservation of the 'civility' so dear to articulate minorities. Indeed, one sector's 'autonomy' and 'civility' can easily be reinterpreted by another as elitist privilege that needs to be levelled.

The return to office, via competitive elections, of no more than lightly 'reformed' communist parties in various East European neo-democracies highlights this persistent tension between the rival claims for allegiance of civil society and political democracy. Similarly, in his analysis centred on capitalist democracy, while Schmitter tends to present civil society as normally and in the long run positive for democratic consolidation, he nevertheless acknowledges the separateness of the two processes and the potential for friction between them: 'civil society, however, is not an unmitigated blessing for democracy. It can affect the consolidation and subsequent functioning of democracy in a number of negative ways.' Among these he includes:

2. It may build into the policy process a systematically biassed distribution of influence . . .
3. It tends to impose an elaborate and obscure process of compromise upon political life, the outcome of which can be policies which no-one wanted in the first place and with which no-one can subsequently identify (. . .)

5. [It] 'may prove to be not one but several civil societies—all occupying the same territory and polity, but organizing interests and passions into communities that are ethnically, linguistically or culturally distinct—even exclusive.[14]

We are thus dealing with strikingly counterposed normative images of the relationship between civil society and democracy. In the first, 'civil society' is the bearer of liberty and is threatened by the mechanical application of majoritarian politics in a society with a still prevailing uncivil inheritance. In the second, the consolidation of political democracy is taken as the desirable goal, and 'civil society' can therefore be scrutinized and evaluated according to the quality of its potential contribution, which could be negative. On the first view, the stronger the civil society is the better, even if it is inherently 'denser' in some social locations than others.[15] On the second, only those forms of civil society that contribute to the consolidation of a high quality of political democracy are clearly desirable. Other forms may be too inegalitarian, too distorting, or even too 'uncivil' to be desirable. Indeed sound democratization could require far-reaching reform, and perhaps even the weakening, of inherited systems of dense associative life.[16]

[14] Schmitter, 'On Civil Society', 14. Note that these negative potentialities tend to run counter to the positive attributes emphasized by Schmitter's initial definition. Here non-usurpation becomes policy bias; deliberation becomes opacity; and civility becomes tribalism. It is difficult to sustain an idealized image of civil society, while also reflecting its multiple and ambiguous manifestations and its lopsided impact on the workings of the larger polity.

[15] In *Conditions of Liberty* (London: Allen Lane, 1994), Ernest Gellner trenchantly sets out the two rival theoretical claims to validation, and asserts his clear choice: 'Theorists of democracy who operate in the abstract, without reference to concrete social conditions, end up with a vindication of democracy as a general ideal, but are then obliged to concede that in many societies the ideal is not realizable . . . Is it not better to state the conditions that make the ideal feasible, or even mandatory, and start from that? Civil society is a more realistic notion, which specifies and includes its own conditions . . . Because it highlights those institutional preconditions and the necessary historical context "Civil Society" is probably a better more illuminating slogan than democracy' (pp. 188–9). But Gellner's imprecise specifications relate only loosely to the ideals of democratic theory.

[16] Carlos M. Vilas provides some striking illustrations of this viewpoint in an overview of the neo-democracies of Central America, 'Prospects for Democracy in a Post-Revolutionary Setting: Central America', *Journal of Latin American Studies*, 28/2 (May 1996). He portrays local oligarchies founded on tight inherited structures of social exclusivity that have learnt to parade the rhetoric of market democracy as a public discourse masking their continued supremacy, while their more intimate social practices perpetuate deeply undemocratic values. Compare E. Gyimah-Boadi on the weaknesses of civil society in Africa: 'preliberal or antiliberal values . . . tend also to pervade the modern and secular civil associations . . . tendencies of some key

The first account makes the implicit assumption of an overbearing state. Civil society therefore needs strengthening against that source of threat to its 'dual autonomy'. In the second, the state is implicitly assumed to lack strong authority. It is therefore the capture of civil society by particularistic interests that presents the main threat to 'dual autonomy'. Since these two possibilities are both theoretically and empirically plausible, we may conclude that the moral significance we can assign to civil society is indeterminate at this level of abstraction. A reasoned evaluation will depend in part on where the observer is located in the social structure, and on how a particular civil society functions and relates to the broader political system. Perhaps it would be better for US democracy if people did all go out to bowling clubs together more often. While on the Upper East Side of Manhattan the natural focus of community deliberation might be excessive tax and wasteful social spending, in the Bronx a rather different form of 'civility' would emerge.[17] The impediments to effective collective action would also prove quite different in these two cases.

One way to cope with this diversity is to say that any collective deliberation that is not subversive, and that does not fall outside the law, is as legitimate as any other. In order to achieve positive results within a liberal constitutional framework, it would be necessary to win over many diverse interests. Some forms of deliberation will therefore be more successful—either more persuasive or better targeted—than others. Still, ineffective and unpersuasive forms of deliberation are also permitted, provided they do not infringe a small number of clearly defined legal prohibitions. In principle, this is the way democratic regimes should define the scope of tolerated deliberations.

Now, can this criterion be used to delimit the scope of debate within 'civil society'? Not according to the approach to 'civility' adopted in this chapter, according to which some forms of discussion that are not illegal in a democracy are nevertheless 'uncivil' and threatening to such crucial norms as non-usurpation and interpersonal toleration. Thus various forms of religious fundamentalism may have to be tolerated within a democracy, but cannot be regarded as part of a modern liberal 'civil society'. A rich family can plot to buy up a

civil associations . . . to refuse to establish "rational" bureaucracies; to "anoint" rather than elect (including those involved in prodemocracy work) their executives; and to endow their leaders with "life" chairmanships'. 'Civil Society in Africa', *Journal of Democracy* (Apr. 1996), 129.

[17] Robert D. Putnam's latest restatement of his thesis about social capital in the USA includes a chapter on its 'dark side'. See *Bowling Alone*, ch. 22.

newspaper, and then use it to discredit its enemies, and this may be carried out within the law. Yet this could fall outside the scope of 'dual autonomy' and 'civility'. Indeed, the very question of how rigorously the law will be enforced in various settings may also be subject to uncivil manipulation, albeit within the bounds of constitutionally permitted action.

In short, in the realm of collective discourse as much as in the realm of social structure, there is a gap between straight talking that properly pertains to our various conceptions of 'civil society' and the coded language of the democratic polity. The precise boundary between the civil and the uncivil may be hard to define in principle, let alone in practice. Alliances of convenience can be expected from time to time, spanning that boundary, just as when the least civil of media barons are courted by the most respected of liberal institutions on an issue of common interest, or when fundamentalists seek the protection of civil libertarians. However, a boundary there must be if 'civil society' is to carry any of the moral or sociological connotations assigned to it by its theorists. If this is so, then the activities which lie on the other side of that boundary can be critical for the quality and stability of the democracy as a whole. If this is so, even in well-established Western democracies, one should expect that in neo-democracies such activities will occupy a much larger social space, often greater than that occupied by an emerging civil society. In order to analyse the scope for democratization in such societies, we therefore need to attend to the political manifestations of 'uncivil' society in emerging democracies. We also need to consider how the scale and power of this 'uncivil' society may affect the content and characteristics of the 'civil society' that accompanies it.

Theory and Experience

When traditional family and particularist loyalties are defined as the central problem to be overcome, 'state strengthening' strategies may seem acceptable, particularly those that strengthen the 'public sphere' by guaranteeing impersonal civic rights and reinforcing the rule of law. Yet when—as in post-communist neo-democracies and in Latin American neo-liberal discourse—the overbearing state is regarded as a greater menace, then deregulation, privatization, and state shrinking will be preferred. In principle these may also involve enhancement of some kind of 'public space' where autonomous agents can interact without manipulation, and so here too it could be said that impartial legality and rights are implied. However, it makes a great difference that such rights are asserted against the state, rather than under its protection, and that the justice system is liable to be subjected to the same austerity and market testing as the rest of the state bureaucracy.[18] In such conditions the resulting 'rule of law' will be above all responsive to the requirements of commerce, rather than to those of state-directed rationality.[19] In the language of Habermas, this would lead to cultural impoverishment and the 'colonization of the lifeworld' from which modern civil society is supposed to emerge.

As the norm of 'dual autonomy' makes clear, civil societies are under pressure from both sides, from traditional particularism and the intrusive state. The preservation and enlargement of an autonomous realm requires a steady flow of resources and recruits, directed with vigilance and continuity of purpose. Civil society consists of multiple self-perpetuating centres of association, competing as well as cooperating in order to promote their interests and project their own conceptions of autonomy, civility, and self-preservation. Some such centres will shrink from particularism but will hope to benefit from enlightened state activism; others will firmly resist state direction, but see little harm in allying with aspects of social traditionalism. Within each civil society, alternative perspectives and priorities will compete for ascendancy with fluctuating success as the external environment is perceived to change.

Still, the main threat to civil society could come—or at least be perceived to come—neither from statism nor from traditional particularism, but from a majoritarian incivility generated by democratization itself. This could arise out of the gap between civil society and the emerging citizenry, and the experience of many neo-democracies confirms its plausibility. Elements might include the impersonal irresponsibility of modern commercialized mass media, the impulsiveness of an uprooted and disoriented electorate, the

[18] Compare the Czech debate over 'civil society' in which President Havel tried to promote the concept as a corrective to excessive emphasis on purely market relationships, while Prime Minister Klaus equated democracy with individual freedom, including freedom from social engineering in the name of civil society. Václav Havel, Václav Klaus, and Petr Pithart, 'Rival Visions', *Journal of Democracy*, 7/1 (Jan. 1996), 18–20.

[19] Recall the liberal pluralism of Durkheim for whom it was the state which 'creates and organizes and makes a reality' of the individual's natural rights, indeed its 'essential function' was to 'liberate individual personalities', by offsetting the pressure on them of local domestic, ecclesiastical, occupational, and other secondary groups (while the latter were also needed to offset the potential tyranny of the state). Steven Lukes, *Emile Durkheim* (Harmondsworth: Penguin, 1973), 271.

short-termism of speculative financial markets, as well as the insecurity arising from such forms of organized crime as arms trafficking,
money laundering, and the drugs trade. Norms of dual autonomy,
rational deliberation, and civility may all come under siege from
potentially majoritarian incivilities of this kind. Evidently this third
challenge to civil society can be found even in the most secure and
developed of liberal democracies. Some theorists stress global integration and the erosion of the authority of the nation-state as the
source of this challenge. Yet, particularly in neo-democracies, it is
often the manner in which the authoritarian regime foundered and
the legacy of incivility left behind that may be more critical than the
erosion of the nation state as such.

Emerging civil societies are, obviously, incipient and untested in
most neo-democracies. The norms of dual autonomy, independent
deliberation, and civility remained uncultivated under authoritarian rule, except perhaps among some very privileged minorities
under what Linz calls 'limited pluralism'. Frequently, such norms
had to be promoted and defended in the face of official repression.
This may have provided an intense learning experience for activist
minorities, but at best these were a select group. Their influence
may have exploded after the authoritarian regime was deposed,
but not all were deeply socialized in the norms of civility, whilst the
helter-skelter of democratization typically dispersed them into
widely scattered activities. The virtual disintegration of Solidarnosc
is a case in point. Competing with activists for influence in post-
transition public life would be many other formations schooled in
less civil norms: pragmatic defectors from the authoritarian power
structure; revanchistes, chauvinists, and fundamentalists from
other sectors of the opposition; the new rich, often engaged in 'prim-
itive accumulation'; carpet-bagging foreign advisers with no
durable commitment to the local society; and so on. Whatever we
understand by 'civil society', it will be a fragile entity under pressure from all sides, contending with actors in a democratic polity
whose commitment to civility may be either questionable or absent.

Long before this 'civil society' can be stabilized and entrenched, as
Walzer would require, the new democracy will have to commit itself
to a succession of foundational decisions that will heavily constrain
subsequent patterns of political interaction. Certain forms of constitutional engineering may improve the prospects of a viable civil
society through a well-crafted bill of rights or even the adoption of
parliamentarism or federalism (see Chapter 4). Similarly, some
strategies of economic modernization are likely to be more supportive than others, such as law-based schemes of open regionalism,

deregulation, and some forms of privatization. Yet there is no single or guaranteed prescription applicable to all cases, nor should the health of civil society be the only point for consideration when choosing between these alternatives. Equally, there is no single way in which leaders of an incipient civil society will respond to the internal contradictions and external constraints they face. The range of alternatives compatible with survival and eventual growth is sure to be limited and inhibiting. Strong civil societies may be erected over the longer term, but not necessarily under conditions of their own choosing. In short, to appropriate Gellner's language for a purpose he did not intend, the conditions for a realistic civil society may not permit the realization of the civil society ideal.

Constitutional government based on universal suffrage would normally imply that those who wish to realize an ideal of public conduct should promote their cause through a political party, or at least via the electoral process. However, the norms of 'dual autonomy' and 'non-usurpation' would exclude from civil society political organizations that compete for public office. In many neo-democracies, the most effective vote-winning organizations often lack a tradition of commitment to 'civility', and/or permit little 'deliberation' over their internal affairs. There is therefore, in general, no compelling reason to expect an 'elective affinity' between a vigorous civil society and electorally successful political parties. Certainly there are some cases where the emergence of a more broadly based civil society is followed by the establishment of democratic political parties which proceed to legislate in accordance with a civil society ideal. However, two other models are equally plausible, namely (i) an antagonism between the architects of civil society and successful party leaders; or (ii) a compartmentalization of the two spheres.

Contemporary Mexico provides some illustrations of both possibilities. Following the revolution, key components of the old structure of associative life were weakened or disrupted. For example, the Catholic Church, with all its extended network of civil associations (educational, charitable, and representational) was subjected to a fierce anti-clerical onslaught. The system of private property rights that had been consolidated before 1910 was subjected to drastic *de facto* modifications during the violent phase of the revolution, followed by *de jure* alterations thereafter. Schools and universities were redesigned in accordance with the emergence of the post-conflict political settlement. This all took place in a context of social struggle, and not just by governmental *diktat*. Thus, new post-revolutionary forms of civic association were developed, under official sponsorship, to displace—or at least rebalance—

many pre-revolutionary expressions of 'civil society'. These new organizations—*ejidos, sindicatos*, business associations—were loosely 'corporatist' in structure. That is to say, they were granted sectoral monopolies in representation by the dominant party which, from 1928 to 1997, held a virtually exclusive control over official positions at the federal level of government.

In reality the verticalism and statism of these arrangements varied greatly from sector to sector, and over time. In the main cities, the business community and the educated classes had enjoyed a large margin of associative freedom from very early days. In some elite circles pre-revolutionary structures and networks of social organization remained intact throughout the entire period from 1910. But for large sectors of the population, especially those rural and urban workers most dependent upon the protection and favours distributed by the ruling party, the margins of permitted autonomous self-organization were, until the past decade or so, much more constrained. In the least favoured locations, such as *ejidatarios* on unirrigated land, urban marginals, and the sites licensed by street sellers, few voluntary associations could survive long without striking a deal with a powerful *patrón* or protector in the upper spheres of the power structure. This is not to deny the persistence (in many indigenous communities) or emergence (among urban squatter groups) of unauthorized forms of association, but only to stress that for security and survival reasons these soon relinquished any illusions of independence and self-governance. Until the early 1980s, therefore, much of Mexican 'civil society' was differentially subordinated to, and limited by, a remarkably cohesive post-revolutionary state bureaucracy.

The past decade or more has witnessed a cascade of changes in Mexico, which in principle open the way to a freer and more diversified system of associative life. Economic liberalization, privatization, political pluralization, and perhaps even democratization exemplify these developments. The important point for our purposes is to note that, in an unequal, heterogeneous and segmented society, the lifting of restraints on independent voluntary association will result in highly uneven (and potentially conflictual) forms of social organization that are equivocal in their attitudes to electoral politics and the emerging democratic political system.

A recent collaborative study of civil society in democratizing Mexico examined five case studies: coffee growers; community activists in a small provincial town; conservative elites in Mexico's second largest city; citizen consultations in the capital city; and a 'clean vote' movement. These were all evaluated and compared as part of a twenty-two-nation comparative project. The study generated two conclusions of particular relevance to our concerns. First

Contrary to the widespread assumption that civil society is a homogeneous cluster of social actors, it turns out to consist of a complex and contradictory range of actors that are heterogeneous not only in the political but also in the social and cultural realms; moreover they move and interact in a diversity of arenas, and the material and symbolic interests that they express cannot be reduced to a single interpretative schema.

Second, 'There are three essential governance functions of Mexican civil society . . . to stabilize the rule of law . . . to expand the public space for autonomous communication . . . and to promote a culture of tolerance . . . Mexican civil society is still very weak, and has not yet achieved an irreversible advance in any of these three areas.'[20]

An additional example of a newly autonomous and broad-based civil society in Mexico would be the *Barzonista* debtors movement.[21] This recent, vigorous, and independent form of self-organization brought into the political community large sectors of society that had been voiceless or dependent until the advent of democracy. The emergence of a strong associative network structured in protest at the inequities of a top–down system of credit distribution, created tensions with some already well-structured sectors of civil society—the Bankers Association (ABM) was particularly affected—and with the major political parties. Such tensions are not necessarily insurmountable and can be fed into the democratic system so as to reinforce it. Yet, as with Olvera's five cases, there is no automatic congruence between the emergence of this type of 'civil society' and the consolidation of a democratic institutionality.

The *Barzonistas* apart, the more autonomous and diversified system of associative life now emerging in contemporary Mexico includes many other innovations. Some of these are favourable to liberal democracy, such as a more professionally independent and assertive legal profession and a less corrupt community of journalists. Others are quite clearly 'interstitial' in the sense discussed

[20] Tr. from Alberto J. Olvera, 'Sociedad Civil, Esfera Pública y Gobernabilidad', paper delivered to the Latin American Studies Association, Washington, DC, Sept. 2001, based on the Mexican component of a Ford Foundation-funded project carried out by IDS, Sussex University.

[21] According to Gabriel Torres, 'by cutting across the corporatist divisions of Mexican society, *El Barzón* has also redefined the relationship between civil society and the government'. The El Barzón Debtors' Movement in Wayne Cornelius, Todd A Eisenstadt, and Jane Hindley (eds.), *Subnational Politics and Democratization in Mexico* (San Diego: Center for US–Mexican Studies, University of California, 1999), 149.

here, such as ex-policemen purged for corruption who now enjoy full rights of association and political representation, not to mention those wealth-holders who benefited from illicit accumulation and rent-seeking in the past.

The experiences of contemporary Mexico provide some illustrative confirmation of the general argument of this chapter, namely that when democratic political rights are abruptly extended across a previously non-democratic social territory, the consequential flowering of civil society will include a diversity of species. These will consist of weeds and thorns as well as the well-watered gardens and manicured lawns envisaged by much of the 'civil society' literature.

Theories of civil society may provide a convenient framework for summarizing the diverse societal factors that can support or obstruct processes of democratization, but both at the level of theory and in considering the experience of most new democracies, their explanatory power is limited. Those searching for predictive causal theories will not find much to work with here. However, this framework can provide illumination for those of a more interpretavist outlook. A stipulative definition can sharpen the focus on key analytical issues, such as the origin, scope, and limitations of 'civility' in democracy-building. Also, the civil society perspective can direct attention to areas of comparative empirical research that have much bearing on social receptivity to democratic institutions and the formal rules of the game. Such research is likely to highlight the complexity and open-endedness of democratization. As the next chapter will show, it is one thing to design good democratic institutions, quite another to educate or persuade citizens to live by democratic precepts.

On Accountability and Institutional Design

> The idea of just designing a constitution and then putting it into practice . . . treats the whole affair as an engineering problem . . . (and so) is radically shallow.
>
> (Hegel)

This chapter considers the theory and practices of 'accountability' that are associated with liberal constitutionalism, democracy, and especially with contemporary democratizations. This focus of interest directs attention to 'horizontal' and 'downward' forms of accountability, as opposed to accountability upwards (towards superiors). Constitution writing, and institutional design for new democracies, is a vast and growing field of enquiry that encompasses many key areas of political science and comparative politics. A single chapter cannot attempt to do justice to such rich scholarship and such diverse experience. Instead it concentrates on some core theoretical issues arising from the approach to democracy, democratization, and citizenship outlined in previous chapters. Once again it adopts a broad temporal and spatial perspective, with the result that a plurality of alternative approaches and possibilities are highlighted, and processes of accountability-building are presented as open-ended. This is somewhat in contrast to the more typical assumption that, if correctly written, a 'foundational' constitution should essentially settle most of the big questions in this area. This chapter argues that in fact it is possible to have both 'too much' accountability and also the 'wrong sort'. Given that the accountability experiences of new democracies are extremely diverse, and often quite unstable, criteria are required to select empirical evidence bearing on the overall argument. Bicameralism and impeachment have been selected for particular attention, both because of their theoretical significance and because they are relatively tractable, but understudied in comparative politics. Neither are easy to accommodate within an overly scientistic approach to institutional design. Both demonstrate the extent to which really existing processes of democratization escape the narrow constraints of political explanations that rely on supposedly objective 'incentive structures' to determine outcomes.

History and Theory of Accountability

At the most general level of social theory, the very concept of an 'office-holder' presumes some form of accountability to some external authority or officialdom. If there is no such accountability then the post in question is a private appointment, a personal property, or a sinecure, not a public office. In theory officeholding could just involve accountability to one personal superior (with otherwise unlimited discretion), or at the other extreme one might envisage accountability solely to impersonal rules. But experience teaches that neither the sultanistic nor the Prussian extremes of accountability can be sustained in this pure form in any large-scale organization (office-holders need to demarcate horizontal and vertical boundaries which then become routinized as rules; while even the most rule-bound of functionaries require some discretion protected by their superiors). In practice all modern systems of accountability are therefore hybrids containing some potentially unstable combination of both elements. On this basis, the concept of accountability assumes some kind of public/private divide, some specialization of public functions, and some form of hierarchy with associated levels of responsibility and monitoring. These are all indispensable features of the modern state, but they are not social givens. They have to be constructed, and their emergence is historically very connected to processes of state formation. As already argued, most state formation has preceded democratization, and it is self-evidently possible to develop highly sophisticated forms of office-holding, and indeed of public accountability, that are not democratic. It is also not only possible but almost inevitable in large-scale societies that prevailing theories of accountability and public responsibility should represent idealized accounts of how such relationships ought to be conducted, accounts that may well provide some powerful guiding principles, but that are almost impossible to realize in full, in the daily practices of most office-holders. In fact such principles are always injunctions (i.e. part exhortations, part descriptions), and historically there are many examples when they are straightforwardly unenforceable.

For example, under the doctrine of the Divine Right of Kings, it was held that the sovereign was accountable only before God for his actions as ruler. This was a striking affirmation of upward accountability, and it was far from meaningless in a society where both the rulers and the ruled were subject to strong monotheistic indoctrination. But in political terms its main purpose was to free the monarch from more earthly sources of restraint.[1] At a more this-worldly level, the Viceroy of Peru was accountable to the Spanish Crown, but in most normal respects this precept was also practically unenforceable, given the time and distance involved in reporting on and supervising such a relationship in the age of sail. Given the impracticality of detailed monitoring from above in such cases, the main available forms of accountability were pre-selection, mandating, and the rendering of accounts on termination of appointment (judicial review, in the case of the Virrey del Perú). Since the average tenure for the first ninety-two viceroys of the Indies was six to seven years, in between these benchmarks there was only the limited accountability provided by the need to file reports for the distant Council of Indies, and to guard against the jealousy of such local rivals as the church and judicial authorities, who might record criticism through independent channels of communication with Spain. Similar processes of upward accountability can be traced within the Roman legions, the Catholic hierarchy, the Ottoman Empire, and the other European empires which rivalled that of Spain.

---

[1] The English Magna Carta of 1215 provides a celebrated example of medieval political accountability and institutionalized restraint on monarchical power. Although much mythologized, it deserves its reputation, not least because of the precedents for parliamentarianism that is established. In historical terms King John's principal concerns were to reassure the church, the barons, and the towns-folk that royal officials would no longer conduct themselves like 'stationary bandits'. Thus clause 38 pledged that 'no bailiff shall in future put anyone to trial upon his own bare word, without reliable witnesses produced for the purpose'; clause 39 provided that no free man would be imprisoned, outlawed, or exiled without lawful judgment; and clause 40 pledged impartial justice for all. But from the standpoint of executive accountability it was clause 61 that converted these protestations of good intention into something more pregnant with long-term significance. It provided an enforcement mechanism, whereby the King authorized an assembly of barons to secure amends from the royal estate for any transgressions denounced but not corrected within forty days. The solemn pledging to this written principle of accountability—subsequently reiterated by later rulers—was far more important than the transient and largely hypothetical specifics of institutional design provided by the charter. Discourse matters in politics as well as power. In the beginning was the word.

With democracy, issues of accountability became more central, and public officialdom became more explicitly answerable both horizontally (between similar levels of hierarchy with the government) and downwards (towards the citizenry). This was already apparent in classical Athens, where the direct democracy of the citizen assembly demanded its say. About 20,000 adult males over 30 enjoyed these full citizenship rights, and each year they elected about 1,200 magistrates, who were each required to submit themselves to public scrutiny before taking office, and to render accounts (*euthynai*) on leaving it. A much smaller group of active political leaders competed for higher office and delivered more frequent and direct accounts of themselves and their policies to the assembled citizenry. Here too there was no doubt a considerable gap between the principles of accountability on which the system was supposed to rest and the actual practices of account rendering (and score settling) that went on behind the scenes. But for our purposes the important point was the adoption of the principle that the citizen assembly could exercise real power from below (even to the point of ostracism).

Political accountability in its modern form is a relatively recent innovation building on these rather approximate foundations. It is built into the notion of representative government that the representatives must in some way render account to those on whose behalf they claim to act. First, in the course of election, they are expected to establish both that they have the requisite formal qualifications (age, nationality, etc.) and that they stand for some version of the public good which they are required to articulate. Second, as office-holders they are expected to make themselves available to public scrutiny concerning the discharge of their duties, and act in accordance with the rules or conventions attaching to their office (e.g. to attend parliament, to uphold its law, to relinquish office voluntarily on completion of the set term, etc.). Competition for popular support between rival candidates for public office usually imposes a certain degree of discipline in attending to such expectations. Third, if they seek re-election they are expected to provide an explanation for their records of public office, and if they are defeated or stand down they have to answer any retrospective charges of abuse of office. Here too the expectations of the voters acquire some edge due to the presumed existence of continuing competition for office, usually reinforced by some ultimate legal sanctions. All these public expectations are inherent in the conventions of representative government that accompany every contemporary democratization. But, once again, they are still *injunctions* concerning political accountability (mixtures of exhortation and description). Democratic theory entitles the citizens of new democracies to hold such expectations about their representatives, but experience cautions them not to expect too much.

These principles of democratic theory are so well known that it seems tedious to restate them yet again. But on inspection it can be seen that they are quite complex and precise, and that they are likely to seem far from self-evident (let alone rational) to the mass of the population in societies where politics has not hitherto been conducted on this basis. In fact the principles involved are more complex and extensive than has yet been indicated, since so far the discussion has only considered the accountability expected of individual legislators. In practice, as already noted in relation to classical Athens, a much higher degree of public scrutiny may be expected from the holders of key executive offices. Moreover, representative government normally involves a range of collective actors and institutional authorities that can also be held to account by the citizenry: political parties, for example, or ministries, or courts of justice. The simplified model of the individual representative held personally accountable for his actions requires considerable elaboration if it is to be extended to the behaviour of such impersonal corporate entities. Most abstractly, but also most profoundly from the standpoint of democratic theory, all these separate strands of accountability are bound together by the far more intangible notion that all those who govern are ultimately answerable to the governed as a whole. This semi-mystical theory of the 'sovereignty of the people' in a democratic system is far too imprecise to be captured by any 'principal–agent' modelling of political behaviour. But, without the mystique of popular sovereignty, democracy, and democratization both dissolve away into a succession of instrumental transactions lacking any necessary connection or moral claim to allegiance.

Given the approach to democracy and democratization developed in Chapter 1, democratic accountability should be understood as a social construction that combines empirical and normative components, and that needs to be attached to the traditions and understandings of each political community.[2] Depending on time and

---

[2] 'The ideal of just designing a constitution and then putting it into practice is an Enlightenment idea. It treats the whole affair as an engineering problem, an external matter of means and design. But a constitution requires certain conditions in men's identity, how they understand self; and hence this Enlightenment idea is radically shallow.' Preface to Hegel's *Philosophy of Right*, tr. T. M. Knox (Oxford: OUP, 1942), 11. 'This is why one cannot just implant a good constitution anywhere,

place, normative expectations concerning the accountability of rulers can vary widely. Saudi and Swedish attitudes provide one contemporary contrast. Even between liberal democracies there can be substantial variation, perhaps reflecting historical differences, but also expressing the fact that popular sovereignty is only one among a set of overlapping and partially competing democratic desiderata. The protection of minority rights and individual liberties is obviously another, as is the preservation of social order.

Clearly, if the protection of civil, political, and economic liberties is considered a cornerstone of institutional design in liberal democracies, then the promotion of accountability will need to be harmonized with the protection of liberty. But both theory and experience indicate the scope for disharmony here. (Slaveowners were often most assiduous in enlisting public authority to hold their legal rights to detailed account; for his part Hayek always insisted that the constitution of liberty required the sheltering of property rights from intrusive accountability to the will of a fickle electorate.) Liberty, security, popular sovereignty, equality, and fraternity are all potentially competitive normative objectives in a democracy. But whereas all these can be considered plausible *ends* of institutional design, accountability is really only a *means*.

If accountability is viewed as a means to an end, rather than an end in itself, then it is clearly possible to have *too much* accountability, or the *wrong kind*. There are, after all, respectable theoretical arguments for the merits of a certain degree of laxity in the enforcement of sanctions (e.g. the case for 'speed money' or petty corruption to circumvent excessive state regulation of the economy). There could even be a public interest defence for certain kinds of impunity. (It can be heard on the right, in favour of impunity for Pinochet; and on the left, in favour of impunity for Castro; and on the centre in favour of impunity for Salinas and Menem.) In any case, as already mentioned, accountability can operate at various levels. *Upward* accountability can be contrasted to the *horizontal* and *downward* varieties. Thus under authoritarian rule the top political leadership may have been insulated form public accountability for decisions taken with respect to human rights, or the allocation of government resources—but the police and the tax authorities could be held strictly accountable upward to their superiors for the discharge of their duties. Inversely, under democracy,

as Napoleon discovered in Spain' (ibid., para. 274 additon). Compare ch. 1 of John Stuart Mill, *Considerations on Representative Government* (London: Everyman's Library, 1910; 1st publ. 1861).

rulers may be accountable *downward* to their electors, but the institutions below them may be less answerable to above. A classical feature of democracy is said to be the mutual controls exercised by divided institutions—sometimes referred to as 'horizontal' accountability. But accountability can sometimes be too fragmented between competing jurisdictions; in other cases, too aggregate to allow the necessary fine distinctions between different types of responsibility. There is also scope for conflicts of accountability (e.g. accountability to the electorate versus accountability to the courts). On top of this, accountability to persons can conflict with accountability to rules.[3]

In general it is necessary to distinguish between different institutional modalities of accountability—through legal process, through internal administrative investigation and audit, through the interplay of plural institutions (which may or may not be horizontal in character), through electoral sanction, through the supervision of an independent mass media, through international scrutiny, through the monitoring activities of policy networks, through the activities of NGOs, and through feedback from liberalized markets. Each of these modalities has its own logic and may require its own particular variety of institutional design.

Thus, if the courts are expected to enforce some forms of public accountability the nature of the offences will have to be precisely specified, and the required standards of proof will be exacting. This mode of accountability will only be effective if the activities subject to control are narrowly defined, and even then very protracted litigation must be expected. (Obviously the courts themselves must also be efficient and trustworthy, a tall order in many new democracies.) An alternative procedure is to rely on a Controlaría, or equivalent specialized auditing agency. Here too the matters covered will be narrow and technical although it may be possible for fairly rapid and publicly trustworthy judgements to be delivered. By contrast, where elected officials enjoy legal immunity for acts carried out during the discharge of their duties, the main mechanism of enforcement may be a congressional inquiry, backed by the sanction of a possible vote to lift immunity. But this mechanism

---

[3] Such complexities are more fully elaborated by Guillermo O'Donnell both in Andreas Schedler (ed.), *The Self-Restraining State: Power and Accountability in New Democracies* (Boulder, Colo.: Lynne Rienner, 1999), and in Scott Mainwaring and Christopher Welna (eds.), *Democratic Accountability in Latin America* (Oxford: Oxford University Press, 2002). Both volumes contain rich theoretical and comparative support for the points sketched here.

turns enforcement into a political process, subject to the imprecision and partisanship characteristic of such votes. Then there is the broader form of electoral accountability arising from the possibility that incumbent politicians may be voted out of office as a sanction for misconduct. However, this mechanism is very imprecise, since not all wrongdoers will present themselves for re-election, and those who do will try to run on party tickets that shift the issue away from the matters on which they are accused.[4] Electors may either support or reject such candidates on grounds quite other from those required by the logic of accountability. Indeed, charges of misconduct during election campaigns are rarely evaluated on their substantive merits. Similar imprecisions arise then whether the press or the markets hold public officials to account for alleged misconduct.

As this brief listing of possibilities indicates, there are various different modalities of accountability in a liberal democratic system, and each has its own specific logic and limitations. An overall system of accountability will probably require a combination of overlapping modalities, but if so a key problem of institutional design may concern coordination between these alternatives, or at least the avoidance of contradiction between them.

So, on the one hand, the current enthusiasm for strengthened mechanisms of accountability in public affairs arises from a long history of abuses, and is broadly justified on instrumental grounds. On the other side, accountability is itself subject to manipulation and misappropriation. On its own it provides no easy or straightforward solutions to complex public policy dilemmas. Indeed, the concept of accountability requires more thought than it has tended to receive in recent policy debates. For example, 'the conceptual scheme' that politicians use when interpreting responsibility processes makes them misconstrue what actually goes on in them. 'The conceptual scheme is fed by institutions that tell them that governing is forward-looking, and that being held responsible for mistakes is an unwelcome interruption of the main business of governing that should be overcome as quickly and simply as possible. The way to do this is to punish a wrongdoer and then go on with business as usual. But these minimizing accounting processes miss entirely the positive functions of such processes: they provide opportunities for selective steering

---

[4] In V. O. Key's classic formulation: 'The vocabulary of the voice of the people consists mainly of the words "yes" and "no".' *Politics, Parties and Pressure Groups* (Ithaca, NY: Cornell University Press, 1964), 544. For a recent elaboration on this insight see Bernard Manin, Adam Przeworski, and Susan Stokes, *Democracy, Accountability, and Representation* (New York: Cambridge University Press, 1999).

and value discovery'.[5] Mechanistic strategies of accountability that overlook this discursive requirement can produce unintended or undesired effects that are subsequently difficult to correct. Too much enthusiasm for 'accountability' as an orthodoxy might even lead to the opposite of what is expected: an upsurge in demands for strong leadership and unfettered authority, to overcome the defects of institutional pettifogging and enforcement gridlock. But, in the new democracies of the post-cold war era, institutional designs intended to strengthen forms of public accountability have seldom been tempered by doubt about such theoretical issues.

Institutional Designs

'Design' refers to the process of developing plans, as opposed to executing them. A design may take the form of a mental experiment, or a model. It involves planning to produce a coherent and effective whole out of a succession of inter-related parts, which should include consideration of the effect of the whole on those who become involved with it. Engineering design may simply require a record of the appropriate concepts and experiences, whereas in fine art design involves an imaginative process of creation, and in architectural design both may be combined. Although it is fashionable to view institutional design as similar to engineering, the parallel with architecture is closer. However, in contrast to all physical instances of design, social construction depends on persuading the users of the design to cooperate. The idea that human subjects will simply conform to a structure of incentives bestowed on them by designers is untenable. Good institutional designs must therefore be capable of adaptation and legitimation.

Evidently, the overall design of a new democratic order must involve a large range of complex choices and interlocking alternatives—far too many to be considered in a single chapter. Among the options most celebrated in the literature on institutional design there is the supposed choice between a presidential and a parliamentary system; there is centralized versus decentralized and indeed federal

---

[5] Herman van Gunsteren, 'Accountability: Governing by Looking Back', paper presented at IPSA 2000, Quebec City. He thus repudiates 'scapegoating', and argues that in the post-cold war liberal democratic era a positive approach to accountability should become 'a central element of governing in an uncertain world'. In addition to its steering function it also offers other benefits that are currently in short supply: 'context, attention, acknowledgement, stopping, and forgiving'.

systems of representation; there is majoritarian versus proportional systems of electoral representation; there are alternative party systems; and so forth. In this chapter attention will be focused on crucial aspects of the legislative/executive balance that are central to all systems of representative democracy. But other strands of the tapestry merit just as much consideration: for example, the power of the purse; the independence of the judiciary; war powers; the proclamation of states of emergency. Democratization involves the reviewing of a long list of such matters, in order to place them in a coherent system which is more clearly structured in accordance with fundamental democratic principles, including the requirements of public visibility and accountability. Viewed in this light institutional design is likely to be a long-term ongoing process, rather than a 'one shot' game. Since there were 120 competitive electoral systems in existence in 2000 (Annex, Table 2), the range of possible combinations and alternatives is obviously very large. So too is the variety of factors likely to contribute in practice to the operation of any theoretical system of incentives. For the purposes of this section it seems useful to isolate two relatively specific institutional arrangements that have a direct bearing on procedures of political accountability, and to survey comparative experiences available so far in these two areas: bicameral versus unicameral assemblies; and the impeachment of heads of state. Recent Brazilian experience is then considered as a case study. (Other related issues of accountability for economic matters will receive some consideration in the following two chapters which deal with political corruption, and with monetary authority.)

Bicameralism

The question of bicameralism places the issues of political accountability in a representative democracy within the more classical constitutionalist setting of ideas about 'checks and balances'. There is a tension here between a liberal tradition (concerned to divide power and so erect barriers against all forms of political oppression) and a democratic strain which sees the will or sovereignty of the people embodied in a single representative chamber with overriding powers. Montesquieu theorized about the separation of powers on the basis of a rather inaccurate reading of the unwritten British Constitution.[6] The founders of the US Constitution followed him in elaborating on what they acknowledged to be a sketchy theoretical

---

[6] The Anglo-Saxon tradition of hostility to single chambers probably traces back unconsciously to the English Civil War, and the discredit attaching to the unicameral 'Barebone's' parliament of 1649–53.

notion. In France itself Montesquieu was superseded by Rousseau. Consequently the single Chamber of Deputies claimed to embody the foundational authority of the French Revolution. Thus both in political theory and in the paradigmatic practices of the earliest modern democracies two rival conceptions of representation and accountability competed for allegiance, expressed in two inherently opposed institutional alternatives: one legislative chamber or two?

The theoretical issues at stake were clearly specified in *Federalist Papers*. Hamilton was typically vehement:

In republics, persons elevated from the mass of the community, by the suffrages of their fellow-citizens, to stations of great pre-eminence and power, may find compensation for betraying their trust, which, to any but minds animated and guided by superior virtue, may appear to exceed the proportion of interest they have in the common stock, and to overbalance the obligations of duty. . . . A single assembly . . . would be inconsistent with all the principles of good government . . . the probability would be . . . by successive augmentation of its force and energy . . . we shall finally accumulate, in a single body, all the most important prerogatives sovereignty, and thus entail upon our posterity one of the most execrable forms of government that human infatuation ever contrived. (Paper 22, published in the *New York Packet*, 14 Dec. 1787)

In contrast Paper 62 extolled the virtues of bicameralism in somewhat more restrained language (perhaps this was penned by Madison): 'a senate, as a second branch of the legislative assembly, distinct from, and dividing power with a first, must be in all cases a salutary check on the government. It doubles the security to the people, by requiring the concurrence of two distinct bodies in schemes of usurpation or perfidy' (written for the *Independent Journal*). Against such arguments the anti-federalists objected that this doctrine of checks and balances went beyond the separation of powers (between the executive, the legislative, and the judiciary) and introduced an unduly complicated structure of legislative representation that made it difficult for the citizens to determine the location of responsibility for acts of government. They preferred a more truly *representative* system of government (i.e. one that more closely reproduced in miniature the characteristics of the citizens on whose behalf it claimed to rule). They thought that if the assembly more closely resembled the society over which it governed its members would be less likely to lose sight of the interests of the electorate. They regarded the constitution of 1787 with its bicameral structure and the indirect election of senators for extended six year terms as tending toward oligarchy.[7]

---

[7] H. J. Storing (ed.), *The Complete Anti-Federalist*, 7 vols. (Chicago: Chicago University Press, 1981).

As we can see, then, there were two sides to the debate on accountability and institutional design during the foundation of the United States of America. Similarly in France after 1789, in Spain after 1812, and in the new republics of South America from the 1820s onwards, rival doctrines clashed, and intermingled with competing interests. Of course the federalists prevailed in the USA, and their enduring success has shaped American thinking about such issues ever since. It has also marked the constitutional structures of many subsequently created liberal regimes, including most of the large republics of Latin America which, among other things, have embraced bicameralism (without necessarily absorbing all the assumptions about checks and balances that underlay it). By contrast, France has worked its way through five republics, two empires, an absolute monarchy, and the interlude of Vichy, sometimes upholding the supremacy of the National Assembly, at others imposing an overbearing executive, and at others experiencing stalemate as the separation of powers produces political gridlock. It might therefore be concluded that the test of experience had produced conclusive evidence in favour of the bicameral approach to representation and accountability, and against unicameralism.

However, a cross-sectional analysis of the 120 electoral democracies listed in Annex Table 2 cautions against any such conclusion. There are sixty-seven such regimes with unicameral assemblies as compared to fifty-three with bicameral legislatures. For obvious reasons, federal regimes adopt bicameral arrangements, but most new democracies are not federations, not at least in any strong sense. Among the unicameralists there are highly regarded old democracies (Costa Rica, Denmark, Norway, New Zealand) as well as influential new regimes (Greece, Hungary, Israel, Portugal). There are countries with large populations (Bangladesh, South Korea, Turkey, the Ukraine); and there are formerly bicameral democracies that have recently converted to unicameralism (Peru, Venezuela). Whatever the merits of bicameralism as an integral component of the US approach to representative government and accountability, it shows no signs of becoming a universal practice, and at the global level the debate over its benefits and scope of application remains entirely open. For example, an independent Scotland or an independent Quebec might still opt for a unicameral form of government, and an eventual European Federation might also take the same form. For all its prestige and durability, the US formula constitutes a special case rather than the correct template for all existing and prospective democracies. The insights of Hamilton and Madison have not been accepted as universally applicable or beyond question, and the arguments of the defeated anti-federalists still find contemporary resonance and appeal.

Impeachment

The second strand of institutional design considered in this chapter is the procedure for executive impeachment. Here the issue of political accountability appears in its most acute form. Again it was the US Constitution that first systemized these procedures as we now know them, adopting a formula that followed logically from the commitment to bicameralism. As Hamilton expounded in Federalist Paper 65 (the *New York Packet*, 7 Mar. 1788), any trials for impeachment would deal with political offences, and could therefore be expected to agitate the passions of the whole community. Contrary to game-theoretical models of impeachment, Hamilton advocated a design in which the outcome must depend upon 'real demonstrations of innocence or guilt' rather than upon 'the comparative strength of parties'. Since it was generally accepted that the initiative of an impeachment process could only be undertaken by a legislative body, the founders proposed to capitalize on their commitment to bicameralism in the following way. The power to *initiate* impeachment proceedings could be lodged in the more directly representative lower body, the House of Representatives, which was likely to be most sensitive to public sentiment concerning any alleged political misconduct by the executive. But it would be the smaller and more independent body of the Senate, *sitting as a judicial authority*, that would be empowered to decide the case, with the requirement that two-thirds of the Senate must vote to secure an impeachment. Hamilton pointed to the doubtful precedent of the British Parliament, and to the more relevant provisions of certain state constitutions. Against the alternative proposal that the Supreme Court might be entrusted with this duty he argued (i) that it might lack the 'fortitude' of the Senate and (ii) that in any case it would fall to the courts to determine punishment in the wake of a conviction upon impeachment.

Other bicameral presidential systems have tended to follow this model. For example, the Mexican constitution of 1917 provides for the Chamber of Deputies to determine—by an absolute majority—whether a sitting president should be charged (only for treason or 'grave offices against public order', Article 108). In that event the Senate would sit as a court and if necessary determine the applicable sentences by a two-thirds majority (Articles 110 and 111). The writers of Mexico's Constitution were evidently still more doubtful than Hamilton concerning the 'fortitude' of their Supreme Court. The Brazilian Constitution of 1988 took a more extensive view of the range of possible presidential offences against constitutional order, no doubt influenced by the many abuses previously committed (Article 85). It provided that a two-thirds majority in the Chamber of Deputies could send the sitting president to trial by the Senate for any such infringements of the Constitution. But the Chamber could also, by the same majority, send him before the Federal Supreme Court for common crimes committed in the exercise of his office. In either event he would be suspended from office pending the hearing, for a maximum of 180 days. However, his mandate could not be interrupted in this way on the basis of changes related to his private actions (Article 86).

These two prominent examples illustrate the powerful influence of the US example, but also the respects in which it may be subjected to subsequent modification in accordance with the local conditions prevailing elsewhere. While it is important to scrutinize the precise rules of procedure adopted in each new democracy (noting, for example, that in unicameral systems such as that of Costa Rica the courts are likely to acquire a larger role in counteracting political improprieties of the executive), comparative experience indicates a substantial disjuncture between the formal principles set out in each constitutional document and the actual processes at work during most impeachment crises. Since such crises have appeared recurrently in a succession of recent new democracies, there follows a brief consideration of how they really operate.

Impeachment is a procedure found in presidential regimes, where the directly elected executive serves for a fixed term unless legally incapacitated. There are crises of executive accountability in parliamentary regimes, and they too may involve prosecution for abuse of office, so what we have to say here is not irrelevant to new democracies of that type. But in a parliamentary system the administration governs only so long as it can assemble a majority in the legislature (or until some alternative emerges that commands such a majority). So for simplicity we shall confine the discussion to *presidential* impeachments in new democracies. It should also be noted that in some presidential systems (e.g. in both Mexico and Costa Rica) other members of the executive—cabinet ministers, state governors, etc.—may also be held to legal account for abuse of office. Moreover, presidents may find themselves subject to retrospective political justice after leaving office (such was the case of ex-President Roh Tae Woo of South Korea, sentenced in 1996 to twenty-two and a half years in prison and a fine of $350 million, after completing his term as the country's first democratically elected president in 1992). But this discussion is limited to core cases involving the actual or attempted impeachment of sitting presidents.

Between 1990 and 2001 six elected presidents were impeached, two were threatened with impeachment, and two attempted unconstitutional seizures of power in order to block congress from initiating such procedures. This list includes Alberto Fujimori of Peru who closed a hostile bicameral Congress in 1992, rewrote the Constitution but was then declared unfit to govern by the successor (unicameral) Congress after conducting a fraudulent re-election eight years later. The other attempted closure of Congress, in Guatemala in 1993, was unsuccessful. Eight of these ten political impeachment crises took place in Latin America (plus Indonesia and the Philippines in 2001), but of course President Clinton also had to deal with an impeachment threat (concerning an offence that was private rather than political). Although four of the six Latin American democracies had bicameral systems of representation, in none of these crises was it possible fully to establish Hamilton's clear-cut separation between 'the comparative strength of the parties' and 'real demonstrations of innocence or guilt'. Most of these processes were messy, often involving extra-constitutional soundings about the loyalty of the military, the potential threat to public order, and the scope for limiting judicial action so that only some of the wrongdoing would be subject to the full glare of public scrutiny. Rather than reaffirming the integrity of the constitutional order, many of these processes ended by further undermining public confidence in the impartiality of fundamental democratic institutions. Thus, for example, the 1993 impeachment of President Peréz contributed to the erosion of trust in Venezuela's political system that culminated in the election of a former coup leader as a president with a mandate to rewrite the entire Constitution. Under the 1999 rules it is unlikely that Venezuela's current chief executive will be impeached, because the requisite separation of powers has been eroded. Similarly, in 1997 when the recently elected President Bucaram was dismissed from office by the unicameral Ecuadorean Congress (on the grounds of 'insanity', which is not an impeachable offence), the consequence was not to clear the way for a more reliable system of executive accountability. Instead the way was opened to further institutional instabilities, including the forced resignation in 2000 of President Mahaud, when the military withdrew their support from him. A figleaf of constitutional propriety was subsequently re-established when his vice-president took over. In Paraguay in 1999 the opening of congressional impeachment proceedings against President Cubas Grau was followed a month later by the assassination of his vice-president (and therefore prospective successor). The president then fled before impeachment proceedings could be completed, and he was succeeded in office by the head of the legislative assembly that had brought the original charges against him. In short, impeachment crises in new democracies uncover an extremely wide gap between constitutional theory and political practice. However, not all analysts would accept the politics of Ecuador and Paraguay as representative processes of executive accountability in new democracies as a whole. In accord with the principles of case selection that will be set forth more fully in Chapter 8 of this volume, we might consider more representative the apparently 'deviant' but actually highly significant case of Brazil.

Brazilian Presidentialism

The quest for presidential accountability has been a central theme of successive regime crises in Brazil over the past half-century. In 1954 President Vargas committed suicide rather than answer his accusers. In 1961 President Quadros threatened to resign unless granted fuller powers. To his surprise his resignation was accepted and his vice-president installed in his place, but with special constraints added in an attempt to tame his radicalism. The breakdown of that artificial arrangement paved the way for the 1964 coup and twenty years of military authoritarianism. Given these antecedents it is not surprising that the framers of Brazil's 1988 Constitution devoted two carefully constructed Articles (85 and 86) to the grounds on which an incumbent chief executive may be suspended or eventually impeached, and the procedures to be observed in such cases. Within four years these articles were invoked, and the first president of Brazil to be elected by universal suffrage was constitutionally removed from office in mid-term.[8]

---

[8] Ari de Abreu Silva, 'Processos Institucionais de administração de conflitos: O impeachment presdiencial' (Rio de Janeiro, Dec. 1998), sketches an intriguing contrast between impeachment in the US system and in Brazil. He concludes with a paraphrase from Michael J. Gerhardt to the effect that the constitution may explain what is permissible, but it is the political culture which indicates what must be done (quoting *The Federal Process* (Princeton: Princeton University Press, 1996), 178).

At one level the impeachment of President Collor was a striking break with Brazil's institutional past, and a vindication of the claim that the new more impersonal and authoritative state institutions of the liberal democratic era were capable of enforcing accountability, even at the highest levels where it had never previously been applied. However, the circumstances were very unusual (Collor had very little organized support, and it was only when his brother turned against him that the incriminating evidence became available). In contrast to the other impeachment crises discussed above, the Brazilian episode was not immediately followed by a cycle of institutional delegitimation. On the contrary, there followed a rather widespread acceptance that the correct legal procedures had produced a necessary and in some ways heartening outcome that tended to strengthen the democratic order. This positive interpretation was partly attributable to the subsequent election of President Cardoso, and his early success in stabilizing the economy while governing in accordance with the new constitutional charter (which he had helped to draft). But the story of Brazilian presidentialism is not simply a narrative of errors and deviations that were ultimately corrected.

The 1988 Constitution was designed to curb the excesses of presidential supremacy associated with preceding authoritarian and military rule. Hence Article 82 limited the president and vice-president to a single four-year term of office. Moreover transitory Article 2 mandated a plebiscite in September 1993 to determine whether Brazil would remain a republic or restore a constitutional monarchy, and whether the form of government would be parliamentary or presidential. Although the bulk of the political class and the serried ranks of foreign and domestic political scientists favoured a parliamentary system, the Brazilian electorate remained strongly wedded to a presidential republic. So the opponents of authoritarian presidentialism ended up, despite their contrary intentions, with an emasculated form of democratic presidential rule. Moreover, on this basis Cardoso won the presidency, at which point—of course—it became apparent that a single four-year term was too short. Constitutional theory might dictate that any change in fundamental rules should be decided on its abstract merits, and not confused with the conjunctural interests of particular incumbent politicians, but that is not how most new democracies have in practice approached the task of amending the rules for re-election. President Cardoso in fact joined the widespread 1990s practice of promoting a re-election clause that would permit an extension of his own mandate (the distinguished roll-call of practitioners includes Presidents Chavez, Fujimori, and Menem). A substantial amount of his political capital in the first term was expended on securing a second.

It is difficult to interpret this story of Brazilian presidentialism (so far) in terms of stable impersonal incentive structures and predictable rules of the game. Clearly there has been a major improvement in executive accountability to the electorate, but attitudes towards presidential authority and discretionality remain highly distinctive and coloured by national traditions and understandings. The Brazilian Constitution, to quote Hegel, 'requires certain conditions in men's identity, how they understand self', and Brazilian conditions cannot be deduced from first principles without regard to history and context. Institutional designs which assume otherwise are unlikely to succeed.

The Experiences of New Democracies

On a broader canvas, at least in Latin America, the norm continues to be that discredited presidents are hard to remove solely by constitutional means.[9] Recent developments in Indonesia and the Philippines indicate that this is not a purely regional phenomenon. Even when grounds for legal action come to light after an outgoing president has left office, it is widely alleged that neither judicial nor political redress is likely to be sought for fear of the intra-elite conflicts such procedural accountability could precipitate.[10]

Comparative experience shows that during transitions to democracy questions of political accountability often present themselves in a highly conjunctural form. There may well be strong demands

---

[9] In 1985 President Siles of Bolivia stepped down a year early because he could not handle a hyper-inflationary crisis; in 1989 President Alfonsín stood down six months ahead of time; and in Ecuador President Mahaud was recently displaced by his vice-president despite his protests. In December 2001 President de la Rua was forced out of office by popular protests when his economic policy collapsed. None of these changes were achieved by the prescribed constitutional mechanisms alone. The impeachment of Venezuelan President Pérez was constitutional, but followed a failed coup.

[10] No Mexican president since Carranza has been held to account for any wrongdoing during his incumbency, although some have been encouraged to live abroad for a while, in disgrace. This is the worst sanction so far meted out to ex-President Salinas, for example although his brother has been jailed. In the Mexican tradition such figures are referred to as 'intocables' and the long-term ruling party cultivated an informal convention of impunity. But it is important to note that Articles 108–14 of the 1917 Constitution have always contained substantial formal protections for incumbents. Mexico has no vice-president who might rally opponents of the incumbent.

for 'truth and justice' commissions to inquire into the abuses committed by outgoing authoritarian rulers, and perhaps to impose punishments on them. On the other hand, there may be equally pressing arguments of expediency for turning a blind eye on the past undemocratic practices of those whose defection from the old order smoothes the way to a peaceful transition. It may be considered necessary—even appropriate—to allow them to keep the privileges (including advantageous political resources) that they had accumulated through collaboration with the authoritarian regime. Even those most clearly committed to opposition to the old regime may well include many with political pasts that would not stand up to public scrutiny. None of this necessarily prevents agreement in the establishment of a new democratic order under which henceforth office-holders will be reliably held accountable for their actions, and popular sovereignty will be enthroned. But there is clearly a disjuncture between the tactical considerations that are bound to arise in the course of transitional bargaining over the new 'rules of the game', and the foundational principles of public accountability that are presumed in democratic theory, and that are integral to the long-term legitimacy and indeed mystique of regimes of this type. Not surprisingly then, the experience of many new democracies suggests that a single structure of incentives can produce widely varied patterns of actual behaviour, depending on such considerations as the *external sources* of inspiration for the new model (e.g. decolonization, reunification, advisory missions); and the *internal structures* available (professional bodies, legal traditions, state institutions); and the *type* of transition involved (e.g. pact versus rupture).

A few summary illustrations may suffice to indicate the importance of such contextual factors in shaping the procedures of accountability and their actual implementation in different new democracies. For the most part the decolonization of British imperial territories involved some degree of attempted transfer of what was known as the 'Westminster system' of representative government. There were many variations within this broad tendency, and the resulting regimes took a wide variety of forms, many of them not in the least democratic. Nevertheless, over a quarter of the 120 'electoral democracies' listed by Freedom House in 2000 originated in this way (Annex Table 2). They therefore acquired traditions and assumptions about political accountability that were peculiar to the British context, and that filtered abstract reasoning about incentive structure through highly specific institutional practices (the common-law tradition, constituency representation, etc.). Not all of these inheritances were positive for democratic accountability (often the colonial regimes left highly repressive anti-subversion laws available to their successors), and by no means all of them proved acceptable to post-independence governments (e.g. the wish of Anglophone Caribbean democracies to reinstate the death penalty and free themselves from legal supervision by the Privy Council in London). The critical point is that this whole ensemble of external influences on accountability was specific to British decolonization. The French legacy in Mauritius, or the Dutch in Indonesia, is quite different. The argument can be generalized from decolonization to a wider variety of external influences on new democracies, currently including the widespread dissemination of institutional design prescriptions favoured by the American political science profession. The take-up of such influences is also critically dependent on the existence of specific *internal* institutions and interest groups. In post-communist countries the systems of promotion and protection characteristic of the old *nomenklatura* may go far to explain how theoretical 'incentive structures' actually work when transplanted to those settings. In Latin America strong corporate interests and closed legal professions may exercise a similarly distorting effect on abstractly conceived rules of institutional design.

In most new democracies an internationally approved drive for 'good governance' has reinforced whatever domestic demands may exist for strengthened public accountability. This drive has been gathering momentum for a decade or more, and would seem to derive from a variety of partially overlapping sources. Democratization necessarily requires an honest electoral process and a plurality of centres of power. Some forms of accountability follow more or less inevitably from this requirement, and others are natural accompaniments. Economic liberalization also requires various kinds of public authority that must be answerable to rival claimants, and therefore capable of upholding neutral procedures (e.g. with regard to taxation, the regulation of privatized monopolies, the stability and openness of the financial system). Outward-looking policies and regional integration initiatives inject external standards of evaluation into area of public policy that were hitherto a sheltered domestic reserve. Capping such essentially pragmatic considerations is a more essential question of principle. If these new democratic regimes and these liberalized economic and foreign policies are to endure they will need to establish firm bases of social support. One could even say they will need to be 'legitimized'. In order for enfranchised citizens and sovereign consumers to provide such support on a consistent basis, they are likely to need assurance that the major beneficiaries of a liberalized order—the party politicians, the private entrepreneurs, the promoters of internationalization—are not merely pursuing their own vested interests. All of these beneficiary groups claim to be promoting policies that serve the public good, but none of them have impregnable reputations for disinterested public service. That is why liberal democratic theory requires accountable institutions, and why the exercise of citizenship involves vigilance, and the monitoring of public authority.

That said, the drive for accountability is also quite problematic. 'Accountability' in the abstract may seem an unobjectionable goal. But as already mentioned, 'upward' forms of legal accountability have existed—at least on paper—long before representative democracy, or even constitutionalism, were in vogue. In most democratizations the real issue is not so much how to introduce public accountability where it had never previously been known, but rather how to redesign, focus, and render effective practices that had previously been subject to manipulation and abuse, and that had therefore under authoritarian rule come to be viewed with cynicism.

In any case more effective machinery of accountability takes time to assemble, and it is unlikely to work well in times of emergency. Thus, in some major new democracies, such as Argentina, Turkey, and Venezuela, there are currently grounds for fearing that economic emergency may throw the whole process into reverse.

In the post-communist states of Eastern Europe the drive for enhanced accountability has come as much from Brussels and Strasbourg as from demands from within. Similarly, the new democracies of East Asia have been subject to strong external demands for improved economic accountability (primarily to the international financial institutions in Washington, DC), demands that have often been poorly coordinated with domestic campaigns for greater political accountability to the newly enfranchised electorates of such countries as the Philippines, South Korea, and Thailand. Therefore when surveying the experience of accountability in new democracies (as opposed to the preoccupations of most theorizing about accountability) it may be important to distinguish between the demands arising from *within* and those from *without*.

From Within

In most new democracies the mainspring of domestic support for enhanced accountability has been a reaction against the arbitrary and unsuccessful policy experiments of the preceding authoritarian period. In the more liberal authoritarian regimes, professional associations (lawyers, journalists, academics), some business interests (especially the more technically advanced, and those geared to international markets), and a broader array of loosely 'middle class' groupings may have long expressed particular interests in improvements in accountability. In the more repressive conditions typical of most communist states, and some anti-communist regimes as well, there may have been less scope for the emergence of such 'civil society' type pressures from professional groupings. But in both cases it is important to recall that the population at large was also involved. The poor and the unorganized can appreciate it when their rights to participation and redress are extended.

However, such domestic coalitions of support tend to be very heterogeneous and unstable. While favouring more accountability than prevailed under pre-democratic conditions, that still leaves great scope for disagreement about which of the various modalities of accountability deserve priority; or about how best to bridge the gap between theory and experience in specific areas of accountability. So it would be unrealistic to assume the continuation of a strong and unified domestic demand for improved accountability, regardless of the results. Where a measure of institutional reform has delivered expected benefits, and in particular has induced the interested parties mutually to adjust their conduct in accordance with the new structure of incentives, a specific coalition can be created that may defend that reform, and indeed press ahead for others. But we have also seen a variety of reasons why the institutional reforms (however intelligent in design) may lack social legitimization. In times of authoritarian rule, broad professional associations of lawyers and journalists may defend the principles of legality, and oppose censorship and repression; but in more relaxed and liberal environment there can be no assurance that the same professional groupings will not champion variants of institutional reform that facilitate 'capture' by their colleagues, or will not resist forms of accountability that put their own prerogatives at risk. The inertia of old institutional practices, and the absence of a clearly defined and self-conscious support coalition in favour of the new, can easily cloud the prospect for further advances in accountability in some major policy areas.

From Without

Self-evidently, major pressures for strengthened accountability have also derived from without. International monitoring of human rights practices may gradually help strengthen the integrity of local justice systems. Both in Europe and in Latin America, regional cooperation, convergence, and integration also expose each country to the best practices of institutional accountability achieved by its neighbours. Similar patterns are beginning to emerge in East Asia as well. A succession of international pressures, influences, and examples of this kind may all tend to upgrade the overall standards of the public accountability over time.

However, here too it is necessary to note some qualifications. First, international convergence favours higher standards of accountability in some policy areas far more than in others. Narrow special-interest versions of accountability may be privileged by international pressures, at the expense of broader and most socially embedded domestic variants. It is possible to have 'too much' externally imposed accountability as well as the 'wrong sort'. Second, transmission effects may operate in both directions. (There is, for example, a serious possibility that cumulative institutional failures in Paraguay could produce damaging consequences in the rest of Mercosur or that misgovernment in new European democracies could destabilize their relations with the enlarging emerging European Union.) Third, and most fundamentally, international liberalization and convergence is often associated with a restructuring of social and power relations in ways that may reduce or erode the efficiency of the nation-state. Yet if accountability is to be strengthened it will have to be done through the instrumentality of the nation-state. Directly international forms of accountability, bypassing the state, are unlikely to work well except in very restricted circumstances. Therefore, we have to consider the interplay between two types of external influence—those promoting accountability versus those weakening state capacity.

Conclusion

In conclusion, therefore, it is clearly possible to have both 'too little' accountability and 'too much', as well as the 'wrong sort'. If is it viewed as a means rather than as an end in itself, that may allow more scope for adjustments in keeping with local traditions and understandings. More generally, institutional design for new democracies needs to be seen as an exercise in social construction and persuasion, rather than in terms of the importation of internationally approved and standardized 'right' answers to all the problems of constitution-writing. While the rewriting of constitutional rules may be largely completed in most new democracies there remains a larger and more open ended task of democratization to be completed. Strengthening accountability needs to be understood in terms of the promotion of democratic values—as a product of resocialization as much as of institutional design. From a normative perspective procedures of accountability need to be promoted within an 'ethic of responsibility', in a context of democratic deliberation. Recent developments in Argentina, the Philipines, and elsewhere serve to demonstrate that such behaviour can in no way be taken for granted. Indeed, only about half of the democratically elected presidents of Latin America have been content merely to serve out their prescribed terms of office. Some have changed the constitution in order to secure their own re-election; some have been removed by impeachment; and some simply quit ahead of schedule in the face of popular protest. (This third category of deviation from the rules is particularly striking, since it seems to violate the basic 'political survival' postulate that drives all rational choice modelling of political behaviour.)

Democratic accountability presumes not just that there is 'only one game in town', but also that most players do not demonstrably cheat at it, and that citizens can trust their representatives for the most part to defend the rules. Otherwise, what motive short of compulsion does anyone have to obey, or to consent? Thus, democratic accountability can only develop through a protracted process of training in self-restraint. Democratization cannot be just about the interlocking of hard and narrow self-interests. It has to include a collective, expressive, and indeed symbolic dimension in order to generalize the mutual steering and monitoring behaviour required of all participants. From this perspective the main impediment to strengthened accountability may not be the difficulty of building new institutions, but that of breaking the inertia of the old ones.

The essential case for strengthened accountability is that the good use of public resources requires the establishment of effective errorcorrection and damage-limitation procedures. In theory, institutional design has always recognized this case, and on paper such procedures have always been available. So the challenge is not so much to invent totally new institutional forms, but rather to promote innovations that will (i) bridge the gap between official theory and social reality, (ii) generate intelligible rational and effective forms of accountability rather than institutional gridlock, and (iii) deliver benefits and generate support coalitions that legitimize an institutional framework often still currently lacking reliable support. This chapter has drawn attention to the gap between the theory of political accountability and the practice of politics in many new democracies, directing attention to questions of institutional design. The following chapter underscores this persisting disjuncture, approaching the gap between theory and experience from an alternative perspective, namely that of 'rent-seeking' and corruption.

....

5

....

On Political Corruption

> In republics, persons elevated from the mass of the community,
> by the suffrage of their fellow-citizens, to stations of great pre-
> eminence and power, may find compensations for betraying
> their trust, which . . . may appear to exceed the proportion of
> interest that they have in the common stock . . .
>
> (Alexander Hamilton)

Theory

'Corruption' is probably the most successful and enduring of all the
vitalist metaphors that have been applied to political life. Whereas
'the body politic' now sounds archaic, and the 'head of state' has
become no more than a figure of speech, the idea of a healthy political organism undergoing some progressive, but perhaps potentially
reversible, degeneration still retains some of the analytical appeal
that made it so influential in political theory.

Thus, the Greek ruler, Lycurgus

> took the view that every type of constitution which is simple and founded
> on a single principle is unstable, because it quickly degenerates into that
> form of corruption which is peculiar to and inherent in it. For just as rust
> eats away iron, and woodworms or ship-worms eat away timber, and these
> substances even if they escape any external damage are destroyed by the
> processes which are generated within themselves, so each constitution pos-
> sesses its own inherent and inseparable vice. Thus in kingship the inher-
> ent vice is despotism, in aristocracy it is oligarchy, and in democracy the
> brutal rule of violence.

> So Lycurgus sought to save Sparta from this 'corruption' by adopt-
> ing a mixed constitution, in which each element would be counter-
> balanced by the others.[1]

---

[1] Polybius, *The Rise of the Roman Empire*, 6 (Harmondsworth: Penguin, 1979),
310.

Machiavelli took up the theme of political corruption in his *Discourses on Livy*, adding broader elements of social and psychological explanation that expanded the range of possibilities of counteracting tendencies towards the decay of political structure. For example, he highlighted the role of secular religion in extending the life of the Roman republic. He also interpreted its eventual decline in terms of the competing effects of inordinate wealth and power, which transformed leading figures from citizens into destructive partisans. This perspective connects with a second classical theme of corruption—the diversion of personal energies from the higher goals of philosophy and the common good to the baser purposes of immediate self-interest.

These classical theories were then recycled in a more patriotic guise by the American revolutionaries. Thus, in *The Federalist Papers*, 22 (*The New York Packet*, 14 Dec. 1787). Hamilton expressed his distrust of ordinary politicians by arguing that

one of these weak sides of republics, among their numerous advantages, is that they afford too easy an inlet to foreign corruption . . . in republics, persons elevated from the mass of the community, by the suffrage of their fellow-citizens, to stations of great pre-eminence and power, may find compensations for betraying their trust, which, to any but minds animated and guided by superior virtue, may appear to exceed the proportion of interest that they have in the common stock, and to overbalance the obligations of duty. Hence it is that history furnishes us with so many mortifying examples of the prevalency of foreign corruption in republican governments.[2]

In this chapter we are mainly concerned with political corruption in newly established democracies, and in particular with the enhanced potential for monetary corruption when untried representative institutions are established in a context of acute economic inequalities. The recent wave of democratizations has been accompanied by a strong international trend in favour of economic liberalization, a trend which can be seen as the economic counterpart to the political and ideological defeat of 'really existing' socialism in the USSR. Consequently contemporary theorizing about political corruption focuses far more on the corrosive potential of unbridled money power than on the more traditional themes of constitutional

---

[2] Hamilton's theory curiously foreshadowed subsequent political experiences that proved all too personal. In 1804 Hamilton was killed in a duel occasioned by precisely such allegations which he had directed against then Vice-President Aaron Burr. Burr went on to collaborate with a secret agent of the government of Spain in a disloyal conspiracy that earned him trial for treason (although he was eventually acquitted by the Supreme Court).

decay and subversion by foreign powers. So this is where we shall start the discussion, although some of the older preoccupations of the theoretical literature will be reintroduced later on.

Since its earliest manifestations money has always been *a* source of social power, but never *the* sole source. Historically, poor monarchs could coerce moneylenders, cash-strapped landowners could mobilize their labourers or try to fall back on the self-sufficiency of their farms, and clerics could threaten retribution in the next world against those who abused their wealth in this one. During the era of state socialism private money power was subjected to unprecedented restraints in many countries, and even in those countries never touched by the direct threat of expropriation, moneyed interests were to some extent politically constrained by the fear of bolshevism. But in a post-cold war secular democratic globalist world all these constraints on the unfettered power of private wealth have been weakened or destroyed. Thus Berlusconi can first buy a media empire in Italy, and then use his wealth and power to entrench himself in the premiership from where he might rewrite the rules so that his business empire becomes unassailable. In 1992 Ross Perot was able to use his personal wealth to found a political movement capable of bypassing the century-old two party structures of the United States, and briefly catapult him to a 19 per cent share of the presidential vote. Rupert Murdoch has established a global satellite communications system that is capable of elbowing aside more parochial or less well-funded media enterprises and that engages in direct political bargaining with the communist regime in Beijing over how much truth and pluralism will be allowed to intrude onto the Chinese airwaves.

In a liberal democratic institutional environment there are supposed to be two remaining great checks on the abusive power of private wealth. These are the rule of law, and the civil and political rights of citizenship. The theoretical basis for trusting in these counterweights is derived from two venerable strands of the Western tradition of social thought that have competed with economic reasoning for ascendancy—namely, constitutionalism and secular republicanism. Here we shall briefly review the strength and limitations of each of these defences against unbridled money power, before turning to an alternative source of consolation derivable from economic analysis itself. This is the idea that competition between rival wealth-holders can serve the cause of freedom and underpin the initiatives of pluralism necessary to generate authentic alternatives of citizen choice.

This chapter tackles a topic which lies at the heart of any realistic discussion of the logic of democratic representation. On the republican view of politics, money power perverts the logic of democratic representation. Alternatively, Marxists used to say that our object of study is the process that bridges the gap between the formal equality of constitutional rule, and the substantive realities of bourgeois power. Either way the relationship between voting and using financial power to secure a public policy outcomes is central to our understanding of how democratic politics really works, and what is needed to make it secure.

The first line of defence against the abusive use of money power in democratic politics is likely to be the *rule of law* in a liberal constitutional order. Some ways of using money to promote political objectives are legitimate, and indeed necessary. Others are illegal. So long as the boundaries are clearly drawn and the judicial authorities are impartial and authoritative, isn't that enough to settle the matter of principle? From time to time, of course, the law may have to be adjusted—trade unionists may be asked to sign up for a political fund, rather than just check it off with their union dues, etc.—but these adjustments can be made after public debate and in a democratic manner.

The trouble with this defence is that, even if the judicial system is indeed impartial and authoritative, it is only the most flagrant cases of violation that will come before it, if even they do. The great bulk of boundary-enforcing will have to take place through tacit compliance, implicit respect for underlying norms, a civic ethos, a sense of decency or the 'civility' discussed in Chapter 3, or the self-restraint discussed in Chapter 4. Yet it is in the nature of interparty competition, and in the nature of the market economy, that those with money and power are always under pressure to gain as much advantage as they can—to go as close to the line as possible without breaching it—or at least, without so flagrantly breaching it that they get caught. Thus, behind the formal defence of the rule of law must lie an informal structure of self-monitoring and controls or implicit rules, which will always be under stress. Indeed, in neo-democracies and in deregulated market economies, we have to enquire most carefully into what might generate the creation or establishment of such supportive norms?

This is where the *second* supposed area of defence against abusive money power makes its entry. The *citizenry* or the *electorate* in a democratic society should be able to monitor the behaviour of their politicians through a free and competitive press, for example, and through all the established mechanisms of democratic control and accountability that accompany the electoral process itself. Recent financial scandals in various established democracies suggest a fairly standard pattern. After initial complacency there may come a crisis followed by a wave of popular indignation. But it is most unusual for the indignation to be based on a full and precise disclosure of who did wrong, and who acted with integrity. Indeed the very boundaries involved are likely to be disputed, and even those most at fault are likely to have their supporters in high places, and their media power. So they will do their best to spread around the discredit. As a general rule, all democratic politicians may end up more or less splattered by the discredit arising from a party financing scandal. This is not to say that the citizenship defence is worthless—Chapter 4 discussed the impeachment of Presidents Collor and Carlos Andrés Pérez—it can be a powerful sanction. But it is also a very imprecise form of control. Democratic integrity can be affected, and those who are the most guilty may get off lightly, even benefiting relative to their accusers.

The *third* theoretical defence can be derived from economic reasoning. It is the competitive nature of the democratic market place itself. A single unified bloc of money power might be able to overwhelm the rule of law and citizen indignation. But, say exchange theorists and liberal optimists, that neglects the discipline arising from consumer sovereignty, which generates incentives for the less corrupt to break away from and compete with the more corrupt, in the hope of displacing them. We have some interesting examples of this—in South Korea lately, and in Mexico, and perhaps in Colombia. But this is far from being the socially optimal consumer sovereignty assumed by theorists of atomistic competition. It is by no means clear that those with cleanest hands will win the electoral contest or secure political power. In South Korea even the most veteran democratic leader turned out, perhaps inadvertently, to have received some precautionary funds from the presidential slush fund of his predecessor in office.

The Costs of Electoral Competition

At this point it may add clarity if we focus on the financing of political parties, rather than political corruption more generally. There are of course both legitimate and illegitimate ways of funding political parties. To get a clear grip on our subject we should start by considering what political parties need funds for. The principal answer is probably that they need money in order to propagate their message, counter their critics, and thus to secure electoral success. Admittedly, there are other possible motives. Parties might try to survive periods of repression—a common enough case in Latin America—and they might need funds for that. Parties might wish to support like-minded organizations in other countries—again that needs money. Parties might serve the interests of specific social groups—trade unions, churches, farmers, and so forth—and might raise money for the direct benefit of those groups rather than for their own electoral purposes. Parties might even accumulate funds with the aim of capturing the state apparatus and stifling democratic competition (there is a long tradition of this kind in parts of Latin America). But in modern competitive democracies the fundamental and indispensable purpose of party finance is to put up an effective show in the electoral arena. All other purposes are likely to founder if that is not achieved, and that is an increasingly costly and demanding priority. So let us focus our discussion there.

Fund-raising for political parties, and to finance election campaigns, has its own clear rationale. Under authoritarian rule political parties were often supervised or even banned, and electoral contests were frequently manipulated by those in power. But even then, most countries held periodic elections and these were often rather expensive affairs. Typically the incumbent authorities would favour a particular party or slate of candidates, and would provide abundant resources to pay for the associated campaigning and publicity. Such resources would come in part from the public sector, and might include the secondment of public employees, deductions from employee payrolls to finance more or less compulsory party membership subscriptions, free advertising and unrestricted access to the (normally censored) media, the loan of official premises and vehicles, and so forth. Approved parties could run very well-financed election campaigns, while opposition parties were generally denied official resources and were often starved even of private funds. Whereas private donors were officially encouraged and rewarded if they contributed to approved campaigns, they were liable to penalties if they supported opposition candidates. The ARENA party in Brazil, Mexico's PRI, Indonesia's Golkar, Taiwan's KMT, and the Colorado Party of Paraguay all exemplified this authoritarian style of electioneering.

Following the transition to a more authentically competitive and genuinely multiparty electoral democracy, new systems of party fund-raising and campaign financing would necessarily be required. But old reflexes and assumptions, and the vested interests created by the previous history, were not likely to disappear overnight. Nor was it usually a straightforward matter to agree on a new 'level playing field' of rules governing political financing, let alone to establish the effective monitoring and reliable implementation of such rules, once they were adopted. When, for example, the Colorado Party of Paraguay mounts a strong and well-financed election campaign under democratic auspices, it is hardly surprising if some sections of the electorate find it hard to believe that all its campaign contributions are now voluntary and above board, especially considering that many contributors and beneficiaries continue to be the very same people who previously engaged in collusive and anti-democratic styles of electioneering.

In addition to the legacy of suspicion and distrust that may arise from pre-democratic experiences of party fund-raising, new sources of unease about election finances may arise during a democratization from the emerging post-transition incentive structure. As elections become more competitive the stakes rise for the rival contenders. Incumbents may fear that, if they once lose office, their chances of return will be severely impaired by the emergence of new options. Opposition politicians may also regard defeat in a competitive election as far more damaging to their reputations and prospects then previous defeats incurred against overwhelming odds. Thus early post-democratization elections may arouse more hopes and fears than conventional campaigns in stable balance of party contests. This may help to explain why allegations of high-level corruption linked to campaign financing have proved a recurrent feature of democratization experiments in many new democracies.

The cost of campaigning varies greatly from country to country, and over time. It also differs according to the type of party. For example, a party with a very well known tradition ('brand name') and prominent public leaders may need less money than a new party whose founders might need to be well remunerated in case it disappears after just one contest, leaving them no long-term influence.

Democratic politicians are supposed to face a permanent condition of 'institutionalized uncertainty'. At every successive election even the most effective and commanding political leaders are exposed to the criticisms of their rivals, and if their performance slips or their luck runs out, they risk rejection by the electorate. In many new—and some old—democracies the consequences of expulsion from power can be most unpalatable. Decisions which look justifiable (or can be covered over) so long as one remains in office, may be viewed in a rather different light once the aura and levers of state power have been removed. Ex-presidents and ex-premiers may be not just an embarrassment to their former supporters, not just unemployable, but actually liable to legal sanctions for their conduct in office. Those whose careers they promoted, or whose material interests they sheltered, may also stand to lose heavily. Not surprisingly, then, many democratic office-holders find themselves under intense pressure to perpetuate their incumbencies, and to diminish their exposure to the institutionalized uncertainty of the electoral process. One obvious strategy is to accumulate such a war-chest of contributions that those in office are able to heavily outspend any challenger in the competition for electoral popularity. To put the point bluntly, ruling parties and ruling politicians may actively raise funds not just in order to win *one* election, but with the aim of establishing a position of impregnability from which they can hope to win an indefinite succession of elections, and thus postpone *sine die* the moment when they could be held accountable for their acts of government.

This 'top–down' or ruling party conspiracy theory is not the only way of modelling abusive relationships between money power and the electoral process. But it is a plausible logical construct, and it does seem to have a number of contemporary empirical referents. For example, the Kuo Min Tang party in Taiwan is reputedly by far the richest political party in the world, having accumulated an extraordinary array of economic assets during its forty years as exclusive dictatorial power on the island. Once it had been converted into a competitive party within a democratic system, it sought to use its accumulated wealth to reinforce its chances of continuity in office secured through electoral success. Until 2000 the PRI in Mexico (after no less than seventy years of authoritarian rule) hoped to follow a similar trajectory, as illustrated by the fundraising event that President Salinas hosted in Los Pinos at the beginning of 1994, in which he apparently solicited multi-million dollar contributions from each of an assortment of leading Mexican businessmen. Perhaps the most spectacular attempt to minimize electoral uncertainty was the massive fund-raising scheme operated by President Collor de Melo of Brazil between 1989 and his impeachment trial in 1993. This episode is difficult to understand unless one considers that the first Brazilian president ever to have been elected by universal suffrage may have been minded to use his victory to create a network of partisan and financial complicities strong enough to ensure a permanent political power base to last for the rest of his natural life—recent revelations about the Fujimori regime and its methods of fund-raising in order to perpetrate itself in power provide lurid documentation of extremes to which this method can sometimes be pressed. President Menem's administration can also be viewed in this light. In general, then, this 'top–down' perspective on party financing is not just a theoretical construct, but a credible hypothesis for those undertaking empirical research.

In practice few specific empirical inquiries are likely to uncover such simple and clear-cut anti-democratic conspiracies as those outlined above. The heuristic model may provide a convenient starting-point, but it should not be allowed to obscure the fact that all 'really existing' party finance scandals contain a multiplicity of overlapping and badly coordinated activities. Monocausal attributions of intention or blame may serve the cause of political simplification, but they are unlikely to capture the full dynamics of real scandals. The opacity of the empirical evidence makes straightforward comparisons of scandals between countries, or even over time within the same country, highly problematic. Judgements about whether such problems are more severe now than in the past, or are worse in Latin America than, say, in East Asia, are further complicated by the characteristic disjunctions that arise between the magnitude of the transactions uncovered and the scale of the public indignation they elicit. Often there is a considerable time lag between the period when the scandal was at its most acute, and the period when the political reaction to it is most severe. Intervening variables may include the role of the media in first damping down, then later stoking up, public concern; the protracted and convoluted nature of many of the judicial and political trial processes triggered by such scandals; and the convenience of blaming on a past administration failings that would be too explosive for public scrutiny if attributed to current incumbents. Another possible consideration is that in some countries parties of the left may attract far greater hostility (because their money scandals reveal the hypocrisy behind their proclaimed ideological discourse) than parties of the right. In new democracies the opponents of authoritarian rule may attract special opprobrium if they are found behaving in office in the same ways that they used to denounce in their undemocratic predecessors.

This 'top–down' dimension of abusive party financing in modern democracies must be balanced against an alternative hypothesis. Modelling from the 'bottom–up' would focus attention on the economic rationality of buying favours through financing a political party. This is an inter-disciplinary topic which must be informed by data collection and case studies (see below). But it is also an area where simplified economic modelling can be quite illuminating— uncovering the basic logic and rationality of the transactions involved, and therefore generating broad estimations of likely social costs. Such modelling procedures deserve consideration in the study of political corruption, since if there is *any* sphere of political life where this approach is likely to be particularly relevant, it is in the realm of corporate financing for political parties. Here, at least, a priori deduction may be helpful, given the difficulties of direct observation. And here, at least, political actors are free to reveal by their actions—the granting and receiving of money—what they may never wish to confess in their words.

So let us consider the economic rationality of the corporation which seeks to buy political favours:

1. The money could otherwise be invested elsewhere—so there is a basic opportunity cost, say the standard cost of capital to the firm, or the expected rate of return or pay-back on an investment.

2. There is also the question of scarce management time. Political brokerage is a management-intensive activity. So the real cost to the business is greater than just the financial opportunity cost— possibly a good deal greater.

3. There is also the risk of adverse consequences if the political party chosen for support loses the election and the donor becomes identified as a partisan opponent by the rival winning party.

4. There is the compliance problem—what is to stop the political party taking the money, and then not fulfilling its (implicit) pledge of favourable treatment?

5. There is the 'free rider' issue. It is most unlikely that all the economic benefits of the favour purchased by the firm will accrue to the purchaser. Indeed it is more than likely that *some* benefits will accrue to its rivals and competitors. A large portion of the resources redistributed through the policy shift may well be 'lost' to organized interests—diffused through the community at large.

From all this it follows that it is only economically rational, in a market economy, for a business to seek to buy influence with a political party when the expected benefits to the purchaser if all goes well are very large, and very clear-cut, and very quick to arrive, compared to the costs. (One might go so far as to suggest that something like a 10 to 1 expected return on investment may be required to justify the extra costs and risks involved.)

Now let us turn to the other side. How does the corporation generate the resources to justify its corrupt investment? One possibility is that the firm purchases a policy improvement that would not otherwise have been adopted. On this 'altruistic' view, the firm gets some of the benefits that its policy influence has bestowed on the community at large. According to a standard economic analysis, this possibility is unlikely to arise very often, if at all. Why should individual corporate donors be privy to altruistic public policy ideas

that would not otherwise be available to competitive political entrepreneurs in search of good ideas and attractive policies that can
generate votes? If a businessman did have such an altruistic
insight, why should his firm pay to have it adopted, rather than simply donate it to the political community?

On this analysis, it is far more likely that a firm will pay for a
policy change that redistributes benefits from other (less well-
connected) political sources towards itself. Thus the cost will have
to be borne by politically ineffective losers. This social cost is likely
to be high—not just 10 to 1 but say 100 to 1 (considering the low proportion of total redistribution that accrues to the donor). Moreover,
the donor may even use his influence to promote policies that reduce
total well-being (provided they boost donor well-being). Two possible sources suggest themselves—either consumers can be made to
pay, or the taxpayer. A little more indirectly, the corporation's main
objective may well be to acquire insurance—political insurance or
regulatory protection from the vagaries of the market that must be
borne by all other players.

One implication of this stylized economic analysis might be to
favour state funding of political parties, associated with effective
policing of their accounts to shield them from corporate predation.
But for state financing to work, and to create an effective barrier
against the abuse of money power in political parties, it would still
be necessary to rely on an effective rule of law, a vigilant and well-
informed electorate, and an ethos of responsibility. Since these are
precisely the theoretical defences against political corruption that
were found wanting earlier in this section, at this point in the argument we pass from theory to experience.

Evidence

Unfortunately there are serious impediments to empirical work in
this area. Individual, sometimes spectacular, episodes of high-level
corruption may sometimes be well documented through investigate
journalism, congressional hearings, and indeed judicial processes.
But even in the most visible and well-documented of cases, large
areas of unclarity typically remain.

Objective and dispassionate data collection on the topic of political corruption is an inherently problematic enterprise.[3] The very

---

[3] Consider e.g. the problem of the time lags that may separate the commitment
of an offence from its public exposure. To take a recent example, following the military coup of 1964 one of the key conspirators used his privileged access to the

term 'corruption' denotes passion and subjectivity, and the charges and countercharges surrounding each case are infused with partisanship. This is hardly surprising when the stakes are so high for the powerful actors involved, and when the control mechanisms are controversial and distrusted, as is often the case in new democracies. In relation to almost every case it will be possible to find well-informed sources that will claim defamation and the planting of evidence, together with equally articulate exponents of the doctrine of the cover-up. Such polemics over the monitoring and control of public office-holders more or less ensure that, for every convincingly proven case of high-level corruption, there must be multiple others which could not be conclusively documented. Some observers will tend to conclude from this fact that most unproven allegations are also probably true, whereas others will argue that in such circumstances unfounded accusations of corruption constitute a virtually costless instrument of political warfare.

From a comparative politics perspective it is not necessary to reach a definitive conclusion about the accuracy and detail of specific political corruption allegations. This is just as well, since even where a full-scale trial has led to a clear-cut verdict, alternative interpretations may not have been conclusively refuted to the satisfaction of all political tendencies. The impact of high-level political corruption allegations on processes of democratization can be gauged in more general terms by consulting the following four sources of comparative information, and by cross referencing them: the public record of overtly investigated cases; the 'corruption perception index' assembled annually by Transparency International; comparative data on party financing and its irregularities; and the corruption monitoring procedures of the international financial institutions.

Each of these sources of information is highly approximate and vulnerable to distortion and manipulation. All of them concern

authoritarian regime to build up a major Brazilian private bank. For twenty years under the shelter of impunity and immunity, this enterprise seemed to prosper. But with the return to democracy its advantages ceased. By 1986 it was effectively bankrupt. Yet, through the negligence or connivance of its regulators and the inexperience of new democratic actors, it continued to take deposits and to roll over debts for a further ten years. It was not until Feb. 1996 that the Central Bank uncovered the fraud (which by then had snowballed to around US$5 billion of unbacked liabilities, currently loaded onto the Brazilian taxpayer). Thus the scandal that broke in 1996 referred to offences committed perhaps decades earlier, but the political fall-out accrued to the present democratic administration. No one can be sure how many other long-buried corruption scandals await exposure in other Latin American market-based neo-democracies.

'perceptions' that may not be either accurate or fully comparable. Taken together, however, they should provide a rough approximation of the scale and incidence of high-level political corruption in new democracies, or at least of that proportion of these activities that has become visible, and that has therefore contributed to collective understandings of the quality and dynamics of contemporary democratizations.[4]

Reported Scandals

A glance at the grossest manifestations of political corruption, as indicated by the public record should be sufficient to confirm that this is a widespread, recurrent, and destabilizing phenomenon. As already discussed in Chapter 4, since 1992 heads of state or government have either been legally impeached or otherwise ousted amidst apparently well-founded allegations of gross abuse of public office at the highest levels of the state in the following major new democracies: Brazil, Ecuador, Indonesia, Pakistan, the Philippines, and Venezuela. This list may not be exhaustive. In any case, the governments of Argentina, Colombia, Mexico, South Korea, and Thailand have also reportedly been almost paralysed for extended periods of time by alleged scandals of a similar kind, although in these cases incumbent chief executives have not been directly ousted. In addition to these twelve countries where over the past decade corruption allegations have at least temporarily disrupted the central functions of government, it would be easy to list at least as many where similar problems have lurked just below the surface.[5] The Russian Federation under President Yeltsin probably provides the most spectacular and extreme example, but most ex-CIS republics are apparently in the same league. Oil-exporting states and narcotics-trading countries also tried to display deeply entrenched problems of governmental corruption. Indeed, even on the restrictive definition proposed by the World Bank ('abuse of public office for private gain') something like a quarter of its 180 member states seem to be deeply affected by clear-cut and high-level political corruption. Approximately half of these are currently 'new

---

[4] For the fullest available cross-tabulations see Robin Hodess (ed.), *Global Corruption Report 2001* (Berlin: Transparency International, 2001).

[5] France, Italy, and Spain have all witnessed extensive and very high-profile cases of political corruption in recent years, although without such system-threatening repercussions as in the countries listed above.

democracies' and something like a quarter of this subset of countries are similarly affected.

Perception Index

Similar conclusions may be drawn from the 'corruption perception index' published annually by Transparency International. In 1995 only fourteen new democracies were ranked by this procedure. But by 2001 coverage had been extended to forty-two new democracies, as well as to twenty 'old' democracies and nineteen other countries (a total of ninety-one in all). Each country is scored on a scale of 1 to 10, using a minimum of three and a maximum of eleven different sources. A score of 10 signifies that the sources consulted perceive no significant political corruption in the system. A score of 1 signifies the opposite. The Annex Table 3 presents recent rankings for the fifty-two new democracies surveyed in 2001.

Although details of this table should be treated with caution, the general exercise is of some interest. For example, it suggests a wide dispersion between the new democracies that are perceived as relatively less corrupt, and those where this problem is viewed as very severe. The lower half of the table contains most of the countries where corruption scandals reportedly gave rise to major political crisis. Those at the very bottom might be regarded as the new democracies most likely to revert to authoritarian rule. The relative stability of the country rankings over time is also worth noting. The presence of Venezuela near the bottom of the list and of Botswana near the top indicate the potential costs and benefits of alternative political choices. Even the most highly regarded new democracies fall well below the ratings of most 'old' democracies, which occupy all top fifteen slots (including Finland with a 'perfect' score of 10.0).

Campaign Financing

These first two sources of comparative information on political corruption are very broad brush. They focus on high-level abuse of public office which certainly undermines the citizen trust required for representative government. But not all political corruption is undertaken solely for purposes of personal enrichment. As explained above, electoral democracies generate their own distinctive incentives for abuse of office, which may have more to do with political survival than with private appropriation. Comparative information about party financing can add value here. The political rationale and institutional logic for, say, amassing hidden funds that can be used to influence election outcomes, should not be confused with other potential patterns of illicit behaviour that can be either curbed or facilitated by relatively specific public policy decisions. Admittedly, in practice, the recently uncovered scandals in Argentina, Brazil, Mexico, Peru, Russia, and the Ukraine indicate how easily one variety of high-level political corruption runs into another; how readily electoral corruption can lead on to money laundering, then to complicity with *narco-traficantes*, and eventually to court-rigging, and perhaps even political assassination. But even if there may well be a corrosive logic to the dynamics of complicity and impunity which often over-runs the neat boundaries that analysts try to erect between one type of illicit practice and the next, party financing is worth isolating as a distinct field of inquiry, with its own specific logic and potential for regulation.

It needs to be stressed at the outset that there is no one-to-one relationship between success at fund-raising and success at vote raising. On the contrary, when Mario Vargas Llosa secured the unstinting generosity of the Peruvian right, the way the money was spent confirmed the worst accusations of his opponents. He started his campaign with 60 per cent voting intentions, and by the time his US election managers had run through their vast budget his support had halved. In the 1996 Republican primaries in the US, multi-millionaire nominee Steve Forbes spent $10 for every vote he received—perhaps an all-time record bad buy. So money does not always suffice to win votes. But in many cases it certainly can help. In 1992 Ross Perot, for example, was able to secure 19 per cent of US presidential votes and came closer than anyone in the twentieth century (including ex-President Teddy Roosevelt and Governor Wallace) to breaking the two-party system—at least in part because he had a bottomless reserve of personal funds from his own private wealth, and so was not hedged around with the restrictions on campaign spending that constrained his competitors.

That said, the following Latin American examples indicated the magnitude of the sums allegedly misappropriated for this purpose, and the widespread nature of the phenomenon. These examples refer to the national levels of party leadership, but regional and local party financing would also repay careful scrutiny.[6]

By the time impeachment proceedings forced his resignation, in December 1992, President Collor de Mello of Brazil was accused of

[6] For more on the Latin American evidence see Eduardo Posada (ed.), *Party Finances in Europe and Latin America* (London: ILAS, 1998).

amassing secret funds, reportedly in excess of one billion dollars, through a systematic programme of commission-taking on public contracts organized by his financial henchman, P. C. Farias (the treasurer of his 1989 presidential campaign). Lacking a strong party of his own, or a solid base in Congress, the president never-theless may have expected to build up a loyal political following and secure passage of his preferred legislation presumably by making judicious payments from this slush fund. Brazilian election cam-paigns have become both frequent and costly, and party discipline is weak. One of the most plausible uses for these secret funds was thought to be to bankroll the election of candidates who would undertake to vote as the president required on key measures. Compare Venezuela. When he was forced from office in May 1993 President Carlos Andrés Pérez of Venezuela was no longer on good terms with the party he had headed since the 1970s. Acción Democrática was a well-funded mass social democratic party which had repeatedly mounted lavish and often highly successful cam-paigns. Venezuela was accustomed to competitive elections, but not to transparent rules on party financing. The charge against Pérez was that he had diverted $17 million of secret government funds intended for security and defence into the black market, where they had been used to finance the president's political campaigns, thus freeing him from dependence on his party machine. Compare Mexico. In February 1993 the Mexican PRI's secretary of finance organized a private dinner, attended by President Salinas, at which the twenty-five prominent guests were allegedly 'invited' to con-tribute $25 million to the funds of the ruling party, in order to cover its expenses in the forthcoming 1994 election campaign. Compare Colombia. In July 1995 the treasurer of the Colombian Liberal Party was arrested and admitted to receiving $6 million from the Cali drugs carted as a contribution towards the second round cam-paign of Ernesto Samper, the party's standard-bearer who had secured the presidency after a close race in June 1994.

As these miscellaneous examples make clear, various elected presidents of Latin America seem to require control over large sums of money of questionable provenance, in order to win elections and to reward loyal followers. Here we are not dealing with funds col-lected in small tranches from the rank and file of the ruling party. On the contrary, part of the object seems to be to free a head of state from undue dependence upon independent party structures. When individual donations are for sums in excess of a million dollars a piece it is difficult to believe that they express unrequited loyalty alone. Especially when the funds are secretly managed and are only provided to incumbents, a presumption of high-level political corruption is difficult to avoid. What could wealthy donors hope to obtain in return for secretly financing the election or re-election of certain candidates or parties? All the four leaders reviewed above were identified with policies of economic liberalization and state reform in their respective countries. It is difficult to escape the inference that wealthy donors might hope to profit from inside information or privileged access regarding such liberalizing reforms.

There is parallel evidence on party financing and political corruption in the new democracies of East Asia, and the role of the 'oligarchs' in funding recent Russian election campaigns is also well-known. More generally, those with financial control over the mass media have frequently seemed capable of swaying electoral outcomes in order to serve their business interests. It is, however, important to stress that serious issues concerning the corrupt funding of political parties have also arisen in numerous older democracies, not only Italy, Spain, and Germany, but also in France, Britain, and the USA.

International Monitoring

Our fourth and final source of empirical information on the incidence of political corruption in new democracies comes from the international financial institutions. For operational reasons, the World Bank, the IMF, and the regional development banks have always sought to monitor bribery, agency capture, and abuse of public office in the countries and sectors where they disburse their loans. This case-by-case information gives them a broad sense of the relative incidence and structure of political corruption across a large number of member states, half of which are now new democracies. In recent years the World Bank Institute has proceeded to systematize and supplement such information, for example by surveying foreign investors to track the prevalence of 'kickbacks' on public procurement contrasts in different countries, or the perceived incidence of 'state capture' by private interests. One comparative study of post-communist economies asked office-holders which public-sector jobs were 'sold'. For example, in Albania it found that 60 per cent of customs inspector posts were sold, but only 5 per cent of ministerial posts, whereas in Latvia the respective proportions were 41 and 19 per cent. Another World Bank Institute attempt to measure 'overall corruption over time' tracked El Salvador and Russia in the first six years after democratization. Russia began with an overall corruption index of 5.5 in 1992 (on a 0–10 scale with zero signifying no corruption) and rose to 8 by 1998. El Salvador began with an index of 8 in 1992, which fell to 4 by 1998.[7] Indicators of this kind are of course very sensitive and controversial. The international financial institutions may have access to more accurate information, and more opportunities for cross-checking, than the other sources considered above. Whether or not these perceptions are more soundly based, they matter more, because increasingly decisions affecting the disbursement of funds are influenced by such factors. As a consequence, such indicators are subject to considerable feedback, and pressures of verification.

In 1996 incoming World Bank President James Wolfensohn announced that 'countries that are fundamentally corrupt should be told that unless they can deal with that they are not going to get any more money'.[8] IMF Managing Director Michael Camdessus followed that up with the directive to member countries: they 'must demonstrate that they have no tolerance for corruption in any form'.[9] Thus, for example, in August 1997 the IMF cut off its lending to Kenya, citing failure to tackle corruption as the cause. That month the Fund also released new guidelines just approved by its Board, and warned that other countries could suffer the same fate as Kenya if they were disregarded. 'Financial assistance from the IMF . . . could be suspended or delayed on account of poor governance, if there is reason to believe it could have significant macroeconomic implications that threaten the successful implementation of the programme, or if it puts in doubt the purpose of the use of IMF resources.' The guidelines also take care to condemn the corrupters as well as the corrupted, and assert that all this can be done without interfering in the domestic or foreign policy of any member state. The WB warned Kenya that, in view of the IMF cut off, its Bank aid would also be 'substantially reduced' and in September 1997 it also approved an anti-corruption policy document (*Helping Countries Combat Corruption: The Role of The WB*) and staff guidelines. More generally the WB has focused on preventing fraud and corruption within Bank-financed projects, and on providing advice on anti-corruption measures. But, notwithstanding research undertaken by the World Bank Institute, WB staff have also been

---

[7] Examples taken from Daniel Kaufmann, 'Civil Liberties and Accountability for "Good Governance" and Anti-Corruption', Atlanta, Ga., 17 Oct. 2000.

[8] *The Financial Times* (London, 2 July 1996).

[9] *The Financial Times* (London, 2 Oct. 1996).

informed that there is no intention of linking bank lending in a mechanistic way to some standard measure of corruption in any member country. Countries ratings are crudely aggregative. There may be institutional 'islands of integrity' the WB can support, even in heavily corrupted political regimes.

Conclusion

In conclusion, this chapter has reviewed some traditional ideas about 'political' corruption, and has presented some evidence about its prevalence and corrosive power in many new democracies. In principle, political corruption might refer to the erosion of public spiritedness, or to a propensity to betray the republic to its enemies, but in contemporary conditions the focus is much more concentrated on deviations of public policy attributable to bribery, or to the direct exchange of money for covert political advantage. In theory there are three main defences against such political corruption— legal, electoral, and market-based. But the evidence suggests that such defences are easily breached.

The key point is that behind a façade of public interest procedures, substantive policy outcomes are secretly sold to those willing and able to pay for what they might not obtain by more visible political lobbying. Corruption in this sense exists to some extent in all regions—authoritarian, totalitarian, newly democratizing, and also in old democracies. It can no doubt be modelled using the rational choice framework of 'principal–agent' theory. But for the purposes of this volume a higher level of aggregation is required. It is not so much individual transactions that matter from the standpoint of democratization viewed as a long-term process, but rather the cumulative propensity covertly to sell public policy to the highest bidder, instead of deciding it on the basis provided by constitutional and democratic procedures. From our interpretavist perspective, what matters for the quality and legitimacy of a new democracy is not just this propensity as measured by some objective indicator, such measurements being in any case extremely problematic and unreliable. (It is interesting to note that even the World Bank became 'interpretavist' on this point.) Rather it is the public *perception* of the propensity for corruption that matters most; a perception that may be only loosely related to the objective situation. In fact the perceptions that should concern us involve not just the *scale* of political corruption, but its *social meaning*. How far does it reflect tacit understandings about the normal ways to proceed?

Have some conventional limits been overstepped? How is the responsibility/blame to be apportioned? This takes us a long way beyond the transactional precision of principal–agent theory, and so leads from a narrow focus on corruption to broader concerns about civil society/social capital, institutional design/public accountability, and the proper role of political leadership versus the depoliticized 'guardianship' provided by courts, general accountancy offices, and bank supervisors. In other words the comparative politics of political corruption is intimately related to the other facets of democratization considered in Chapters 3, 4, and 6 of this volume.

If democratization is viewed as a long-term, open-ended, process of resocialization, and if political corruption is understood as a broad preoccupation heavily shaped by collective perceptions that extend beyond judgements about specific individual transactions, then periodic 'eruptions' of concern over this topic are to be expected. Each 'corruption scandal' will have its own specific *petite histoire*, and will unfold according to a largely unpredictable specific dynamic. The closest analogy may be a wave crashing against a rock and scattering foam in all directions. The general significance of such episodes is not to be sought in their often arbitrary details.

In *some* new democracies, over time, each crisis can be isolated and absorbed. The systems of administration, representation, and rule of law are seen as normally unaffected. Public opinion gains confidence that, despite individual scandals, an underlying 'ethic of responsibility' can be discerned. In fact specific scandals may serve the cause of demonstratively testing and reconfirming the basic non-corruptness of the system. They may dramatize the dangers that the community needs to counter. But, as the evidence in this chapter makes clear, in a *significant proportion* of democracies (perhaps a quarter, old and new), cycles of political scandal are not so easily absorbed in this way. They may even multiply, spread to the most trusted institutions, and eventually undermine public confidence in the democratic system as a whole.

The typical case is neither a unilinear progression to full confidence in the integrity of all institutions, nor an indiscriminate collapse of public trust. In accordance with the general standpoint of this volume, political corruption should normally be viewed as a long-term, complex phenomenon, an associate of the democratization process which is more likely to sap its quality than overwhelm it altogether. Periodic episodes of anti-corruption reform may well be followed by periods of stagnation or lost ground, particularly in a climate where 'money politics' tends to rein supreme. 'Islands of integrity' may be established in certain parts of the state apparatus, but equally well other parts of the political system may remain structurally dependent upon the persistence of political corruption. The typical experience may therefore be of an extended period of ebb and flow, with no clear or final outcome.

Political corruption may in general be understood in this way. But this pitches the discussion at a very high level of abstraction. Chapter 6 focuses the analysis on one crucial realm of economic power where public confidence is most vital, and where democratic procedures to protect the public interest are most problematic (or even indeed dangerous, if we follow Hamilton's point of view). The specialized area in question is that of monetary authority, an area where not too much can be expected from the standard defences (legal, electoral, and market-based) that are supposed to shelter democracies from political corruption.

6

On Monetary Authority

You cannot in a democratic society have an institution which is either fully or partially disassociated from the electoral process, and which has the powers that central banks inherently have.

(Alan Greenspan)

This chapter explores the relationship between processes of democratization and the establishment and/or reinforcement of trustworthy and credible systems of monetary authority, with particular emphasis on central banks. As elsewhere in this book, a long historical perspective is included, and the evolving experiences of old democracies are used as reference points for assessing the more recent and incomplete experiences of neo-democracies. Some theoretical issues are considered, but the emphasis is placed as much on recent experience. The 'delicate balance' between monetary authority and democratic legitimacy, the underlying rationale for central bank independence, the scope and limits of 'consent' in monetary affairs, are all theoretical issues of relevance to new democracies. This chapter is equally concerned with the need for feedback from experience to theory, as when the granting of central bank independence is followed by unanticipated financial crises that inflict heavy redistributive costs on the society, and may even weaken the legitimacy of its fledgling democratic institutions.

The governments of many new democracies are heavily dependent upon access to international capital markets in order to maintain the economic stability necessary to address the other demands of the electorate. In such conditions it becomes a high political priority to design and manage a system of monetary authority that can command 'credibility' in financial markets. Inherited monetary arrangements are seldom adequate for this purpose, since most predemocratic monetary systems were prone to the abuses of power that are characteristic of authoritarian rule, and many displayed additional dysfunctionalities from a global market perspective—interventionism and financial repression, etc. Thus, new democracies have frequently found it necessary to place the restructuring of monetary authority high on their list of institutional reform priorities, focusing on provisions intended to enhance 'credibility'. But newly established democracies also face the need to demonstrate to their domestic constituencies that they differ from their undemocratic predecessors with respect to political accountability for the use of public power. This implies a need to design and manage a system of monetary authority that will be subject to constitutional restraints and respectful of the rule of law. Such a system ought in some way to be answerable to the voters, for example, via congress, the elected executive, or at least the courts and perhaps an audit office controlaría. A democratic monetary authority also implies an institution capable of formulating and communicating its decisions in terms that can be understood, and (ideally) accepted, by the major participants in both the financial and the political systems. Here, then, we find two desiderata to guide the necessary restructuring; each is demanding, and together they may well conflict. Such conflict may emerge either at the level of design principles, or—even if that can be avoided—at the level of practice. This chapter will review attempts to balance the two objectives. It adopts a historical, comparative, and international perspective, and evaluates some recent experiences in key new democracies. The conclusion is that neither theory nor experience has yet generated a stable, reliable, and generally applicable formula for handling these tensions. The obstacles appear to be lodged as much, or more, in the international financial system as in requirements internal to the logic of democratization.

In their standard forms both political democracy and modern monetary authority are organized through the nation-state. In order to establish these two systems on a durable and impersonal basis they are based on constitutional principles and upheld by legal systems that are in principle permanent. The temporal and spatial authority of the law is coterminous with that of the state apparatus which promulgates them (hence the Spanish refer to 'estado de derecho', roughly meaning the rule of law within a given state). In this way these authorities are able to lengthen the time horizons covered by their activities beyond the lifetime of individual legislators or bank officials. They can also make long-term commitments that regulate the division of powers between democratically elected politicians and monetary officialdom, and that specify the principles of accountability between them. In a world of nation-states this is the standard formula relating representative government to monetary authority. Each territorial unit reproduces arrangements of this kind, which apply up to the boundaries of the state, but not beyond them.

However, we know that, before the establishment of the modern national state, both constitutional and highly elaborated forms of monetary authority (including sophisticated credit systems backed by force of law) had already come into existence. Moreover, as many analysts assert and as the emergence of the European Union appears to illustrate, the Westfalian model of the nation-state could now be losing its primacy. Even if this proves to be the case, new less state-centric forms of constitutional democracy are likely to be attempted, and new forms of monetary authority capable of generating credible commitment will be required. The balance between these two will need to be regulated in some way or other, whether or not the primacy of the nation-state is preserved. The balance sought in new democracies is partly modelled on various earlier experiences linking liberal constitutionalism with financial confidence-building.

Pre-1914 precedents highlight the delicate nature of the balance that has to be established between the requirements of market confidence, on the one hand, and the need for political and legal cover, including accountability to an impersonal structure of sovereign authority, on the other. The global resurgence of liberalism since the 1970s has meant that these precedents have acquired a renewed relevance, and have exercised a significant degree of influence over debates on institutional design in new democracies. But, of course, these contemporary experiments are far from being mere replicas of their nineteenth-century precursors. For one thing, the gold standard is no longer available as a supposedly automatic financial stabilizer. Hence the term 'monetary authority' must be construed broadly if it is to cover the whole of a long history. On the same basis, today's new democracies are characterized by universal suffrage, mass media, and related features of modern democracy that differentiate them from the more restrictive constitutionalism of their predecessors. Finally, the new democracies are also 'emerging markets', not the lead economies of the capitalist world, in contrast to the pre-1914 innovators.

Long-standing and pre-democratic antecedents link political sovereignty, constitutional rule, and the empowerment of durable and impersonal monetary systems and authorities. This can be seen from the emergence of effective monetary authority in the Netherlands, England, and France from the seventeenth century onwards. By the nineteenth century all these three key European powers had developed dynamic and sophisticated commercial economies, and ended up with complex, broadly 'constitutional' systems of government. But they were also monarchical and expansionist, and they all established extra-European empires. Thus they differed from the democratic and territorially bounded nation-states sketched in the first paragraph of this section. They also constructed their monetary systems on the basis of the stability they associated with bullion. Thus, if we are study new democracies, it is important to consider the history of constitutionalism and monetary authority in the new republics of the Americas, particularly those which used their legal authority to promote paper money.

In general, it seems that, although the establishment of a new constitutional regime might provide the legal and political prerequisites for the creation of a national monetary authority capable of making credible long-term commitments, there was nothing automatic about such an outcome. There was typically a time lag between the creation of the new political regime and the establishment of its monetary authorities. In order to establish itself on a permanent basis a new constitutional regime would require an effective system of self-financing. But not all the interests represented in the new regime would necessarily share a consensual view about the monetary disciplines, or self-limitations, to be imposed. Over the centuries and across the continents merchants and large wealth-holders would seek reassurance that their capital would be secure and that, whatever the constitutional supervision over the monetary authorities, this would not permit meddling by debtors or inflationists. Otherwise they would withdraw their funds. Under the gold standard all constitutional regimes were disciplined by this threat.

Although today's new democracies know the US as prime backer of a standard model of monetary discipline and the 'insulation' of central bank authority, this is not how the USA itself developed from a new democracy and emerging market into the world's dominant liberal power. Nor is it an accurate depiction of how the Federal Reserve presents itself to the American people. In the words of Alan Greenspan, 'You cannot in a democratic society have an institution which is either fully or partly disassociated from the electoral process and which has the powers that central banks inherently have.'[1]

---

[1] Remarks addressed to a London conclave of central bankers on 9 June 1994, and published in F. Capie *et al.* (eds.), *The Future of Central Banking* (Cambridge: CUP, 1994), 253. This categorical statement came after the European Union had already ratified the Treaty of Maastricht, Art. 105 of which specifically prohibits the new 'independent' European Central Bank from allowing political discretion over its policy-making, which is directed exclusively to price stability. Compare Hans Tietmeyer, then President of the Bundesbank, in a lecture at University College,

The era of managed money began shortly after the founding of the Federal Reserve system in 1913. This was a worldwide consequence of the First World War, which meant that by the time the Fed came into existence the international gold standard was on the brink of passing into history. From then until the 1970s both economic and political liberalism were mostly on the defensive. Under conditions of warfare or perceived threats to national security, the the existing monetary authorities were liable to be subordinated to political controls aimed at strengthening state authority over the allocation of resources. In many parts of the world this was accompanied by a rise in economic nationalism, and the imposition of controls over international capital movements. This was the essence of the 'managed money' system (nation-centred and relatively disengaged from automatic forces in the international economy) that prevailed in most market economies for over half a century. Where managed money coincided with mass democracy the problem of democratic accountability arose. Issues of monetary policy are abstruse and arcane, but too important to be left out of public debate. Keynes was himself a great popularizer of such issues, but he recognized the delicacy of the balance that would need to be struck. Here is how he posed the issue to the Liberal Summer School of 1925:

I believe that the right solution will involve intellectual and scientific elements which will be above the heads of the vast majority of more or less illiterate voters. Now, in a democracy, every party alike has to depend on this mass of ill-understanding voters, and no party will attain power unless it can win the confidence of those by persuading them in a general way that it intends to promote their interests or that it intends to gratify their passions . . . With strong leadership the techniques, as distinguished from the main principles, of policy could still be dictated from above.[2]

Oxford on 3 June 1999: 'I believe that there are two preconditions which have to be fulfilled for an independent central bank to be unequestionably compatible with a democratic system. First, the assigning of independence and the mandate have to be arrived at democratically . . . Second, the mandate of the independent central bank must be unambiguous. Political value judgements among various competing aims may be made only by those who have acquired direct democratic legitimacy as a result of elections . . . The decision-making body of an independent central bank, which is not elected directly, may not make any autonomous judgements among various competing aims. An over-riding objective has to be specified in advance. That is precisely what the Maastricht Treaty does. It specifies the primary objective of price stability . . .'.

[2] Unpublished speech quoted in D. E. Moggridge, *Keynes* (3rd edn. Toronto: Torono University Press, 1993), 29.

After the defeat of the Axis powers, in the democracies of Western Europe central banks were nationalized, and more generally private finance was subjected to increased taxation and regulation, and experienced reduced political leverage. These were not propitious conditions for refining the delicate balance between financial credibility and political accountability. Not only were financial markets exposed to political controls, but constitutional regimes were also thrown onto the defensive. Challenges from communism, fascism, and economic populism all involved disregard for the self-limiting principles of liberal constitutionalism. Thus both sides of the balance tended to be neglected.

However, the last quarter-century has witnessed a remarkable worldwide resurgence of economic liberalism, accompanied by a 'Third Wave' of democratizations that has greatly extended the reach of political regimes which are—at least formally—not only constitutional systems, but also ones regulated by competitive elections based on universal suffrage. In all market democracies there is a tension between the requirements of financial stability and predictability, and the pressures of electoral politics. The monetary authorities are charged with promoting the former, but governing politicians must be responsive to the latter. In the US case this tension is managed through an elaborate system of rules under which the president nominates a chairman of the Federal Reserve for a four-year term, but from among seven board members each appointed for a fourteen-year term of office subject to ratification by the Senate. In addition to the seven 'political' board members there are also five votes held by governors representing the twelve districts of the Federal System (these are representatives of the commercial banks). Additional provisions include a six-monthly requirement on the chairman to report to Congress (under the Humphrey–Hawkins Act) and the obligation to publish minutes of the board's monthly meetings (after a six-week time lag). This elaborate structure is designed to acknowledge the principle of political accountability (the Fed was, after all, created by Act of Congress), while erecting barriers between the monetary authorities and the electoral politicians. Details vary from country to country, but similar principles now govern the relations between the British Parliament and the Bank of England, the Bundesbank and the German federation, the Reserve Bank of New Zealand and its parliament, etc. Thus a fairly standard model emerged for OECD democracies.

Just as the new democratic regimes of the 'Third Wave' could draw on a stock of theory, models, and experience derived from the slow

emergence of the 'old' democracies over previous generations, so also
the available models of monetary authority under conditions of economic liberalization could be borrowed from the OECD countries. As
we have seen, institutions like the Bank of England and the Federal
Reserve System had been evolving within constitutional limits for
generations, or even centuries. Some of the theories and precepts of
the pre-1914 international liberal economy had been built into their
foundations. Spurred by the 1950s return to currency convertibility,
the 1960s emergence of the euro markets, and the worldwide
upsurge of inflation in the 1970s, the monetary authorities of the
leading liberal capitalist economies took the lead in directing policies away from national Keynesianism and 'managed money', and
towards international economic liberalization. This 'monetarist' or
'neo-liberal' shift was well under way by the time most of the new
democracies came to consider the appropriate relationship to establish with their national monetary authorities. In many cases their
choices were heavily constrained by the legacies of debt crisis and
inflation arising from previous experiments with economic interventionism. In any case, these new democratic regimes needed access to
international capital markets, and were subject both to explicit conditionalities and the more subtle influence of economic doctrines
emanating from the lead economies. In short, in a large number of
countries both political democracy and neo-liberal prescriptions of
economic orthodoxy arrived at roughly the same time. Both were to
some extent 'imports', hastily adopted in accordance with what was
held to be best international practice. If there is a 'delicate balance'
to be established between them, it would be particularly sensitive
under such circumstances. Moreover, there were international
transmission mechanisms encouraging democratization on the one
hand, and the construction of financially credible monetary institutions, on the other. But they were seldom well coordinated. So, if the
lead liberal economies had acquired useful experience of balancing
democracy with monetary authority, such experience was liable to be
diluted or even lost in the course of international transmission.

Given the speed with which most transitions to democracy took
place, and the pace at which policies of economic stabilization and
adjustment were implemented, it would have been surprising if
the balance between the two had been carefully coordinated. Not
infrequently, constitutions were written, electoral systems were
designed, prices were freed, debt reduction agreements were negotiated, capital accounts were liberalized, state banks were privatized,
and central banks were granted 'independence', all within the
briefest of intervals. In such conditions a lack of coordination

between the various reform initiatives is only to be expected, and there would inevitably be problems of hasty implementation. This is all the more probable when, as was usually the case, such liberalizing reforms were introduced in a context of weak accountability, uncertainties over the rule of law, and instabilities in the emerging 'rules of the political game'. Moreover, despite the strength of external pressures in favour of economic and political liberalization, the external environment was also typically subject to various uncertainties. Different governments and international agencies competed to promote somewhat varied models of reform, and these models also shifted to some extent over time. The volatility of international financial markets was a compounding factor here. (For example, prescriptions on appropriate monetary policy changed significantly in the wake of the East Asian currency crisis of 1997/8, as we shall see below.) In any case, even when a single model was consensually promoted from without, there could be differing interpretations from within of how it might be locally applied (e.g. contrast Klaus and Balcerowitz, or Massad and Cavallo), and sometimes external models were imperfectly assimilated by their local promoters. On top of all this, each individual new democracy found itself in competition with its neighbours for recognition and a favourable international ranking of its efforts. This competitive logic applies both to political reforms and to economic measures intended to attract international capital and to promote investor confidence.

In view of all these factors, the emphasis has been on speed and showmanship rather than on the careful crafting of institutionally balanced arrangements for reconciling public accountability with financial credibility. Whereas the pre-1914 prototypes had emerged slowly under the influence of internal deliberations, and exposure to various kinds of stress testing, the systems of monetary authority established in most neo-democracies have been mass produced in haste, and are mostly more the product of hope and imitation than of experience. Also, although constructed to contain inflation and resist the arbitrariness of the 'managed money' era, they are not subject to the same automatic constraints as prevailed under the international gold standard. And although we presume contemporary democracies to be more broad-based than the restricted constitutional regimes of the nineteenth century, they are not the product of elaborate institutional compromises between diverse regional or sectional interests, as was the Federal Reserve, for example, or indeed the German Bundesbank.

In the new democracies, during the 1980s and 1990s the demand grew for a return to orthodoxy, the strengthening of property rights, and enhanced protections against currency debasement. This was in reaction to the inflationary upsurges and financial instabilities of the 1970s and early 1960s, together with the intellectual reaction against Keynesianism, and the taxpayer revolt against the welfare state. Social power and intellectual prestige shifted from trade unionists to financiers, from public officials to business lenders, and from liberal academics to conservative think tanks. The demand for central bank independence needs to be situated in this broader context. We also need to attend to important national variations. In Italy, for example the political left tended to cultivate a special relationship with the Banca d'Italia, viewed as perhaps the only component of the state apparatus that might act as a counterweight to the clientelism of the perpetually dominant Christian Democrats. Brazilian social democrats campaigned for a more autonomous central bank that might free the economy from the manipulations of the financial oligarchy. The Slovaks sought their own central bank as a way to throw off Czech financial supremacy (and the Czechs reciprocated with a campaign for their own currency and separate financial regulations). Not all democracies establish independent monetary authorities. Not all monetary authorities originate at the moment when a new democracy is established. Some monetary authorities enjoy a 'credibility' established prior to democratization, and which survived in spite of it. Some used to be more independent and more 'market credible' before democratization undermined those attributes. Some new democracies have as yet failed to promote either the market credibility or the political accountability of their monetary authorities. In short, the approximately 120 competitive electoral regimes currently in existence display a very wide range of variance in their relations with their monetary authorities. This chapter cannot cover all the possibilities. The experiences of greatest interest are those of new democracies with at least relatively autonomous monetary authorities, where the logic of democracy is strong enough to set up a demand for some degree of monetary accountability and where the logic of financial market credibility is sufficiently present to create an incentive to establish confidence-inspiring monetary arrangements.

Central bank independence must mean independence *from* some constraint. Reduced dependence on one source or type of imposition may increase the relative (or even absolute) dependence of the institution on rival sources of constraint.[3] Absolute independence is an

---

[3] As Arthur F. Burns put it in 1976, 'In our democratic system the independence of a governmental agency can never be absolute'. *Reflections of an Economic Policy-Maker: Speeches and Congressional Statements: 1969–1978* (Washington, DC: American Enterprise Institute, 1978), 383.

illusion, so behind any campaign for central bank insulation we need to consider not just how sound the public interest or theoretical arguments may be, but also which specific interests are likely to win or lose, and by how much. We might even enquire about the 'pareto opimality' of alternative models of *relatively* independent central banking.

Generally speaking, these new central banking arrangements have contributed to much lower and more predictable rates of inflation, increased financial confidence, and a more neutral depoliticized allocation of credit. Given the severe irrationalities and financial distortions of the previous period, these institutional innovations have been characterized as a necessary and effective restructuring of the rules of accountability applicable in this area. Specialists in central banking and financial regulation were given clear narrow mandates, high salaries, long terms of service, and increased protection from political interference so long as they performed their public services. This at least was the rationale behind the shift to 'central bank independence'. It was the banking equivalent of establishing an incorruptible tax administration, or an institutionally secure and autonomous judiciary.

But in most new democracies there is no short and easy route to the establishment of an incorruptible tax system, or indeed a trustworthy and autonomous judiciary. So why has it been so readily assumed that insulated monetary authorities are so much easy to summon up by decree, or through imitation of foreign models? Considering the huge power that accrues within an efficient autonomous and authoritative central bank, such devices as tying the bank governor's salary to the fulfilment of some single easily monitored contractual target can be no adequate guarantee of his altruism. In fact the logico-deductive theory of personal motivation underlying most of the more elegant arguments for central bank independence is unable to explain why central bankers should be above the sordid mêlée, any more than it can explain why the postman reliably delivers valuables through the mail. In place of a logico-deductive doctrinal approach, we need a historically informed analysis which is sensitive to national variation. As the IMF has recently discovered in Moscow, Kiev, and Buenos Aires, central bankers may not always be immune from the vices of their environments. But if not, then the doctrine of 'insulation' must be subject to one of the oldest interrogations in the history of constitutionalism: *Quis custodies ipsos custodes?* In the 'really existing' Central Banks of many contemporary neo-democracies it is possible to uncover multiple examples of personnel clashes, resignations,

dismissals, accusations of malfeasance, and indeed, criminal con-
victions for corruption. This raises an important theoretical question. What grounds have we for believing that well-insulated
central bankers will act with impeccable professionalism (indeed
public-spirited altruism) when all other agents in politics and in the
market place are assumed to be prone to the temptations of self-
regarding egotism?

Certainly, in their more extreme forms, the arguments for an
insulated, depoliticized and unassailable structure of central bank
management tend to rely upon a one-sided micro-analysis of human
motivations. In these accounts inflexible institutional rules will be
all that stand between monetary stability, order, and the corrosive
perils of the rent-seeking lobbyist, the vote-seeking politician and
the benefit-seeking welfare claimant. But on this model of human
motivation, who is to protect society from the central bank governor
who abuses his protected status to pursue his own self-interest?
Indeed, the more independent well-insulated and rule-justified his
position is made, the stronger the incentive structure for self-
advantage. In this context, it is no use arguing that central bankers
are selected and socialized into a mystique of public service—for
once it is granted that such institutional arrangements can generate a high degree of altruism, other state actors can make the same
case, and then the whole neo-liberal rationale for state shrinking to
eliminate rent-seeking would be put in jeopardy. Nor can the relent-
less majesty of the law be invoked as a sufficient control against
malfeasance, for if judges can be relied on to punish straying central
bankers why not also accept them as an adequate defence against
state-centred, rent-seeking in general? But in that case the need to
insulate the central bankers from all other public functionaries
would be undercut.

Although there are some strong theoretical arguments for
'depoliticizing' control of the money supply, these do not necessarily
trump equally powerful arguments for the democratic accountability of economic rule-givers. Against the arguments about incomplete credibility and time-inconsistency, which were developed in
the 1970s to reinforce older arguments for an immutable rule-based
system of monetary control,[4] can be pitted the case for democratic
control as an 'error correction' mechanism. This is particularly so in
neo-democracies after a long period of authoritarian rule, often

---

[4] Finn Kydland and Edward S. Prescott, 'Rules rather than Discretion: The
Inconsistency of Optimal Plans', *Journal of Political Economy*, 85/3 (June 1977) and
R. Barro, 'Inflationary Finance under Discretion and Rules', *Canadian Journal of
Economics*, 16 (1983).

associated with persistent economic mismanagement. The over-reliance on rigid structures of policy rules seem to reflect an exaggerated distrust of the maturity of newly enfranchised electorates. The Korean and Mexican experiences analysed below confirm that the capacity for sound judgement of the voters may not fall far short of that displayed by previous, securely insulated, technocratic elites. In any case, even if the democratic process does at times generate destabilizing macroeconomic results, we should not underestimate the significance of a second classical argument for democratic control: that the diffusion of political control has a highly educative effect, and over time should tend to convert inherited attitudes of suspicion and hostility to those in authority into an ethic of responsibility. According to this argument, democratic control promotes a diffusion of responsibility and creates a community of involved citizens with a stake in the good working of all institutions. Such a community, and the trust on which it rests, can only be created over a lengthy period, and in the course of a protracted process or democratic learning and invention. But it provides the best long-term guarantee of responsible, effective, and predictable macroeconomic policy-making. If so, then an alternative, more 'discretionary', and politically accountable model of central banking will remain a legitimate alternative to the depoliticized and automatic model that was fashionable until the mid-1990s. On a generous estimate there appear to be about seventy new competitive elected regimes in existence at the beginning of the year 2000 where the twin pressures of democratization and the need for market 'credibility' are strong enough to induce attempts to establish confidence-inspiring monetary arrangements and where at least relatively autonomous monetary authorities have therefore been established. About thirty were located in the western hemisphere, and a further fifteen in East-Central or Southern Europe. Among the most notable were Argentina, Brazil, India, Mexico, South Africa, South Korea, Thailand, and Turkey. (The inclusion of India as a 'new' democracy indicates the breadth of the field covered.) For the purposes of this chapter it is particularly relevant to focus on those larger democracies with weightier economies where the balance between domestic legitimation and international confidence-building is both especially significant and unusually delicate.

During the past decade, each of the eight notable countries listed above has experienced at least one episode of financial crisis that highlighted the systemic consequences of failure to inspire market confidence in the national currency and its associated monetary regime. These countries all have broadly democratic regimes, but in every case the democracy might prove vulnerable if such a financial crisis were allowed to run out of control. For democratic politicians it is therefore a matter of the utmost importance to establish some system of monetary authority that provides at least a reasonable degree of defence against such dangers. It is also a question of considerable importance to investors, the business community, and indeed the taxpayers as well, to limit the economic damage that can easily arise as a consequence of financial crisis. On the one hand, therefore, these new democracies face strong incentives to establish, or restore, the financial credibility of their monetary authorities. On the other hand, however, since the political consequences of a mistake could be so far-reaching, and since the economic cost to the taxpayers (and therefore to the overall balance of public policy) could also be huge, the same reasoning points equally to the need for effective political accountability over issues of monetary management.

The mainstream literature on democratization has focused more attention on the need to avoid 'populism', by 'insulating' the technocrats from short-term electoral pressures, than on the need to 'consolidate' political authority over an area of policy-making that is both highly specialized (requiring expertise) and critically concerned with the core issue of 'who gets what, when, and how' (requiring accountability).

From a neo-liberal perspective, market processes may need sheltering from political intrusion, hence the stress on 'insulating' the technocrats. This could even be a prerequisite for elite acceptance of majority rule, especially in societies where most of the benefits of the market economy accrue to a privileged segment of the electorate. But such a line of reasoning has been brought into question in recent financial crises. For example, in Mexico after the 1995 peso collapse, the newly empowered majority in Congress discovered that the fiscal cost of rescuing the privatized banking system had soared to around 20 per cent of GDP, and that 'insulating' the technocrats involved was difficult to distinguish from the old authoritarian practice of impunity for incumbents. Thus both in Mexico and similarly in South Korea after the 1997 currency collapse, the claims of political accountability have come to rival those of technical insulation. Similar considerations are likely to apply when the financial crises of 2001 (Argentina and Turkey) are subjected to comparable scrutiny, but at the time of writing it is too soon to evaluate these cases. However, it is not too soon to note that the Argentine crisis was accompanied by the forced resignation of the theoretically independent head of the central bank, and the

Turkish crisis by the resignation of the theoretically independent banking regulator. Both these individuals resisted subordination to economy minister armed with emerging powers. There is clearly a *delicate balance* to be struck between the twin imperatives of accountability and insulation, certainly in the two new democracies studied here, probably more widely and arguably in general.

Mexico and South Korea

Mexico and South Korea were both admitted to the OECD in the 1980s. This was in recognition of strength of their respective economies and political systems, and the major strides both had made towards convergence with the old established market democracies. Although both had long histories of authoritarian or semi-authoritarian rule, both had also undergone far-reaching political transformations from the mid-1980s onwards. Elections were increasingly competitive (although the incumbents continued to perpetuate themselves in office) and constitutional checks and balance were becoming increasingly constraining. Rulers were no longer assured of impunity for abuses of power committed while in office, and citizens were more independent and assertive than before. On the economic front Korea had a better reputation for industrial dynamism than Mexico, and both had long track records of state interventionism and close collusion between political elites and favoured groups of 'national' businessmen, but both were viewed as 'graduating' towards more mature and standardized forms of liberal capitalism. Mexico had become the world's largest manufacturer of television sets, for example, and South Korea was the world's largest ship-builder. Membership of the OECD both acknowledged these achievements and offered assurances that liberalization was likely to continue.

However, shortly after entry into the OECD both these countries experienced a dramatic financial crisis which demonstrated that their 'pathways from the periphery' remained far from smooth, and that neither the enthronement of impersonal constitutional principles nor the entrenchment of financially credible systems of monetary authority could yet be taken for granted. In Mexico entry into NAFTA was immediately followed by the implementation of a constitutional reform granting 'independence' to the Bank of Mexico, and then followed in turn by the cleanest presidential elections in living memory (won by the eternally governing PRI). All this took place in the first half of 1994. But by January 1995 the peso was in free fall, the newly privatized banking system was on the brink of collapse, and the outgoing president was hounded into informal exile under an avalanche of accusations of crime and corruption, including large-scale abuses of the financial system.[5] Only the largest international rescue package ever assembled on behalf of a single country sufficed to halt the free fall, and eventually to turn around the situation. Three years later came the turn of South Korea. Again a close fought presidential election (this time won by the perpetual candidate of the opposition) was immediately followed by a currency in free fall, a national banking system teetering on the edge of insolvency, and an IMF rescue package of unprecedented size. Again the outgoing president was disgraced by charges of corruption, including receipt of bribes for arranging loans to a steel company which then collapsed, precipitating the banking crisis.[6] Again, it was the international rescue package (which of course came with various liberalizing conditions attached) that provided the markets with a floor, and that paved the way for the subsequent rebound and recovery of financial confidence. In both cases a newly elected administration with a more or less convincing democratic mandate was well placed to negotiate the post-crisis policy framework, and to establish some distance between past malpractices and a prospective future of political accountability and financial transparency.

There are some striking parallels between these two examples, which are evidently both critical test cases of the emerging relationship between democratization and financial credibility in 'Third Wave' regimes. The various reassuring laws and institutional reforms adopted to an external chorus of approval prior to these crises proved quite insufficient to cope with the scale of the vulnerabilities subsequently exposed.[7] Notwithstanding the strengthening of constitutional checks and balances, the proclaimed improvement in public accountability and official transparency, and the additional monitoring processes associated with economic liberalization, privatization,

---

[5] For a clear reconstruction of 1994 see Sidney Weintraub, *Financial Decision-Making in Mexico: To Bet a Nation* (Pittsburgh: Pittsburgh University Press, 2000).

[6] For a detailed analysis of high-level political corruption in South Korea, see the Oxford D.Phil. dissertation submitted by Bronwen Dalton, 'The Social Construction of Corruption in South Korea', May 2000.

[7] In the wake of the peso crisis the Washington-based financial institutions tried to shift responsibility by arguing that they had been misled by the newly independent Banco de Mexico concerning the real state of Mexico's reserves, although in fact they should have been able to monitor the true position. If they failed this was probably as much due to the IMF negligence as to Banco de Mexico deception.

and internationalization, the monetary authorities (including the Finance Ministry which retained powers to instruct the central bank) still possessed an extraordinary degree of policy discretion. By 'bailing out' favoured banks the monetary authorities were able to commit funds approaching 20 per cent of Mexican GDP to purposes for which no political or legislative mandate was required, at least until the fiscal bills came in retrospectively.[8] The Korean legislature seemed even less capable of monitoring the use of taxpayer funds in the course of that country's bail-out operation. In both countries the monetary authorities (including here not only the central banks but also the government-created bail-out agencies), possessed huge discretionary power, but seemed largely insulated from public accountability, and were indeed sheltered enclaves of elite collusion reflecting the personnel and practices of the pre-democratic era.[9] A third observation is that in both these cases the crisis was so abrupt, extreme, and system-threatening that emergencies remedies had to be adopted without much preparation or consultation (except perhaps with international agencies). These were certainly not propitious conditions for the careful design of institutional procedures that would reflect the 'delicate balance' of competencies that might be expected and desired by liberal theorists.

A fourth observation would be that, despite the serious causes for concern just outlined, and continuing worries about how these crises may eventually turn out, the democratic process does appear to have introduced a countervailing element of real value in stabilizing the situation. Contested elections and divided governments have meant that malpractices have been exposed to public view, malpractices that under previous regimes might never have received official scrutiny. Democratic debate has educated the citizenry on the issues involved, and may have stimulated a sense of collective involvement and responsibility. Electoral alternation has created the space for renovation and reform (whether or not that opportunity has in practice been well used), and whatever the eventual outcome, public accountability over monetary policy has acquired a legitimacy that would otherwise have been lacking.

[8] In a study of the fiscal cost of bank restructuring after financial crises in thirty-four 'emerging' economies the World Bank estimated the average cost in the 1980s at over 11% of GDP, and above 8% in the 1990s. But that was before the Korean and Mexican numbers were available. *Global Economic Prospects and the Developing Countries* (Dec. 1998) 126.

[9] The World Bank report just quoted refers obliquely to 'sometimes flawed' policy-making processes in Korea during the 1997 crisis ('with limited information sharing between the central bank and the Ministry of Finance'), 129.

Those dissatisfied with the outcome now have access to clear procedures about how to challenge and indeed correct it.

Balancing all these considerations, the overall verdict on these two cases has to be both provisional, and also somewhat mixed. Tightening democratic and constitutional restraints, combined with increased citizen alertness to issues of this kind, reinforced by a more independent press and a more vigilant private sector, *might* lead to progressive refinements in the 'delicate balance' between political accountability and financial credibility. But such an outcome is by no means assured. The old collusive practices of the authoritarian and interventionist era are far from totally discredited. Powerful vested interests still have a stake in defending the old ways. In any case, under conditions of acute emergency—which could well recur—priority goes to immediately effective remedies, regardless of the longer term constitutional implications. The legal and political counterweights to money power remain uncertain, especially when so much discretion remains vested in the hands of insulated monetary authorities.

For example, in Mexico the chief author of the Finance Ministry's unsound bank privatizations of 1990/1 who also had lead responsibility in the flawed bank rescue plan of 1995, is currently in post as governor of the independent Bank of Mexico, and cannot be removed until his term of office ends in 2003, whatever the electorate may think. So far all this discussion of a 'delicate balance' has focused on possible counterweights *within* a liberalized national system. But these two recent examples both suggest that the critical dynamics of financial crisis are more likely to be located at the international level. Which brings us to the international dimensions.

The International Dimensions

Not so long ago every modern national state believed it should be equipped not just with its own army, its own law courts, and its own parliament and civil service but also with its own telephone monopoly, its own airline—and of course, its own currency, regulated by its own central bank. These assumptions are all being rapidly undermined by liberalization and globalization. Why should central banks be different from telephone monopolies when the ultimate user of both services is a mobile and restless individual consumer?

The internationalization of economic exchanges and the liberalization of financial markets is beginning to forge a more globalized system of monetary regulation with its accountancy standards, its Basle formula for capital adequacy ratios, and its Financial Action Task Force against non-compliant monetary jurisdictions. Each individual monetary authority has to be viewed in this overarching context, and not merely in national terms. Everywhere the old ideas of national sovereignty are being eroded by commercial and financial interdependence. Viewed from this perspective there are good grounds to doubt the immutability of classical central banks as pillars of the territorial nation-state. But if the monetary authorities of the 'Third Wave' democracies have to be overhauled in the same way that their state owned enterprises have been, it is far from clear what the replacement design principles should be. Thus, for example, the World Bank's 1998 report on *Preventing Financial Crises in Developing Countries* was obliged to concede the inadequacies of previous panaceas (rapid financial liberalization, pegged exchange rates, etc.) and to acknowledge that 'reliance on capital inflows exposes developing countries to external panics that may cause sudden and massive reversals in capital inflows, deep illiquidity, and strong contagion effects. Minimizing these risks and dealing more effectively with such financial crises would require a better architecture of the international financial system.'[10] Four years later no such 'architecture' has yet emerged and the risks of abrupt interruptions in the flows of private capital to emerging markets remain as acute as ever. The same report explained the limitations of financial regulation in individual developing countries in terms that could just as well be applied to the international financial institutions themselves: 'It takes too long to develop supervisory capacity and skills. Moreover, supervisors are often unable to detect risky behaviour and take action against banks because the kinds of behaviour tend to change over time and supervisors are not prepared for them. They may also be prevented by policymakers from taking action.'[11]

The combined banking and currency crises that have erupted in Mexico, East Asia, and Russia since 1995 have given rise to an intensified international debate about the appropriateness of the current mandates of the Bretton Woods institutions in general, and the IMF in particular. There have been high-level suggestions that the IMF took on inappropriate commitments, particularly in Russia, and became involved in tasks that were beyond both its

[10] *Preventing Financial Crisis in Developing Countries* (Washington, DC: World Bank, 1998), 129.
[11] Ibid. 139–40.

mandate and its competence. Fears have been expressed that, if fragile governments come to believe that their monetary policy errors will be corrected by IMF rescue packages, this will induce 'moral hazard'—the temptation to take risks on the grounds that the costs of failure will be assumed by others.

The Bretton Woods institutions derive their leverage from the support of key governments which are willing to replenish their capital if the need arises. But, in addition, unlike the financial institutions of the pre-1914 period, they are not backed by the automaticity of a collective consensus that gold provides the ultimate store of value. Instead they exercise discretion based on their claim to superior knowledge or technical expertise about the nature of modern financial markets. Recent controversies over the purposes and activities of the Bank and Fund arise from the fact that this ostensibly neutral source of authority and correct action is increasingly contested. As private capital flows expand and substitute for official funding and as a wider array of state actors, political interests, and civil society activists react to the consequences of globalization and of IFI prescriptions, these underlying assumptions concerning the Bank and Fund are increasingly contested. In a more democratic era, with official discourse more focused on 'transparency', IFIs (international financial institutions) are being scrutinized not only over their expertise but also over their political legitimacy.

Globally, democracy and liberalized markets may be in the ascendant, but the relationship between them is by no means stable or fully worked out. The new democracies in emerging markets provide a particularly vivid demonstration of the persisting uncertainties. Even when viewed in strictly political terms, these are not fully consolidated regimes that have been stress-tested in adversity. A certain proportion of them are likely to swing from weakly democratic to precariously authoritarian and back for some time to come. If they are subjected to further banking and currency crises of the gravity experienced by Mexico and South Korea, such political fragilities could well be accentuated by economic stress. Argentina and Turkey are currently demonstrating the continuing potential for severe instability.

Both liberal theory and recent experience lend some support to the proposition that financial credibility can be combined with democratic accountability in ways that allow both investors and citizens to extend their time horizons and scope for autonomous choice. However, neither theory nor experience has yet generated a stable, reliable, and generally applicable formula for handling the potential tensions between monetary confidence and political responsiveness. Hitherto the most encouraging evidence was confined to a limited number of favoured national jurisdictions (such as the USA and Switzerland). Now liberal internationalism ambitiously proposes (with some configuration from post-cold war experience) that these two desiderata can be reconciled beyond such national frontiers, indeed throughout a global community of democratic nations bound together through integrated financial markets. But, as we know from earlier, historical experience (notably 1914), even the more promising projects of liberal internationalism can end in failure. The unconsolidated regimes and fragile financial systems of many 'third wave' democracies indicate that such dangers could still destabilize the current international liberalizing project.

The first side of the 'delicate balance' has become clearly understood as financial liberalization proceeds. If local monetary authorities fail to provide the private sector with competitive terms for the placement of their funds capital will flow elsewhere, credit will become scarce, tax revenues will fall, the currency will weaken, inflation will loom. In democratic conditions, sooner or later the electorate is likely to withdraw support from governing parties that allow such conditions to develop. Thus democratic regimes are constrained to generate systems of monetary authority that can command 'credibility' in international financial markets. New democracies may well find that the monetary arrangements they inherit from outgoing authoritarian regimes require restructuring in order to build the requisite market confidence.

There is a second side to this balance, which is of equal importance for legitimizing a liberal order. Newly established democracies also face the need to demonstrate to their democratic constituencies that they differ from their undemocratic predecessors with respect to political accountability for the use of public power. Initial attention may focus on the fiscal accounts, on the legislature's 'power of the purse', and on transparent procedures in the public sector. But, as the Mexican and South Korean examples make clear, and as numerous other recent controversies in the central banks of neo-democracies confirm, the monetary authorities also have great power to allocate (or misallocate) public resources.

In such situations democratization may also require an extension of democratic political authority over arenas of policy-making that had been abusively managed under authoritarian rule and that could easily be open to further abuse after the installations of a democratic political regime. Even granting the need for expertise in the management of monetary affairs, and the advantages of at least partially distancing the guardians of financial probity from the vicissitudes of daily political struggle, an effective monetary authority in a democratic regime is likely to require a degree of legitimation, and therefore will need some way to demonstrate that it has the 'consent' of the governed.

This then invites some theoretical reflection on the notion of 'consent' in general, and more particularly on how it might apply to monetary authority. Whereas democratic theorists worry about consent, financial analysts are more preoccupied with the 'credibility' of monetary institutions and policies. There are parallels and interconnections between these two approaches, but the democratic concern is with *citizen* consent, whereas the economic perspective focuses on *market* confidence. Markets monitor monetary policy with obsessive attention and precisely calibrated evaluations, whereas citizen evaluations are far more occasional and distant. Negative evaluations can force drastic changes of policy and even of personnel, at very short notice, and despite the preferences of political officialdom. In a liberalized market economy the monetary authorities of most new democracies may therefore have to attend to their financial credibility with more urgency than they would devote to the routine implementation of their mandated responsibilities. Small numbers of financial operators, probably anonymous, and possibly not even locally based, may dominate opinion. But in a newly established democracy citizen concern over the management of the monetary system may also become quite insistent. In this case, however, political monitoring of monetary issues will be quite public and visible, with identifiably protagonists who will only exercise influence if they can marshal support from a substantial coalition of domestic constituencies. Whereas financial reaction times operate in hours or days, shifts in political consent take months or years to engineer.

The doctrine of 'consent' is at the heart of much traditional liberal political theory, although there is also a more critical current that views it as little more than a convenient fiction. There is a good case for scepticism about strong versions of the doctrine, even in regard to strictly political issues. So what, if anything, might it involve when applied to the relatively arcane realm of monetary policy and institutions? Here it may be helpful to distinguish between four different manifestations of citizen consent. It may be explicit, implied, withheld, or withdrawn. Under each of these headings it is also important to distinguish between consent on procedural issues, and consent concerning the substantive outcome of monetary policy (although it is not always possible clearly to sustain this distinction in practice, as we shall see).

Explicit political consent arises through such formal and publicly visible processes as the enactment of a law mandating central bank independence, or the drafting and ratification of a new constitution. (Examples include the Argentine convertibility law of 1991; the 1993 reform of Article 28 of the Mexican Constitution; and the Brazilian Constitution of 1988.)

Implied consent covers much more of the normal operations of monetary authority under any system of representative government, and it is here that the critics concentrate most of their fire when describing consent as a convenient fiction. Nevertheless, a good case can be made that *in principle* both the procedures and the outcomes of normal monetary policy enjoy the implied consent of the democratically elected political authorities when they are in accordance with the rules and mandates explicitly approved by the latter. In addition, as indicated by the quotes from Greenspan and Tietmeyer (in n. 1 to this chapter), the sense of implied consent can be reinforced by such monitoring procedures as the (usually delayed) publication of the minutes concerning monetary deliberations; periodic presentation of testimony before congress; executive and legislative vetting of nominees to periodic vacancies in the bank's directorate; and in the last resort by the availability of redress through legal channels in the event of gross misconduct or malfeasance. This is all very plausible theoretically and in principle, but not necessarily so straightforward in practice, least of all in financially fragile new democracies, for reasons to be considered further below. It is important to stress, however, that under proper democratic conditions implied consent is always backed up from two sides: a framework of explicit consent, on the one hand, and the real possibility of withholding consent, on the other.

Withheld consent comes in several forms, ranging from the mildest of sanctions (critical questions in parliament, delays in the appointment of recommended nominees) to much stronger objections that may include the ultimate threat of withdrawal. Perhaps the most regular and significant of these 'withholding' options is the power vested in the elected authorities not to reappoint bank governors when their tenure comes up for renewal (which is typically only at long intervals). A stronger variant would be to 'force out' a controversial individual, that is, persuade someone to resign early on the grounds that he (there are few shes in this business) had lost the confidence of his colleagues. What recent financial crises in emerging markets suggest is that, while emergency powers may become necessary, and 'normal' monetary operations may therefore be brought into question, such examples of the 'withholding' of democratic consent from a monetary authority does not necessarily lead to heightened political control. On the contrary, given the need to re-establish market 'credibility', and to secure additional endorsement for the international financial institutions, replacement appointees may well be more strongly insulated from domestic political pressures than their predecessors. For all that, it would be an error to conclude that only convenient fictions of consent, or counter-productive episodes of political interference, constrain the autonomy of monetary authority in new democracies. The ultimate sanction of the withdrawal of consent cannot be excluded from the menu of theoretical possibilities available to a democratic polity. Its existence (albeit at a cost that would normally deter most politicians from taking it seriously) provides an edge that might otherwise be lacking to the other three manifestations of consent.

What would the 'withdrawal' of democratic consent from a national monetary authority involve? At the most abstract level, it is of course always possible for a democratic regime to convoke a constitutional assembly, and thus to rewrite its fundamental charter. But to go further we must consider some examples. This was, for example, what the Venezuelans did in 1999, and arguably it was done in accordance with democratic principles. It certainly resulted in a constriction of the institutional autonomy that had been (formally) granted to the central bank by the 1992 law. Admittedly, Venezuela's oil resources make it a very special case in financial terms, and its politics are also quite unusual. Not everyone would accept this as an example of the withdrawal of consent by a democratic regime, nor can it be assumed that the results of this example will be such as to inspire imitation. Nevertheless, it shows that withdrawal of consent is not just an entirely theoretical notion. A second example may suffice to confirm that this is so, while also underscoring the exceptional circumstances likely to be required before a theoretical possibility turns into a serious prospect. There is a genuine likelihood that, within a generation or so, the two Koreas may be reunited. In such circumstances both the locus of power within the Korean political system, and the fundamental economic priorities of the Korean state would be drastically altered. An independent South Korea central bank devoted to tasks of inflation control and financial stabilization would surely be hard-pressed, in such circumstances, to continue operating according to its existing guidelines. In such dramatic, but nevertheless foreseeable circumstances, a profound reorientation of the objectives and procedures of Korean monetary authority is only to be expected. If this reunited Korea is to be a democratic regime, then it is more than just a theoretical possibility that the existing consent to the established monetary authority may have to be withdrawn and replaced by an alternative (hopefully coherent and consensual, but in any case distinct) system of regulation and control.

However, all these variations on the theme of consent assume the existence of authoritative monetary institutions within a framework of impersonal constitutional government. Yet Chapter 4 has drawn attention to the limitations on public accountability in many new democracies and Chapter 5 has highlighted the related problems of corruption control. One clear implication of these chapters is that the theoretically neat distinction between 'process' and 'outcome' may often be difficult to sustain in practice.

If impersonal institutions are less than fully authoritative, then more personal forms of authority and leadership are likely to fill the resulting policy space. Thus, for example, Brazilian voters associated the price stability and other disciplines of the 1994 'Real Plan' not with any constitutional or institutional arrangements, but with the persona of President Cardoso. There were similar confusions between Argentina's convertibility plan, and the economy minister (Domingo Cavallo) whose prestige was entangled with it. Even in the USA it is sometimes difficult to determine how far the Federal Reserve System's credibility rests on its abstract structure, and how much is dependent upon the personal reputation of Chairman Greenspan. The European Central Bank's failure to inspire more market confidence (so far) is sometimes attributed to the poor leadership skills of Wim Duisenberg. But if a system of monetary authority becomes identified with an individual leader, this dislocates the theory that impersonal monetary authority should be both permanent and lastingly credible. In practice, all individual officeholders follow career cycles that are time limited and subject to tarnishment.

Under conditions of weakly institutionalized authority, and especially during episodes of financial crisis, the theory of democratic consent outlined above will require various modifications. For example, it is only if constitutional authority trumps all other sources of political power that the doctrine of explicit consent can deliver the full benefits of credibility and autonomy assumed by liberal theory. Otherwise a central bank president may find himself over-ruled or dismissed regardless of his constitutional status, as seen in various recent democratizations (e.g. in the central bank of Indonesia in 2000, etc.). Similarly, the delicate signalling mechanisms and processes of mutual adjustment and tacit consultation presupposed by the theory of implied consent presuppose a stable division of powers, and a broadly respected system of 'checks and balances'. In executive dominant, 'delegative', or other illiberal forms of democracy, such understandings are likely to atrophy or be subverted. But in the absence of a reliable framework of explicit consent backed up by elaborate practices of tacit mutual accommodation, contending interests and factions are likely to resort far more readily to methods of pressure and threat in order to make themselves heard. Thus, examples abound in many new democracies of attempts to withhold consent from the constituted monetary authorities, or even to withdraw their mandates. Such public recriminations (sometimes well-founded, but often based on misunderstanding and opportunism) may in turn reinforce the 'siege mentality' of the financial technocrats, who would then seek ever stronger forms of 'insulation' in order to shore up their 'credibility'. To complete the cycle, unaccountable technocrats lacking assurance of their democratic legitimacy are more likely to behave in ways that reinforce social demands to over-ride their constitutional prerogatives, and perhaps even to withdraw political consent from their activities.

Fortunately, despite the tendencies just outlined, there are also some strong countervailing forces at work. For one thing, many newly enfranchised citizens still have vivid recollections of past periods of monetary disorder, and will not easily condone any relapse. For another, academic and financial interests have united into a strong 'epistemic community' backed by considerable resources devoted to the training, recruitment, and protection of those with what is regarded as the greatest 'expertise' in sound monetary management. Given that other priorities are of greater concern to much of the electorate (e.g. see Chapter 7 on citizen security) and that their grasp of financial issues is seldom very strong, it may be hard to sustain any coalition of citizens around a policy concerned with holding financial authorities to public account. Campaigns against individual acts of gross corruption might be a different matter however.

Finally, most new democracies inherit what may be called 'inferior currencies', and their citizens know it. They would rather receive their incomes and hold their savings in dollars or euros than in national money, and understandably so. For this reason if the national monetary authorities are seen to be failing in their responsibilities, and the prospect arises that consent may be withdrawn from them, citizens are likely to react more quickly and effectively through the market than through the political process. The alternative may not be an effective national monetary authority under democratic control, but rather the abandonment of monetary sovereignty and the unilateral embrace of 'dollarization', a 'currency board' system, or some other international guarantee of monetary stability. This is often presented as a dangerous manifestation of 'globalization', and there is some merit in that line of argument. But from the standpoint of this volume the key point to note is that it may also reflect a legitimate choice made by the citizens of a new democracy, when they judge that their political regime is incapable of delivering some minimum level of monetary stability and financial responsibility.

The theoretical point requiring emphasis here is that last-resort control through democratic processes can provide a vital 'error correction' mechanism, to protect society from an unstoppable persistence in a course that no longer commands support or delivers on its promise of benefits. Authoritarian rule may sometimes deliver real benefits, but when it goes wrong the absence of countervailing restraints allows the costs to mount without limitation. An unaccountable monetary authority may also deliver highly valued public goods, at least for a time, but again the potential exists for the social costs to mount unrealistically, when insulated power-holders wedded to an unrealistic doctrine cannot be restrained by democratic feedback.[12] Experience clearly demonstrates that too much democratic interference with monetary policy may also prove damaging, so some 'delicate balance' must be struck. But there are grounds for doubt whether a permanently acceptable balance has yet been struck in most of the new democracies that were encouraged to embrace central bank independence in the 1990s. With the benefit of hindsight it may well turn out that overall shifts in priority from state to market, and from production to finance, were reaching a cyclical peak at precisely the same period as the democratization wave was cresting. The enhanced power and self-confidence of monetary authorities, both in old democracies and in new, could reflect a lagged response to the inflationary surges of the 1970s, and might therefore be followed by a counter-trend once fears of inflation have been offset by other policy preoccupations. This cyclical rather than linear hypothesis concerning the development of monetary authority has some historical plausibility and also some theoretical foundations.

---

[12] The Chilean central bank tried to stay on the gold standard even after Britain had been forced off, thus precipitating one of the worst economic downturns of the great depression. In the 1982 debt crisis Chile's so-called 'Chicago Boys' attempted a near repeat of this experiment, with similar results. In both cases dogmatic economic technicians relied on the backing of an inflexible dictatorship.

Experience suggests that independent monetary authorities are sometimes tempted to extend their policy reach beyond the narrow confines of some supposedly technical mandate. Feeling more secure on the narrow front of price stabilization, and enjoying enhanced prestige because of that success, central bankers and other relatively unaccountable monetary authorities are inclined to extend their prescriptions into ever wider areas of economic policy, where they may encroach progressively on the prerogatives of elected politicians. Thus, a properly authorized concern to defend price stability can easily lead to recommendations concerning exchange rate policy, fiscal discipline, privatization, labour market deregulation, pension reform, and so on. However, unless a delicate balance can be struck between technical expertise and democratic legitimation, the logic of this mission creep would be to depoliticize more and more of the policy areas that had previously been assigned to democratic control. If this is the underlying logic at work it is eventually liable to provoke a backlash, at least in some democracies, including some new democracies.

Rather than a linear progression we might do better to analyse such tendencies in cyclical terms. The following rationale suggests itself: (i) the recent convergence on an idealized model of monetary policy autonomy could reflect a wide but shallow negative consensus (a reaction against previous failed experiments in interventionism) rather than a deep and durable positive commitment to a universally valid economic doctrine; and (ii) such cyclical shifts may take a long time to work themselves out, and may introduce all kinds of rigidities intended as guarantees against reversal that can serve to extend the life of the cycle, although not necessarily to pro vide absolute guarantees against its eventual reversal.

Some ongoing experiences in contemporary neo-democracies seem to correspond to the expectations of a cyclical theory. Consider the 1991 convertibility law in Argentina. This has tied Argentine monetary policy to the dollar, regardless of whatever surprises may arise either from the evolution of the economy or from the political realm. The commitment is supposed to be permanent and effectively irreversible. (In theory the Argentine Congress could repeal the law, but in practice long before it had completed its deliberation the very fact that this was being considered would produce a disorderly collapse of confidence.) As this volume goes to press, the government of Argentina is failing to sustain its pledge that this monetary system will never break down or have to be redesigned. But the method chosen does introduce a high degree of rigidity into the system, meaning that although a cyclical reversal will still come about, it can only occur at a very high cost, not only to the financial system, but also to constitutional order and the democratic system as a whole. Whether Argentina or Ecuadorean experiments with the 'irreversible' expatriation of monetary authority prove to be step-changes or cyclical extremes remains to be seen, but whatever the outcome the consequences are as important for democracy as for monetary stability.

In conclusion, this chapter about monetary authority in new democracies has echoed a number of points that are made elsewhere in this book about other aspects of democratization. Building 'consent' for monetary authority is a complex and long-term process that involves striking a 'delicate balance' between the requirements of efficiency and the need for legitimacy. New democracies come to this process from a diverse range of backgrounds and with distinctive resources and inheritances. As the process unfolds there may be convergence towards a relatively standardized model of central bank autonomy, financial market liberalization, implied consent through carefully controlled channels of accountability to constitutional authority, and integration into an international 'epistemic community' of financial expertise. But convergence should not be confused with final closure.

No single ultimate model of monetary authority has been discovered that provides the unique 'right solution' for all countries in all situations. Even in the democracies there are major differences of emphasis between the Federal Reserve and the European Central Bank of Japan, with no one expecting the relatively successful US model to be universalized. The European System is a controversial experiment and international arrangements governing monetary issues are fragmenting and unstable. So it is hardly surprising if in neo-democracies convergence is fitful and uneven, with several alternative outcomes still possible. Dollarization may prove the answer in some countries, but is unlikely to work equally well for all. Others may require relatively discretionary management of monetary policy, and perhaps also moderately close supervision by elected politicians. Some may enjoy strong protection from the main international centres of financial powers, but others will be more dependent on regional initiatives that may respond to a rather different logic, and still others may depend upon the patronage of a single state, or may indeed lack strong international allies of any kind. All these variations signal the persistence of pluralism in a world of new democracies. This pluralism is likely to be accompanied by various forms of instability: for example, when further financial crises hit certain emerging market democracies; or when the balance of domestic forces shifts for an against monetary orthodoxy; or as technical change transforms the nature of financial transactions. Democratization leaves open the scope for imaginative innovations in the structure of monetary authority as in other areas of public policy, such as the topic of the next chapter namely— citizen security.

7

On Citizen Security

Upon the impartial administration of justice depends the liberty of every individual, the sense he has of his own security.'

(Adam Smith)

The caesura between the minimum requirements of democratic theory and even the very best performance of 'really existing' democracies provides an organizing framework for this whole volume. Nowhere is this more striking than in the area of citizen security. Much theorizing—not only about democracy but also about democratization—takes the basic security of the median citizen as a datum, a presupposition upon which liberal and constitutional systems can be founded, rather than as a problematic social construction. This chapter reviews the theoretical issues, both from a traditional rule of law standpoint and in the light of more 'sociological' approaches to the question of citizenship. It then presents case studies from Latin America to demonstrate the gap between theory and experience, and concludes by drawing out the implications for our understanding of democratization.

Standard political theory holds that in a democracy all citizens should have a voice on public affairs. Although not obliged to participate, if something concerns them they have the right to be heard by those in authority; and to ensure that their concerns are taken seriously they can even choose to change their rulers at predetermined intervals. Yet there is a counterpart to this right to be heard: all citizens in a democracy are also subject to constraint. In liberal constitutional theory, which antedates democratic theory, citizens are viewed as individual agents with consequent equality of rights and responsibilities before the law. The rule of law protects critical aspects of their personal and collective security, and in return they are obliged to abide by its provisions. The following two paragraphs from Samuel Pufendorf's 1673 treatise convey a sense of the balance involved in classical rule of law doctrines:

The overriding purpose of states is that, by mutual co-operation and assistance, men may be safe from the losses and injuries which they may and often do inflict on each other. To obtain this from those with whom we are united in one society, it is not enough that we make agreement with each other not to inflict injuries on each other, nor even that the bare will of a superior be made known to the citizen's: fear of punishment is needed, and the capacity to inflict it immediately. To achieve its purpose, the penalty must be nicely judged, so that it clearly costs more to break the law than to observe it. . . .

There must be easy access to those who are charged with the administration of justice; they must protect the common people from oppression by the powerful; they must give justice equally to the poor and humble and to the powerful and influential; they must not drag out legal cases more than necessary; they must abjure bribes; they must show diligence in hearing cases and put aside any prejudices that would mar the integrity of their judgements; and they should not fear any man in doing what is right.[1]

If certain provisions of law are objectionable to good citizens they may seek to change it by legal means, but until it is changed they should observe it. Thus citizenship involves an exchange: more security in return for less freedom of action. But of course this argument presupposes the existence of an effective and impartial justice system capable of interpreting legal principles as they apply to the messy particulars of individual cases. As our initial quotation suggests, Adam Smith makes just that assumption in the *Wealth of Nations*.[2]

In addition to this formal-legal strand in liberal political theory, there is also a more sociological perspective on citizenship and citizen security. However fair and thorough the justice system, only a small and unrepresentative set of cases can be attended to. For the great majority of acts by individual citizens the rule of law is only enforced to the extent that groups and individuals practise appropriate forms of self-limitation. The rights and restraints of citizenship are thus internalized rather than imposed. From this perspective, good citizens are those who learn to behave with civility towards each other, and with restraint towards the public authorities that uphold their rights.

Among the theorists of democracy, Durkheim was especially notable for his sociological perspective and exploring the connections between the development of democracy and the evolution of

---

[1] These passages are taken from the translation by Michael Silverthorne (the original was in Latin). Samuel Pufendorf's *On the Duty of Man and Citizen According to Natural Law* (Cambridge: CUP, 1991), 139–40, p. 176.

[2] Adam Smith, *The Wealth of Nations*, book 5, chapter 1, final paragraph of Part II.

collective sentiments about punishment. He classified political systems along a continuum ranging from those that were isolated from the rest of society to those where communication between state and society was at a maximum, at which point democracy itself was maximized. 'A people is more democratic in so far as deliberation, reflection and the critical spirit play a more considerable role in the conduct of public affairs. It is less democratic in so far as unawareness, unconsidered practices, obscure sentiments and, in brief, unexamined prejudices are predominant.' For Durkheim, the moral superiority of democracy arose from the fact that it was 'a system based on reflection, it allows the citizen to accept the laws of his country with more understanding, and thus with less passivity'. In accordance with this view of democracy, which he associated with the emergence of modern industrial society, Durkheim sketched a sociological account of changing collective attitudes towards law, punishment, and morality that suggested that, as social complexity and individual autonomy advanced, the degree of repression (the 'intensity' of punishment) would decline. Moving along the continuum towards a maximization of democracy there would be an associated move towards increasing collective respect for justice equality of opportunity, and individual dignity.[3] Among political theorists, R. G. Collingwood developed this perspective with particular emphasis on its classical foundations, situating it in the broader context of 'civilization' or becoming more civil. 'Where it refers to a man's relations with his fellow men it indicates abstention from the use of force . . . Being civilised means living, so far as possible, dialetically, that is, in constant endeavour to convert every occasion of non-agreement into an occasion of agreement.'[4]

Michel Foucault's perspective on liberalism and security recasts this discussion in more fashionable language. He accepts that the essence of liberalism is the internalization of restraints that hitherto were outwardly imposed. Individuals are set free to pursue their interests, but then for Foucault the art of government involves not only guaranteeing the resulting liberty but manufacturing it at each instant. This change of perspective assigns a far more active role to the authorities under liberalism. They continually produce, maintain, and also limit the freedoms exercised by their citizens, but they must also allocate the costs arising from this public activity.

[3] This account of Durkheim's views is digested from ch. 13 of Steven Lukes, *Emile Durkheim: His Life and Works* (Harmondsworth: Penguin, 1975), esp. pp. 258 and 272–3.

[4] R. G. Collingwood, *The New Leviathan* (Oxford: Oxford University Press, 1992), para. 39.15, p. 326.

Moreover, and most fundamentally for Foucault, the production of such liberty involves a formidable extension of procedures of control, constraint, and coercion. This apparently paradoxical feature of liberalism arises from the view that the production of liberty is indissolubly linked to the management of danger. Mechanisms of freedom and security are thus seen as interdependent; indeed, the two words are viewed as virtually synonymous, just as 'administration' is equated with 'police'. What may induce civility and restraint among liberalized individuals is their awareness of the dangers accompanying their freedom, and the art of liberal government is therefore to manipulate that constraining calculus of interest.[5]

Such restraints and civility are necessary components of democratic citizenship, in part because the gap between the regulatory principles of the justice system and the specific circumstances of individuals and groups in conflict is inherently large. Not even the most ideal system of police and courts can deliver justice to more than a small fraction of the parties in contention. Yet all parties are obliged to observe the rule of law (not take justice into their own hands), even when their disputes cannot be officially adjudicated. This is why goodwill and civility are necessary components of citizen security in a strong democracy. It is also why confidence in any justice system is as much a function of *perception* as of objective performance. Obviously, a well-functioning justice system is better placed to generate citizen confidence than an ineffective one. However collective perceptions of justice and security are shaped by media reporting and other forms of discourse and representation as much as by direct personal experience. Thus, the several broader strands of Western political theorizing about citizenshp and democracy direct our attention to such issues as education and socialization into norms of civility and self-limitation, the role of such agencies as the media in shaping collective representations of authority and justice, and the eternal dialogue between official discourse and direct popular experience over how to interpret social dangers and how best to provide security against them.

Within such traditions of democratic theory, self-limitation is required of the state as well as of the citizen. In order to protect citizen security, the public authorities may well need a strong and well-focused capacity to penalize both criminals and enemies of the

---

[5] 'Michel Foucault et la question du libéralisme' (in *Le Monde* special supplement *Horizons-Documents Le Siècle*, 1 Jan. 2000), 18. This is an otherwise unpublished extract from a lecture to the Collège de France (24 Jan. 1979) as part of the course 'Naissance de la biopolitique'.

republic, as well as to cope with other threats to collective well-being. A powerful security apparatus and a penetrating system of intelligence may thus be required. Still, according to liberal political theory a democratic state must also be regulated by law and be respectful of the rights and freedoms of citizens. The formal/legal strand of this theory emphasizes such constitutional features as the separation of powers, the independence of the judiciary and a bill of rights as crucial guarantees of state power being used to protect citizen security, not to subvert it. More sociological or extra-institutional strands emphasize constraints on the absence of state power arising from an independent 'civil society' (as discussed in Chapter 3) and from learnt norms and values of citizen autonomy.

This more sociological strand to the analysis of the self-limiting democratic state directs attention to what is sometimes called the 'public sphere', where citizens can associate and deliberate autonomously, free from fear of state coercion. From this standpoint public authority needs to be structured not just to *protect* citizen security, but to *promote* open collective debate about the sources of insecurity and how best to defend citizen security. Such defences may be built around community self-organization as well as through more top–down official interventions. There are, of course, alternative points of view within this general framework. For example, one venerable strand of Western social theory, prominent in the Scottish enlightenment, associates the growth of trust with the rise of the market and of commercial prosperity, whereas the 'civil society' and 'public sphere' approaches tend to see market forces as a potential threat to republican virtue. This is the point at which liberal theories of democracy begin to approach what more radical critics regard as the real requirements for democratization in a society based on class division and economic exploitation. Yet even those who believe that liberal democracy is not enough, and that a substantive or social democracy is required, will face the problem how to establish the norms of self-limitation, civility, and restraint that are required of all citizens—not just the privileged classes but all classes.

In contrast to those who emphasize such societal restraints on arbitrary power, conservative and realist theorists emphasize a narrower conception of the threats to security, privileging the state apparatus as the definer and guarantor of 'order', even at the expense of freedom and justice. Such views were influential in many Western democracies during the cold war, and could well enjoy a resurgence if 'global terrorism' is seen as an equivalent security threat. There are versions of this position that are both venerable and defensible, and that need not necessarily take an anti-democratic form. It is hard to ignore the Machiavellian dictum that 'security for man is impossible unless it be conjoined with power'. President Jefferson used his first Inaugural Address of 1801 to tackle this difficulty head on: 'I know, indeed, that some honest men fear that a republican government cannot be strong; that this government is not strong enough.' Yet he dismissed this as a 'theoretic and visionary fear,' asserting that 'I believe this, on the contrary, the strongest government on earth, I believe it is the only one where every man at the call of the laws, would fly to the standard of the law, and would meet invasions of the public order as his own concern.'[6] In a similar vein, for Collingwood,

Law and order mean strength. Men who respect the rule of law are by daily exercise building up the strength of their own wills; becoming more and more capable of mastering themselves and other men and the world of nature. They are daily more and more able to control their own desires and passions and to crush all opposition to the carrying out of their intentions. They are becoming day by day less liable to be bullied or threatened or cajoled or frightened into courses they would not adopt of their own free will . . .[7]

Of course the 'problem of order' has always been a foundational preoccupation for Western political theory: how to overcome the risks of anarchy and factional strife, or the need for authority to regulate violence and the clash of uncoordinated wills. However, if we recall the nine 'procedural' conditions for democracy reviewed in Chapter 1, these consist of minimum 'citizen rights' and constitutional powers in the absence of which democracy is not possible. For example, 'citizens have a right to express themselves without the danger of severe punishment' and 'popularly elected officials must be able to exercise their constitutional power without being subject to overriding opposition from unelected officials'. On the face of it, these constitute two strikingly high thresholds of citizen security that are far from universally observable even in secure polyarchies.

---

[6] As quoted in Joseph J. Ellis, *American Sphinx: The Character of Thomas Jefferson* (New York: Vintage, 1996), 218.

[7] R. G. Collingwood, *The New Leviathan* (1992 edn. of a book 1st publ. in 1942), 332. This book may have been unduly influenced by the author's intense reaction to the threat of Nazism and its glorification of strength of will, but its view of citizen security founded on a law and order which are in turn grounded on a classical Western philosophy of civilization (and, in his terminology, civility) still offers a striking synthesis of the liberal and realist perspectives. In contrast to Jefferson, Collingwood considers socialization with civility to be an ongoing and incomplete process (he was a Hegelian, after all). So he has to face the problem of how to apply the rule of law impartially both to those schooled in it and those who resist it. (See also the final chapter of this book.)

Perhaps this schematic theoretical review is enough to show that, even within the framework of liberal political theory, as practised in the long-established Western democracies, there is considerable scope for debate about the nature of citizen security and how to preserve or advance it. The debate widens further when we turn to processes of democratization.

For the most part, citizen security lurks in the background of most democratic theory. It tends to get included—if only tacitly—in the definition of 'democracy'; it is often assumed, taken for granted, or even enters as an unstated presupposition. By contrast, theories of democratization need to include some explicit account of how citizen security can be constituted or constructed out of conditions in which it is normally absent. There are, of course, various degrees of insecurity possible in the pre-democratic period. In a few cases, such as colonial Hong Kong, the civic rights dimension of citizen security may be highly developed and protected even though universal suffrage (and the additional elements of security arising from exercising such authority over one's rulers) is lacking. More frequently, either authoritarian rule, or the absence of securely constituted authority, is associated with personal insecurity—the risk of arbitrary arrest, absence of stable rights of association, denial of the information necessary to evaluate public affairs, and more general failings to promote or uphold democratic standards of 'citizenship'. These deficiencies are particularly flagrant in those countries where the pre-democratic period was marked not just by authoritarianism but by protracted civil war, as we see below in relation to El Salvador.

The construction of citizen security out of initial conditions marked by its absence or denial is a major, but under-theorized, component of most processes of democratization. Here we are concerned if not with the construction of 'citizenship', then at least with the provision of the basic conditions of personal and collective security required for its creation: protection for those willing to live within the constraints of the democratic constitution, habeas corpus and due process for those officially accused of infringing the rule of law. In the absence of such basic conditions, neither citizenship nor democracy can be regarded as secure. These are necessary, if not sufficient, conditions for democratization. They are also complex and artificial social constructions.

If citizenship is understood as an outcome of socialization, as the renegotiation of social identities in accordance with constitutional precepts and democratic values, then the majesty of the law (the 'top–down' approach to security) has to be harmonized with the subjectivity of the people (a 'bottom–up' approach). In this case, the definition of what should count as 'citizen security' and the priority to give to the protection of its various components cannot simply be derived from the statute book or from case law. The citizens must have their say on this, and the more democratic a society becomes the more weight their opinions should carry. In some societies they may opt for a thoroughly traditional or restrictive interpretation in accordance with conservative theories of order. Threats of external attack or internal subversion could emerge as the sole contingencies requiring a public policy response so far as public opinion is concerned. Still, this is not a typical pattern of citizen expectations in most new democracies, where a broader conception of citizen security is required. Citizen security could include the right to assistance in the event of natural disasters; it could extend to expectations concerning public health or focus on such mortal hazards as road safety or domestic violence. The relative importance of these various public policy concerns will vary from society to society in response to specific risks and the outlook of the citizenry in each case. In general, the wider the range of demands, the greater the gap between perceptions of citizen entitlement and the capacity of the authorities to deliver. However, while this is certainly a source of tension and instability in new democracies, the consequences are not all negative. In a democratic setting, the authorities are in a position to explain that they cannot deliver everything at once, and that they will need the participation of communities if citizen security, broadly construed, is to be advanced. Civility and self-limitation would thus become integral to the management of the inevitable tensions.

Such theorizing about citizen security and its relationship to democratization can doubtless be extended and refined. At this point it is more germane to measure what we have said against the experience from a selection of new democracies. Given the emphasis placed on social perceptions of citizenship and security, our discussion of how citizen security is perceived in 'really existing' democracies must tackle the problem identified at the outset, namely the wide gap between the minimum demands of theory and the maximum achievements of experience. The Freedom House listing of current competitive electoral regimes (Annex Table 2) provides the universe from which to extract our evidence. In most of these countries, citizen security is perceived to fall so far short of the demands of theory that we are dealing with a gulf rather than a gap. The question is not whether some minimum conditions have been satisfied, but the developmental processes that would be required to bring them into the range of possibility. In such circumstances, a key issue for democratization is how to begin to establish respectable standards of citizen security.

When attempting to specify such thresholds—what counts as a 'respectable standard' in a particular context?—realism is needed concerning both sides of the dividing line. Beneath it are countries classified as democracies but where the reach of the state does not extend across the whole of the territory, or where it is present it fails to provide much by way of security to the population. Where security is provided it may come from sources with no constitutional standing or with little interest in democratization, such as the operators of natural resource enclaves, local landowners, or even insurgent forces and crime cartels. A substantial number of putative new democracies are located well beyond the line at which the average citizen can claim security from an autonomous and authoritative state. In such countries, Adam Smith's 'impartial administration of justice' is even more distant a prospect than in the remotest corners of the Scottish Highlands when he was writing.[8] All that can be said here is that 'democratization' requires the prior establishment of a more extensive and effective system of formal administration that involves countrywide coordination.

Referring to countries above the dividing line, we need to introduce the essential but elusive distinction between public insecurity perceived as *a* problem *for* the government and a state of insecurity judged by the public to be *the* problem *of* government. In the United Kingdom, for example, there is widespread recognition that in much of Northern Ireland over the past thirty years, if not longer, local *de facto* powers have been strong enough to resist the rule of law, to intimidate sections of the electorate, and to bring strong extra-legal forms of pressure to bear on elected politicians. It may now be that minorities in certain inner-city areas on the British mainland would also feel that their basic security had become a problem of government. Yet even on the most negative assessment, neither the distribution nor the undesirability of these concerns would change the generally held opinion that the United Kingdom is a well-established democracy with a long tradition of promoting and protecting the security of its citizens. Ulster may be *a* severe problem *for* the government in Westminster, but that does not disqualify British democracy as a whole. Similar observations could be made about France (notwithstanding Corsica or the *banlieues sensibles*), or in Spain (with the insecurity emanating from the Basque

---

[8] Adam, Smith *The Wealth of Nations*, book 5, ch. 1, part 2 (1st publ. 1776).

provinces or associated with some of its immigration problems). Equally, the same can be said of the United States, even at the height of its inner-city riots. This is not the place to extend the list; the point is simply that, if we accept this degree of citizen insecurity without doubting the democratic credentials of a regime, then our theory of democracy and democratization fails to generate a clear-cut criterion or empirical indicator for determining where the threshold between incidental and fundamental citizen insecurity is to be located. A complex and potentially subjective exercise in judgement may be involved.

The rest of this chapter focuses on the large band of intermediate cases. These are countries where putative democracy may be characterized by perceptions of such widespread and chronic citizen insecurity that it is straining democratic theory to the limits to screen out such realities. Yet, they are also countries where there is sufficient evidence of an authoritative and effective state presence for it to be meaningful to discuss the security that the authorities could reasonably be expected to provide. Following the theoretical points made above, this discussion is couched in the language of 'perceptions' and 'expectations'. So the question naturally arises as to whose opinions count in this context, and how we are to discover them. As indicated in Chapter 1, the views of citizens must be given close consideration not just by academic analysts but by those who claim to be their democratic leaders. Yet, we also said that these views may be subject to debate and revision in the light of comparative evidence, and that we need to be aware that the conditions for free deliberation may not exist uniformly across the whole society.[9] Consequently, a combination of indicators needs to be assembled and critically evaluated. Perceptions are critical to the analysis of citizen security issues in new democracies, and these need to be painstakingly and critically evaluated. The study of perceptions also involves the study of local contexts and specific histories, since every new democracy can draw on a prior experience of pre-democratic, anti-democratic, or even totalitarian practices in the realm of citizen security. Citizens can only formulate judgements about what constitutes a problem *of* government—versus what must be classified as *the* problem *of* democratic government—on the basis of such comparative judgements.

[9] Guillermo O'Donnell extends this argument by referring to the 'brown areas' of society, specific sectors and regions where political freedom may be highly constrained despite an overall national framework of civil rights. Habermassian critics direct attention to media manipulation of perceptions elsewhere in society, where traditional restraints on freedom of enquiry are not an issue.

Most of the material that follows is drawn from Latin America, a score of new democracies in which almost all have experienced widespread and sometimes severe public dissatisfaction with their police and justice systems.[10] Evidence from South Africa and Eastern Europe shows that Latin American democracies are not alone in this respect. There are thus many 'new democracies' in which citizen insecurity comes close to being regarded as *the* problem *of* government.

Brazil is one of the largest and best established of these new democracies, a country with a strong administrative capacity and a consistently poor record of delivering on its promises of citizen security. It provides a major and representative example of the realities under discussion in this chapter, although we should not seek to disguise its distinctiveness—for example, as a country where slavery was only abolished in 1888. Central America provides other examples of countries where such phenomena present themselves in an exceptionally strong and clear form. Guatemala and El Salvador are recently constructed democracies that have emerged from acute civil conflicts; they therefore test notions of citizen security under democratization in a severe manner. Costa Rica—perhaps the most durable and exemplary democracy in Latin America—can be included for the sake of comparison. Here we focus on the acute problems facing El Salvador, where there is a widespread perception that the key problem for democratization is the need to overcome massive failures in the area of citizen security. It is a paradigmatic case in that the prospects are quite finely balanced, and that the success or failure of current efforts to tackle such problems will have important implications for other new democracies with similar problems albeit in less acute form.[11]

---

[10] Latinobarometro produces annual attitude surveys on a standardized basis in eighteen republics. Between 1997 and 2001 these surveys showed substantial declines in overall confidence in most institutions apart from the Church and the media. Confidence in the police fell from 36% to 30% and in the judiciary from 36% to 27%.

[11] Representative, critical, and paradigmatic cases are all examples of what Flyvbjerg classifies as 'information-oriented' cases, i.e. cases selected on the basis of expectations about their information content, rather than on the basis of some sampling procedure. His definition of a 'critical' case is more exacting than mine ('to achieve information which permits logical deductions of the type' if this is (not) valid for this case, then it applies to all (no) cases). His definition of a paradigmatic case is close to my conception ('to develop a metaphor or establish a school for the domain which the case concerns'), *Making Social Science Matter* (Cambridge: CUP, 2001).

Turning first to Brazil, Article 5 of the 1988 Constitution contains the most comprehensive listing of fundamental citizen rights and guarantees, both individual and collective. The seventy-seven clauses of this article constitute an equivalent of a 'bill of rights', norms that are supposed to have 'immediate application'. Although the article refers to 'rights and duties', the text only contains promised rights for citizenry and assumed duties for the state. Among the long list of citizen rights designed as guarantees against the arbitrary practices of the past, clauses 42 and 43 deserve our special attention, documenting as they do the distance between liberal theory and social practice in key areas. Clause 42 outlaws the practice of 'racism', which is punishable by imprisonment without rights of bail. Clause 43 classifies torture, drug trafficking, and terrorism as 'heinous crimes' not subject to pardon or amnesty. This provision applies not only to the authors of such crimes, but those in a position to act but who fail to prevent them.

With reference to clause 42, Peter Fry reports that the Special Police Station for Racial Crimes, established in São Paulo in 1993, opened only eight dossiers in 1996, suggesting that the new law has been no more effective than the old in stemming racism or punishing 'racist practice'.[12] His explanation for this invokes distinctive features of popular perceptions of race in Brazil, features that powerfully determine the way formal rules and legal provisions are implemented in practice:

most contemporary Brazilians deny racism, hold racist beliefs . . . and yet deny that they themselves practice racial discrimination against those who are darker than themselves . . . [hence] the police, the technicians of the judiciary, magistrates, juries, judges, the accused, and even at times, the accusors, share a reluctance to allow conviction unless there is incontrovertible proof of racism. They would prefer to maintain racial discrimination as an abstract evil rather than a real concrete fact of life.[13]

Obviously such divergence between a theoretical equality of citizen rights and a practice with discriminatory consequences for social categories with adverse markers (skin colour, poverty, 'indianness' or other minority or outsider status, etc.) is not unique to

---

[12] Peter Fry, 'Collor and the Rule of Law in Brazil', in Juan E. Méndez, Guillermo O'Donnell, and Paulo Sergio Pinheiro (eds.), *The (Un)Rule of Law and the Underprivileged in Latin America* (South Bend, Ind.: Notre Dame University Press, 1999), 194. He notes that complaints may end up classified as defamation rather than as racial crimes.

[13] Ibid., 200 Fry's chapter also supplies evidence of the 'real and concrete' nature of this fact of Brazilian life, a large topic on which there is an abundant scholarly literature.

Brazil, nor to new democracies more generally. Indeed Brazilian democracy may deserve some credit for recognizing the problem and attempting to confront it. However, given the high proportion of Brazilians whose security could be undermined by racism, the extreme inequalities of Brazilian society and the deficiencies of the Brazilian police and justice system, the apparent inapplicability of clause 42 is of more than passing significance. It provides a telling illustration of how the attractive language of democratic theory can cohabit with 'really existing' practices that negate the rhetoric of universal citizen security and therefore deprive a democratic regime of its theoretical rationale. With respect to the constitutional protection of habeas corpus, it is important to bear in mind that 'in São Paulo, when the military police kill a suspect, in order to remove most forensic evidence, they commonly take the victim to the hospital as though he or she were still alive'.[14] Similar observations apply to other areas, such as child labour and gender relations. Here we have the social foundations for our expectation that there will be demands for 'democratization' (in the sense of the fulfilment of the moral claims on which democratic theory is founded) which persist long after stipulative definitions would tell us that democracy has already been 'consolidated'.

Clause 43 provides a second, perhaps more generally compelling illustration of the same argument, concerning the banning of torture. If citizens are at risk from torture (or summary execution or forced labour), and if those responsible enjoy effective impunity, then the basic rights enshrined in the rhetoric of 'citizen security' must be void, with troubling consequences for all claims on a democratic order. Here is how Human Rights Watch summarizes the recent situation in Brazil:

Our research for this report confirms that torture is still a routine practice in police precincts throughout Brazil, a practice that is widely accepted, particularly when the victim is a poor, criminal suspect. Torture is practised by members of all police forces in Brazil—state, civil and military police, as well as federal police . . . The reasons for this widespread practice are varied. Most analysts agree that the lack of adequate training often leads police to use torture rather than more sophisticated investigation techniques. Also, no doubt, the impunity that police torturers frequently enjoy plays a key role in the continued practice.[15]

---

[14] Paul Chevigny, 'Defining the Role of the Police in Latin America', in Méndez *et al.* (eds.), *(Un)Rule of Law*, 57.

[15] Human Rights Watch, *Police Brutality in Urban Brazil* (New York: Human Rights Watch, 1997), 29–30. This report is mainly concerned with extra-judicial executions by the police, but it draws on a wider range of research as well. Ironically

This brief discussion only focuses on one narrow component of citizen security in Brazil. As agents of the state, the police may have specific legal responsibility but they are caught up in a much wider network of power interactions. Wealthy citizens may hire private security guards for their gated condominiums, so that there is one police service for the rich and another for the poor. Organized crime may acquire such concentrated local power that it can effectively administer its own (rough) justice within the framework of an ostensibly constitutional regime.[16] If the courts and the prisons fail to administer justice, then the only punishments received by many genuine real criminals may be those directly administered by the police who first detain them.[17] Social perceptions of criminality, insecurity, and the appropriate scope of police action may be as distinctive and complex as those outlined above with reference to racism. In summary, the realities of ordinary life in democratic Brazil constantly challenge the assumptions of liberal theory concerning citizenship and citizen security. In such conditions, democratization demands that the lived realities of the median voter are brought closer to the normative pretensions of constitutional and liberal democratic theory.[18] Any democratization worthy of the name has to curb police torture and extra-judicial killings, and has to win police consent for the view that such practices are intolerable. The

the high incidence of extra-judicial killings occurs in a country which has outlawed the death penalty (Article 5, clause 67).

[16] A recent ethnographic report on four *favelas* in Rio de Janeiro describes the ways in which the drug traffickers have increasingly legitimated their local control through the administration of quite elaborated (and very harsh) forms of local justice, which fill a void left by the absence of official justice. Enrique Desmond Arias and Corinne M. Davis, 'The Role of Criminals in Crime Management and Dispute Resolution: Understanding Drug Traffickers' Control in Rio's *Favelas*' (LASA, Sept. 2001).

[17] On 7 Feb. 2001, the Brazilian weekly *Veja* published the following data comparing crime and punishment in Brazil and the USA: per hundred violent crimes reported 24 led to an arrest in Brazil (40 in the USA); the suspect went to trial in 14 cases (38); the trial resulted in a prison sentence in 5 cases (19); the sentence was served to completion in 1 case (15). Citizen frustration with ineffective official justice stimulates resort to extra-official sanctions.

[18] Another ethnographic enquiry in São Paulo concluded that 'the public knows they have rights, but these seem to be "floating in the air"'. Interviewees were unable to define these rights and to build logical connections between the duty of the state and their citizen rights. Therefore, the perception of rights expressed itself as a matter concerning isolated individuals and intertwined with feelings—as if rights had more to do with feelings than with the rational logic of citizenship.' Luciana Gross Siqueira Cunha, *Access to Justice and Judicial Assistance in São Paulo* (LASA, Sept. 2001).

material presented here from Brazil—which could be replicated for numerous other new democracies)[19]—suggests that democratization understood in such terms can only be a long-term, complex, and open-ended process.

In post-conflict Central America, El Salvador provides a paradigmatic example of democratization. Once it was clear to domestic and international opinion alike that the old forces of order had contributed to and aggravated the civil conflict, it followed that an externally monitored compromise peace settlement would involve a far-reaching restructuring of El Salvador's police and justice systems. This was indeed a key element of the 1992 Chapultepec peace agreement and of the democratization process that followed. Since one-fifth of El Salvador's population now lives in the United States and has direct exposure to a broad and effective system of citizen protection, there is widespread appreciation of what citizen security means. However, this leads to demands to which it is well beyond the traditional capacity or disposition of the Salvadoran state to respond adequately.

Seen comparatively, the Salvadoran democratization has involved a more explicit recognition of the need for citizen security than elsewhere in Latin America, or indeed further afield. Most western hemisphere new democracies have not radically reshaped their police forces, or indeed removed from positions of command officials associated with previous episodes of repression. Perhaps only in Haiti and Panama, both of which restored electoral processes in the wake of US invasions, did the recasting of the old forces of order go so far. El Salvador has also become something of a model of how UN mediation can contribute not just to conflict resolution but to the construction of a post-conflict democratic regime in which a reformed police plays a new and more positive political role. Yet, a decade after the arrival of the first UN mediator, citizen security remains far from assured, and the long-term success of the

---

[19] According to Paul Chevigny, 'Torture is reported in the Dominican Republic, Honduras, Nicaragua, Paraguay, Peru, and Venezuela. Torture also appears in relatively quiet places, such as Chile, Ecuador and Uruguay. Torture is notorious in Mexico. . . . In some places such as Colombia, Cuba and Peru torture is reportedly used against political dissidents, but for the most part victims everywhere are accused of ordinary crimes. Clearly, torture is used against those who are "torturable" . . . it is used as a form of punishment just as it is used to seek information. It is rarely used against middle class people. . . . Having been tortured by the police is a badge of poverty and degradation. . . . However . . . the use of torture is decreasing'. Chevigny, 'Defining the Role of the Police in Latin America', in Méndez *et. al.*, *Un(Rule) of Law*, 52–3.

whole democratization process depends heavily on whether persistent failures in this area progressively can be overcome.

Comparisons with other Central American republics highlight different aspects of the Salvadoran reality. Comparison with Guatemala, perhaps the country with the most similar historical experience, tends to emphasize the more positive aspects, whereas comparison with Costa Rica does the opposite. In her recent analysis of the Guatemalan peace process Susanne Jonas includes a specific set of comparisons with El Salvador. These underscore some similarities, but they also indicate Guatemala's more substantial problems with regard to institutional reform, notably demilitarization and the failure to secure vital reforms during the 1999 referendum on the constitution. She concludes that 'the upshot of this comparison with El Salvador is that the stakes are higher in Guatemala, but the capacity of domestic Guatemalan actors by themselves is lower. (. . .) Nevertheless, it is important not to distort this delicate balance into a (commonly heard) false comparison that belittles or dismisses the Guatemalan experience relative to the Salvadoran'.[20] There is also an interaction between the two cases, such that if citizen security in Guatemala degenerates further, the demonstration effect will be felt in El Salvador. Equally, if the Salvadoran process can be steered onto firmer ground, that example would have resonance in Guatemala.

Crime statistics enable us to compare the proportion of the population in each of the three Central American republics which has been victim to robbery and assault: 55 per cent in Guatemala, 47 per cent in El Salvador, and 33 per cent in Costa Rica. El Salvador is often described as having one of the highest homicide rates in the world, but there are no credible comparative Guatemalan statistics. Whereas the reported rate peaked above 100 per 100,000 in El Salvador, the reported rate is only about seven in Costa Rica, the country with probably the most accurate data. Although this puts Costa Rica at about

---

[20] Susanne Jonas, *Of Centaurs and Doves: Guatemala's Peace Process* (Boulder, Colo.: Westview Press, 2000), 229. However, the gravity of the current situation in Guatemala is underscored by Caroline Moser and Cathy McLlwaine, *Violence in a Post-Conflict Context: Urban Poor Perceptions from Guatemala* (Washington, DC: World Bank, 2001). The authors carried out an 'urban appraisal' exercise in nine poor communities in Guatemala in spring 1999. They report that 'the severe lack of confidence in the government's capacity to provide adequate police or judicial protection fosters development of alternative informal social cleansing justice systems such as lynching. Nevertheless, the new Policia Nacional Civil is held in much higher regard than the former Policia Nacional—with associated lower levels of delinquency, robbery, and violence in communities severed by the PNC' (p. 9).

the same level as the USA, its citizens express intense concern at their perceived vulnerability to crime and insecurity.[21]

Even in Britain and the USA voter perceptions that crime and violence are growing problems put pressure on elected governments to take stronger measures. As Table 7.1 indicates, El Salvador's homicide problem is several orders of magnitude worse than in the Anglo-Saxon democracies. Even in these, there are pockets of severe citizen insecurity, and statistics for parts of Detroit or most of Compton, Los Angeles, bear comparison with the Salvadoran data. This suggests that processes of democratization and the construction of citizen security are never fully complete. The idealized democracy of liberal political theory is an unattainable end state. Comparative analysis shows that the nature and scale of the threats to citizen security vary enormously both between and within 'really existing' democracies. Even so, this type of political system responds to the same logic across the board. If the voters care enough about what they perceive as poor governmental performance in this area, they can pressure their political leaders to take corrective action on pain of dismissal.

This data shows how severe and generalized the problem of citizen insecurity in general, and criminal violence in particular, has become in El Salvador. In May 2000, 49 per cent of the adult population rated crime and delinquency as the country's main problem (CID/Gallup). Such circumstances feed perceptions that can stimulate authoritarian and anti-democratic reflexes among significant sectors of the electorate. Hence the institutions that have been reshaped or refounded in the course of democratization receive no

TABLE 7.1. *Homicides in Three Democracies at the End of the 1990s*

	Total Population	Police Numbers (Officers)	Prison Population	Homicides
El Salvador	6m	17,000	8,000	6,000
Great Britain	59m	130,000	66,000	600
USA	282m	640,000	1,400,000	15,500

[21] In a May 2001 opinion survey, violence and crime were rated the most serious public concerns in Costa Rica, well above economic problems, poverty, and corruption. Two months later the professional assassination of an investigative journalist generated intense public debate, indicating a widespread perception that Costa Rica was slipping towards the insecurity of its neighbours, although in statistical terms this still seems totally unfounded.

more than provisional and conditional public approval. Their continued authority will depend on their success in delivering expected benefits, and these are far from guaranteed at this stage.

However, while opinion and victim surveys reveal a very bad objective situation, they also contain some encouraging signs for those interested in crafting a democratic strategy towards crime prevention. One concerns the growing importance of local government. El Salvador's 1999 Auditoría de la Democracia reports high and rising levels of citizen petitioning to the municipal authorities, with 12 per cent of those surveyed claiming to have made such representations in 1995, rising to 18 per cent in 1999. One-quarter of respondents identified delinquency and lack of security as the most serious problems facing their municipality. Those who had been victims of delinquency were more likely than others to take part in municipal affairs.[22] Local government was rated more favourably than other branches of government, with the rating increasing further since 1995. Respondents therefore supported the devolution of tax revenues to local administrations.

Despite the quantity and quality of recent empirical research on citizen security in El Salvador, there remain major limitations to the data, although given the breadth of the concept and the scale of the problems it could hardly be otherwise. Such limitations mean that opinions continue to be formed on the basis of rumour and suspicion. With citizens increasingly dissatisfied about the generalized nature of insecurity, and the regime's apparent inability to address the situation, the legitimacy of the current political order is threatened. Perceptions of failure in the area of law and order are fed by frustrated expectations in other areas. For instance, the January 2001 earthquake showed that the regime was unable to protect the citizenry from natural disasters. It also fails to meet minimum expectations in the protection of public health, the avoidance of traffic accidents, and the restraint of domestic violence. Such broader deficiencies reinforce collective disillusion and resentment about law and order failings more strictly defined, such as kidnappings, gang control of the streets of marginal *barrios*, and disclosures of criminality and impunity among the security forces. The contrast between this climate of insecurity and the image of democracy in the USA (where so many Salvadoran families now have relatives) simply increases dissatisfaction. Still, perceptions are volatile, and if reforms begin to generate improvements, the tide of expectations could change.

---

[22] UNDP/University of Pittsburgh, *Auditoria de la Democracia* (San Salvador: UNDP, 2000), 34–42.

It may be argued that Brazil and El Salvador represent extreme and atypical experiences. Even a casual inspection of the literature from other new democracies should suffice to rebut this objection. For example, the following passage closely resembles the Central American experience:

One of the major challenges of the South African Police Service is how to change it from an instrument of oppression into a community resource. The crisis of legitimacy that currently faces the police service is the consequence of a deep-rooted institutional complicity or organizational deviance which over the years has inhibited the SAP's capacity as a police organization to become a protector of communities, especially of black communities. Throughout the apartheid era members of the South African Police service were trained and motivated to control rather than protect communities. In order to change this attitude, much more than legislative intervention will be required. More innovative processes which emphasize 'culture change' and dedication to community protection will have to be evolved.[23]

Similarly, in post-communist Eastern Europe, a contrast is often drawn between policing practices—including police violence, lack of accountability, complicity with organized crime, and inexperience in community policing—and the standards promoted by the European Union (although not all EU countries are above reproach in such respects).[24] Examples could also be found among new democracies in Asia. Further research would undoubtedly contribute to uncovering the wider aspects of citizen security that go beyond policing.

Disenchantment with the quality of public life is thus widespread. Corruption, impunity, lack of accountability, and failure to deliver on election promises figure prominently in public indictments. Alarm over the seemingly uncontrollable expansion of common crime—both organized and petty—along with distress over the weakness of the police and justice systems, features recurrently as a major aspect of citizen discontent. Survey data, crime statistics, victim reports, and press coverage all underscore the gravity and ubiquity of the phenomenon. The term 'citizen security' refers broadly to all these concerns about criminality and the rule of law.

[23] Medard Rwelamira, 'Democracy and Policing', in F. Nel and J. Bezuidenhout (eds.), *Policing and Human Rights* (Cape Town: Juta & Co, 1997), 61–2.

[24] András Kádár (ed.), *Police in Transition* (Budapest: Central European University Press, , 2001). In Nov. 2000, the vice-president of Italy's National Association of Magistrates denounced the Camorra (the Neopolitan mafia) for still controlling illegal immigration, human trafficking, and systems of extortion and social control based on intimidation and murder, and all organized from Rome (*Il Messagero*, 19 Nov. 2000).

As we have seen, it includes other aspects of public policy that affect the physical security of the population, such as the response to natural disasters. Arguably, technological advance gives modern governments greater control over nature than in the early days of democracy. Citizen security is expected to extend to coping with such disasters, as well as regulating conflicts between citizens.

Contemporary notions of citizenship rights are also more extensive than before. Carlos Sojo (of FLACSO, Costa Rica) recently argued that, in democratic Central America, 'the concept of citizen security is expanding as governments and security officials recognize that crime and social violence are linked to broader social and economic issues, such as the lack of education, health, and economic opportunities'. To this, Laura Chinchilla (of UNDP, Costa Rica) added that 'citizen security needs to be perceived as a condition to wider political and economic development, and not an end in itself. Improved security on the streets and in the home is a joint responsibility of the local government and the citizens themselves and should not be viewed as a service to be provided by the government alone.' These are strong arguments in favour of an expansive concept of citizen security. Yet the problem arises of being too ambitious in a setting where the reach of the state is often quite uncertain. This is particularly the case where traditionally neither 'citizenship' nor 'security' have been promoted or respected, and where the right of the state to monopolize the legitimate use of force remains in dispute due to the legacy of past injustices and actual conditions of social inequality.

This chapter has indicated that in new democracies such issues of citizenship and citizen security can easily become volatile and unstable. Instead of being *a* problem of *the* government, perceptions can change until they are viewed as *the* problem *of* government. These are societies in which stable conceptions of citizenship may not have been fully internalized by all the population. In some cases, like El Salvador, the pre-democratic authorities may have used the language of constitutional rights, but without any intention of upholding them for all citizens in all circumstances. In others, such as Brazil, democratic regimes may have proclaimed constitutional rights that are spectacularly out of line with citizens' daily experience. In such conditions, it is hardly surprising that many individuals remain sceptical about the reality of such rights, and that they feel insecure and unprotected as the bearers of citizenship. They may be forgiven for entertaining corresponding doubts about the need to fulfil the duties theoretically associated with citizenship rights. It is not so much a question of the *absence* of citizenship, but uncertainty about its scope and reliability. So, even if there is a clear understanding of the theory of citizenship and a desire to achieve it, there may be grave doubts about whether it is attainable. In a large number of 'really existing' new democracies, an authentic sense of citizenship can coexist with the perception that in real life such pretensions are incomplete and unstable. This can only be overcome through long-term, complex and dynamic processes of citizenship construction. Just such processes lie at the heart of the democratization project, correctly understood.

This chapter has also reviewed some comparative indicators revealing the wide variety of experiences of citizen security to be found within the large universe of existing competitive electoral regimes. Even though this evidence is merely illustrative and more extensive work needs to be done, it should suffice to demonstrate the magnitude of the issue and its significance for regime legitimacy in a large number of new democracies. It also highlights the need to distinguish between objective indicators and citizen perceptions in individual societies, since it is perceptions that have most bearing on the standing of a democratic regime. In El Salvador, the objective indicators are so poor that one might wonder how the democratic regime can hope to endure. Yet given Salvadoran history and traditions, expectations of citizen protection are much lower than in, say, Costa Rica. The Salvadoran regime may therefore be able to generate considerable new support for its democracy by policies that improve perceptions of its effectiveness, even though crime and violence remain extremely high by international standards.

More generally, this discussion of citizen security illustrates key issues of comparative method that arise in democratization studies. The next two chapters take up these methodological questions for a broader perspective. They pay particular attention to the problems of comparison across large regions like Latin America, Eastern Europe, or East Asia, whilst also highlighing the utility of paired comparisons like those presented above for El Salvador/Costa Rica and El Salvador/Guatamala. Chapter 9 considers Chile as an exemplary single case, pursuing the same strategy of comparative analysis used for El Salvador in this chapter.

8

On Comparing Democratization Processes

> If therefore, even one or two of these few instances be insuffi-
> ciently known . . . and therefore not adequately compared with
> other instances, nothing is more probable than that a wrong
> empirical law will emerge.
>
> (John Stuart Mill)

Issues of Method

This volume is concerned with the comparative analysis of a
particular type of long-term historical process. As such, it has
drawn on a diversity of theoretical and empirical sources, and has
included some extended discussions of key methodological issues
(such as the meaning of critical concepts, the role of metaphors in
theory building, and the merits of an 'interpretavist' approach to
theorizing about historical processes). This chapter aims to provide
a more focused discussion of one methodological issue that is particularly central to the approach of this book, namely how to undertake the comparative side of the analysis.

The standard approach to comparative work may be labelled the
'reporting unit' approach. Here the procedure is to identify the
universe of units included in the study, and then to assemble standardized objective indicators for each unit. This permits such statistical procedures as sampling the universe, measuring distributions
of relevant characteristics within it, and investigating correlations
between the indicators, calculating probabilities of outcomes. The
120 competitive electoral regimes listed in Annex Table 2 can
clearly be analysed in this way, and a substantial amount of academic energy has been devoted to such efforts, sometimes yielding
revealing results.[1] Comparison requires a minimum of shared

---

[1] A. Przeworski and F. Limongi, 'Democracy and Development', in Axel Hadenius
(ed.), *Democracy's Victory and Crisis* (Cambridge: Cambridge University Press,

methods and concepts, and where cultural differences tend to generate misunderstandings and cross-purposes, that makes it all the more important to spell out clear meanings and to insist on objective procedures of verification. The citizens of fragile new democracies deserve clarity and precision about how far their regimes match up to 'best practice' in the most solid and advanced democracies, and if they fall short, why? In at least some areas of comparative politics it is possible to uncover reliable regularities (e.g. concerning the foreseeable consequence of adopting alternative systems of electoral rules), and that universal technical knowledge should be spelt out and made available to the designers of new constitutions wherever they may be located. So the standardized reporting unit approach is an indispensable component of comparative studies.

However, all this requires discrete and comparable reporting units which generate sufficiently informative objective indicators to provide reliable information on the topic under investigation. Those with most confidence in this procedure even recommend that the names of the reporting units should be suppressed, so that only the associated variables (as measured by the indicators) will be taken into consideration. This rigorous and parsimonious procedure is intended to screen out subjective associations and to ensure that the investigator examines this material with an impartial gaze. In principle all such findings should be strictly replicable, with no scope for subjective individual interpretations. Moreover, each statistical observation should refer to a given reporting unit at a single moment in time. While this clearly favours cross-sectional comparisons (assuming the units are in fact comparable) it can only cope with historical processes to the extent that a time series of standardized indicators permits the accurate tracking of dynamic processes.

This volume has characterized processes of democratization as long-term, complex, dynamic, and partially open-ended. It has also asserted the importance of contextualizing them, on the grounds that the critical concepts are social constructions with some variations in meaning over time and space. It has argued for an 'interpretavist' perspective on democratization, and for a recognition of the normative as well as empirical content of such processes. All of this involves degrees of complexity and subjectivity that are not congenial to the reporting unit approach. Following Mill, unless

1997); T. Vanhanen, *Prospects of Democracy: A Study of 172 Countries* (London: Routledge, 1997).

these features of democratization are taken into account many of the instances under investigation will be 'insufficiently known', with the risk that a 'wrong empirical law' will emerge.[2] In fact, if the standard method depends for its reliability on the quality of its analysis of the least known instances, then it is almost certain to fail, given the poor data available on some of the countries listed in the Annex tables.

So the reporting unit approach needs to be tested against alternative strategies of comparison. It screens out much of the history, geopolitics, and linguistic-cum-cultural variation that may need to be considered if we are to account for social meanings and consequent outcomes arising when democratization is imagined and attempted in different contexts. Very few analysts or observers have access to sufficiently full information and understanding to make serious international comparisons about the quality of democracy in more then two countries, let alone in over one hundred countries across five continents. For example, how many English-speaking political scientists can convincingly rank and compare the quality of democracy in Britain and the USA, or in the USA and Canada, or Canada and Australia, let alone in France and Spain, or in India and South Africa? The empirical tabulations that are offered in substitution for this contextual knowledge often rest on such crude and approximate systems of measurement that they are bound to contain gross inaccuracies. While welcome as the starting-point for a comparative enterprise, they can hardly be put beyond the reach of feedback from alternative sources. Finally, and perhaps most fundamentally, the standardized reporting units approach to comparative democratization requires fixed point observations. Yet, as argued elsewhere in this book, it may be more appropriate to view democratization as a long-term, complex, dynamic, and open-ended process. If so, alternative strategies of comparison will be required.

To avoid 'selection bias' the reporting unit approach requires each observation and each case to be of equal standing with every other. In effect it assumes simple causation, and also causal homogeneity within the domain of cases under investigation. Yet some historical processes involve long complex chains of causation, and causal heterogeneity across cases. How can these be studies comparatively?[3]

[2] J. S. Mill, 'A System of Logic' (1843), in *Collected Works*, ed. J. M. Robson (Toronto: University of Toronto Press, 1973), vii. 917.

[3] See David Collier and James Mahoney, 'Insights and Pitfalls: Selection Bias in Qualitative Research', *World Politics*, 49/1 (Oct. 1996), and Dietrich Rueschemeyer and James Mahoney (eds.), *Comparative-Historical Analysis* (New York: Cambridge University Press, 2002).

Thus when studying comparative processes of democratization is it an inadmissible bias to identify certain individual cases (and regions) as exemplary or paradigmatic? For example, the democratization of Spain after the death of Franco occurred early in the recent sequence, and took nearly all observers by surprise. Much of the discussion of democratization in South Europe treats Spain as the indispensable core case, with Portugal and Greece as possible reinforcements or add-ons. The outcome in Spain captured the imagination of political elites throughout Spanish America, and so altered the terms of debate in many subsequent democratizations. There are those who would agree that we should only analyse the characteristics of blondes in general, never considering the case of Marilyn in particular. Yet, in social life, this self-denying ordinance can be blinding rather than illuminating—if, for example, the collective imagination of what blondeness signifies can only be understood by attending to how Marilyn Monroe was perceived.

When contending with such circumstances the notion of 'bias' may need reconsideration. It could be biased *either*: (i) to treat Spain as just one unit in a universe of something approaching 100 cases, all denuded of their specificities and paired down for objective comparison *or* (ii) to treat Spain as paradigmatic, to call it by its name, to examine its inner specificities in detail, and to judge other processes by comparison to the Spanish yardstick. There are no doubt biases implicit in both of these procedures, each of which may be appropriate for certain designated purposes. Alertness to the potential bias of each method may be preferable to the disqualification of one and the sanctification of the other.

If this argument about selection bias holds for Spain, it also holds for large areas such as Latin America. When virtually the whole of the subcontinent democratized that changed perceptions and raised new questions in other large regions of the world. Moreover, when one refers to the influence of the whole of Latin America one need not necessarily give equal weight to every country within that continent. The democratization of Ecuador had little resonance beyond that country, whereas the democratization of Brazil was an event of continent-wide significance. The suggestion that we should drop the names of the countries involved, and replace them with more abstract variables (e.g. semi-industrialized countries, or whatever) wilfully deprives the analyst of vital information for evaluating the true weight of each case. If Nigeria or Indonesia succeeds in stabilizing a new democracy, that alters the entire balance in sub-Saharan Africa or in East Asia. Those countries, and those regions, deserve to be singled out by name so that we can use our normal standards of practical judgement to evaluate how much, or how little, each case means to the wider world.

If shared symbolic meanings or cultural contexts make a difference to behavioural responses, then comparative explanations of behaviour may only prove adequate when bounded within appropriate cultural or regional limits. For some explanatory purposes the appropriate 'universe' of cases may therefore not be unlimited by time or space. Explanatory range and depth may only be attainable if, for example, we confine ourselves to contemporary Latin America. Within those geographical and temporal confines, comparisons may invoke shared understandings of such key terms as 'constitutionalism' 'democratization', and 'reform'—whereas in the post-communist states, or sub-Saharan Africa, or even in post-independence Latin America that would be less of the common ground upon which effective comparisons must be founded. This is perhaps just a heavy-handed way of denying that 'case selection' restricted to one socio-cultural region or time period is necessarily arbitrary or anti-scientific. Again, the force of the argument depends upon the particular analytical task at hand. It must always be a question of demonstration, not mere assertion or a priori definition, that the relevant 'universe' for comparisons needs to be bounded. The effectiveness of broad shallow comparisons in contrast to narrower and more focused ones can only be established by attempting best practice in both, and then comparing the results. On this basis, this chapter considers two alternative strategies of comparison that may be particularly appropriate for democratization studies. The next section considers comparisons across large regions (such as continents), and this is followed by a section on 'paired' national comparisons.

Comparing across Continents

Democratization can be imagined, and attempted, in all corners of the globe. Liberal democracy and constitutionalism are familiar traditions with centuries-long histories in Europe and the Americas, whereas in Asia and Africa they arrived more recently and may be associated with Western expansionism, or with decolonization. In much of the Middle East democratization may be harder to imagine, in part because of the apparent strength of oil-financed monarchies (such as the Saudi regime), but also because of the conflict with Israel, and most basically because of an asserted incompatibility between Islam and Western liberalism. But none of these large regions is now immune from the contagion of democracy. In Africa the post-cold war discredit of one-party regimes was quickly followed by the dismantling of apartheid and the democratization of South Africa, raising hopes of an 'African renaissance', based on liberal democratic principles. Both the power and the limitations of these aspirations have recently been underscored by Nigeria's latest attempt at democratization. In Asia the world's most populous democracy—in India—has for all its faults survived its first half-century, thus demonstrating the adaptability and staying power of constitutional and democratic precepts; while in China the student movement of 1989 could only imagine, and not seriously attempt, the adoption of similar principles (although Taiwan has taken up that baton and it retains an imaginative hold in Hong Kong). Even in the Islamic world the most populous countries—Bangladesh and Indonesia—are attempting to construct democratic regimes, albeit in the face of tremendous difficulties. And variants of democracy that might perhaps be reconciled with Islam have been imagined, and indeed attempted, both in Iran and—with more tragic consequences so far—in Algeria. Turkey also struggles to strengthen democracy, conceived in this case as a reorientation of national identity from the Middle East towards Europe. In the same spirit, the post-Soviet republics of Central and Eastern Europe have seized the opportunity provided by the disintegration of the Moscow-centred imperial system to embrace what they see as their long-suppressed European traditions, and to lock in a westward orientation.

So the comparative study of democratization must be capable of tackling all these national, regional, and indeed continent-wide, variants of a common process. However, what is imagined, and attempted, in the name of 'democratization' will vary significantly according to the history, religion, and resource endowments of each region. Geography matters in this context, and so does language. Even in English we know that apparently common terminology carries different resonances in different countries (think of 'the state', or 'freedom of the press', and what these terms connote in Britain and the USA respectively). When terms like 'democracy', 'political party', 'accountability', and 'the constitution', are translated into Arabic, or Chinese, or Turkish, it is all the more likely that subtle changes in meaning will complicate the tasks of comparison.

One intellectual strategy to control for (or suppress) this range of variation is to insist only on the use of precise and standardized empirical indicators, as defined in the master language of political science (i.e. English) and derived from the canonical texts of the discipline (which happen to be imbued with tacit assumptions, mostly derived from a certain interpretation of the US experience). Throughout the world those who imagine democratization will deploy English concepts and US experience as inescapable reference points, whether for purposes of imitation or of differentiation.

Comparisons between large regions of the world, or across continents, must take into account English concepts and US experience, but not to the exclusion of other well-grounded perspectives and traditions. Just as the standardized reporting unit approach is useful for some purposes, but insufficient and potentially misleading if pursued in isolation from other perspectives, so with comparisons across continents. The usefulness of the strategy depends on the questions to be addressed. Some critical issues in comparative democratization studies require large area comparisons, although the biases arising from this level of abstraction must always be kept in mind. Comparisons between the 'Southern European' democratizations of the 1970s and subsequent South American experiences underpinned the 'transitions' debates of the 1980s. With the fall of the Berlin Wall big region comparisons were initiated between Latin American and post-communist East Europe. If the starting-point was decommunization and rejoining the West, how much difference did that make as compared to transitions based on the repudiation of military regimes structured in accordance with anti-communist national security doctrines? Less than one might suppose, has been the provisional answer so far. But there is scope for testing this conclusion more thoroughly, and for thinking through its broader implications if correct. Then, during the 1990s, some of the major 'developmental states' of East Asia, such as Indonesia, South Korea, Taiwan, and Thailand also underwent remarkable processes of democratization. Again the initial conditions (now including the cultural context and the geopolitical balance) were quite different from those affecting Latin America and East Europe. And again, there were apparent similarities of process and outcome despite these contrasting starting-points. So here too large-scale comparisons across regions have something of general significance to teach us. In addition comparisons between large regions of relatively successful democratizations and regions where the process is less successful (sub-Saharan Africa) or blocked (the Middle East) also have the potential to add to our overall understanding of democratization processes.

Here, then, are some representative examples of useful propositions that might be investigated through large area comparisons:

1. Latin America, sheltered by a US security umbrella and distant from most geopolitical conflict zones, has long been a 'zone of

peace' compared with most other large regions. This helps explain the early incidence of democratization in the subcontinent, and its current prevalence. It can also help explain some features of the sequence, timing, and content of democratization processes in this region by comparison with others.

2. Post-communist Central and Eastern Europe, abruptly released from a system of controls based in Moscow, sees democratization as part of a larger 'return to the West' which involves economic and security assurances against a resurgence of Russian control, in addition to the adoption (or re-adoption) of a democratic political model. This helps explain the distinctively bunched timing of the transitions in this large region, and the differential progress of democratization thereafter. Again, these features can be highlighted when this large region is compared with others.

3. The major developing countries of the East Asia region have also mostly democratized, but this region is subject to more geopolitical cross-pressures (the rise of Chinese influence, a demoralized Japan, an intermittently assertive USA) and there is not the same uniformity of direction as in the first two large regions considered above. Again large region comparisons can help clarify aspect of the sequence, timing, content, and stability of democratization that differentiate this region from others.

Propositions of this kind may be thought-provoking but can they provide the basis for a serious comparative analysis? Most social scientists are taught to screen out subjectivity, and to ensure that any conclusion they reach as been arrived at by methods that can be replicated and checked by any other analyst. Only if the dependent and independent variables are much more clearly separated, and the units of analysis are precisely and objectively demarcated, and the number of observations is extended to permit probabilistic measurement and testing, only then would such propositions be objectively testable. Whereas the universal reporting unit approach has the merit of apparent rigour, the identification of units of comparison in large area exercises is liable to appear arbitrary and *ad hoc*. Depending on the comparison chosen, the conclusions may even be partially predetermined. In any case, this method is inductive rather than deductive. The regions identified above are incomplete, and so may be the product of 'selection bias'. Their boundaries are imprecise and not necessarily commensurate. The time periods covered are also unspecified and perhaps arbitrary. In any case, with only three regions under review the 'small N' problem is acute, precluding attaching any statistical significance to variations between the cases. This would be a disqualification even if for each case a clear and unambiguous independent variable had been identified and linked through a strong one-way causal mechanism to an unmistakable predicted outcome (the dependent variable). In fact, in each of the three propositions listed, the postulated linkage is a complex interaction effect with differential outcomes. (For example, despite the US security umbrella, the Latin American regional analysis would have to cope with the Cuban exception; the East European analysis would have to account for Serbia.) Thus, following the King *et al.* recipe book for well-cooked social science,[4] these large area comparisons might well be classed as inedible.

Nevertheless, if the objective is to understand as fully as possible, on the basis of rational inquiry, the genesis and trajectories of the democratization processes actually occurring in the contemporary world, it is legitimate to explore what can be validly concluded about these propositions, and to compare that knowledge with the findings generated by more standard social science methodology.

This section develops the contention that good comparisons across continents *can* be undertaken if the purposes and procedures are carefully specified, and if the analysis is conducted in terms of suitably selected general propositions.

Just as universal data sets should not be 'crunched' regardless of theory, so cross-regional comparisons should be structured around well specified initial research questions. For example, Soviet scholars have questioned whether there is enough common ground between the 'transitions to democracy' that have occurred beyond the reach of communist rule, and the transitions from communism to democracy, to justify a unified examination of the two processes. This is a question of universal theory, but it is also a fertile ground for cross-regional comparisons. It postulates the uniqueness of the post-Soviet regime changes. Can they fruitfully be compared among themselves, but not with non-communist transitions? This question can initially be investigated by comparing the former Soviet bloc (either as one large region—or as two, the ex-USSR states and the East European 'satellites') with all other regime changes. But since Latin Americanists also try to analyse the prospects for regime change in Cuba they too must address the question of how much difference it makes if the starting-point is communist rule, or to what extent is Cuba also subject to regional influences specific to Latin America. Similarly, Asian scholars confront parallel questions about

[4] G. King, R. Keohane, and S. Verba, *Designing Social Enquiry* (Princeton: Princeton University Press, 1994).

the People's Republic of China, and the communist regimes of Vietnam and North Korea. Thus what began as a question of universal theory and was taken up as a specific problem for Soviet area specialists can acquire a cross-regional comparative dimension. What this example shows is that comparisons across continents are not a self-contained activity, an end in themselves. Rather, they constitute one possible strategy of inquiry among various alternatives, they should be viewed as potentially useful components of a broader analysis that will require well specified general research hypotheses, and that may also invoke other techniques of comparison.

Some large regions have reasonably self-evident boundaries (e.g. South America, sub-Saharan Africa), but others are quite artificial or debatable. Clearly cross-regional comparisons will fall at the first step if, for example, some place a reunited German in West Europe while others include the former East Germany among the post-communist democracies of East–Central Europe. Even the 'new democracies of southern Europe' can be interpreted restrictively (Portugal, Spain, and Greece, with Spain treated as the first among equals) or more inclusively (adding post-war Italy, but then why not France, and what about Malta, Cyprus, and even Turkey?) In physical geography South America includes Guyana and Suriname, both challenging cases for the comparative study of democratization, but seldom considered in the political geography of that subcontinent. While South America constitutes a plausible 'large region' for some comparative purposes (e.g. civil–military relations) it is only one of several possible groupings. Latin America as a whole (i.e. including post-revolutionary Mexico, Cuba, and Nicaragua) may also serve, for example if the question of church–state relations or the influence of the US Constitution and the French Revolution are under consideration. If the central concern is the role of European ideas and political influences in the absence of direct rule from the old world, then the entire western hemisphere (including the US and Canada) becomes the relevant 'large region'.

In the cases of Asian values, the delimitation of regional boundaries is far more subject to disagreement. There is a lively discussion about the role of such values in blocking or filtering Western liberal ideas and practices that may purport to universalism. But which values may have these attributes, and where in Asia are they lodged? Christianity is not distinctively Asian, yet there are many Christians all over Asia and in some countries (e.g. the Philippines) they are in the majority. Likewise communism is not distinctively Asian, yet it remains the official ideology of China, Vietnam, and North Korea. Islam also originates outside Asia, despite its prevalence in

Indonesia, Malaysia, Bangladesh, and Pakistan. So which parts of Asia could be identified as the large region inherently resistant to Western values? It seems that the most frequently invoked 'large region' argument in the comparative democratization literatures lacks a clearly defined regional base. In any case, if such values do exist, and do generate a cogent critique of Western liberal assumptions, then it is hard to see why they should not also acquire a following outside Asia.

Nevertheless, even if 'Asian values' lack a clear regional foundations, there could be other more productive cross-regional comparisons that require an Asian component. This is best illustrated by considering the so-called 'emerging market economies' of East Asia in comparison to those of Latin America. Both groupings compete in the international capital markets for equity and bond finance of the same class. Both are therefore under pressure to undertake economic liberalization in order to secure open markets for their industrial exports to the advanced economies. Both have found that this liberal and outward orientation brings them new risks and external conditionalities as well as new benefits. The financial crises of 1997/8 which spread by 'contagion' through the East Asian economies and then into Latin America dramatized this interconnectedness. Most emerging market economies in the two regions have also undergone transitions to democracy in the same period that they have adopted liberalizing reforms. In both regions, therefore, there is debate about how closely, and through what linkages, economic and political liberalization may be connected.

This, then, provides a prima-facie case for investigating the extent to which processes that can be detected region-wide in Latin America parallel apparently similar processes in East Asia.[5] The outer boundaries of Latin America are easily given by the Atlantic, the Pacific, and the USA. The central cases can also be identified quite simply. They are the larger economies with the clearest records of both economic and political liberalization. If one takes Argentina, Brazil, Chile, and Mexico as representative of Latin America for this purpose, that simplifies the analysis without seriously falsifying the regional tendency. Although it is a little harder to apply the same procedure to the emerging market countries of East Asia, there is probably enough to the cross-regional comparison to justify the effort. The most disputable part of this region's

[5] This discussion draws on a more extensive text to appear in Laurence Whitehead (ed.) *Emerging Market Democracies: East Asia and Latin America* (Baltimore: Johns Hopkins University Press, forthcoming).

outer boundary concerns mainland China, which is, of course, a part of East Asia closely linked to Hong Kong, Taiwan, and Korea. The coastal areas of the mainland may indeed be subject to liberalizing processes similar to those at work elsewhere in the region, but for the time being communist-ruled China does not fully conform to an 'emerging market' logic, and can therefore be placed outside the limits of the region. If so, then within the external boundaries of our East Asia region we have eight emerging market economies, enough to constitute a 'large area' that can be compared and contrasted to Latin America. However, none of these eight present themselves as paradigmatic examples that can stand for the region as a whole. Indonesia has the largest population, and is currently undergoing a chaotic process of both economic and political liberalization, but it is an oil-dependent economy, a latecomer, and is subject to exceptionally severe internal problems of cohesion. At the other end of the scale, South Korea and Taiwan are both exemplary emerging market successes, and remarkable instances of democratization, but they are outliers in other respects. Malaysia, the Philippines, and Thailand come closer than the rest to representing what we might regard as the regional norms concerning economic and political liberalization, but they do not dominate the region, and they differ substantially between themselves. From this brief survey it can be seen that emerging East Asia is a substantially less cohesive large region than Latin America, and that comparison between the two will require scanning a wider variety of cases, and coping with a bigger dispersion of experience in the former than the latter.

Nevertheless, the exercise can be instructive, not only for what it uncovers about the similarities and differences between the two large regions, but also for what it clarifies about variance within them, and about the scope and limitations of key propositions in the general literature. For all the dispersion of experience within East Asia, five of its eight 'emerging market' economies have undergone democratic transitions since the mid-1980s, and the three that have not are strongly cross-pressured. In addition, the International economic competitiveness of Hong Kong, Malaysia, and Singapore seems to require levels of education and access to global networks, combined with assurances of personal freedom, that may be difficult to reconcile with undemocratic systems of political representation, particularly if democracy has become the norm in most emerging markets. Similarly, the East Asian financial crisis of 1997/8 and its sequel in other emerging markets has demonstrated that too much is at stake for questions of banking supervision to be relegated to a purely 'technical' realm, and insulated from broader processes of democratic institutionalization (Chapter 6). It also showed that, despite its diversity, the East Asian region needs to be considered as a whole (it would be a serious error to exclude, say, Thailand or Indonesia, given the evidence of strong regional interdependencies). Moreover, as the crisis spread to Latin America (first Brazil, then Argentina) it tested key cross-regional propositions, such as the view that institutional reform had been carried further in the western hemisphere, thus insulating that region from the troubles associated with East Asian 'crony capitalism'. Cross-regional experience encouraged mutual recognition of common problems and processes, and pointed to the need for more precisely refined specifications of similarity and difference, for example, concerning the importance of universal education for the promotion of citizenship; or the connection between extreme social inequality and the legitimacy of any modern political regime. Qualitative comparative work which probes these questions both within and between large regions can add value to the more quantitative but uncontextualized findings that are typical of the 'universal reporting units' strategy of investigation.

The third 'large region' comparison is the post-communist democracies of Central Europe. Here too the first question to consider is the boundaries of this proposed regional grouping. Modern political democracy presumes the existence of the nation-state, but which units in the middle of Europe qualify for that designation, and how many of them belong in 'Central Europe'? By general consent it would seem that all proposed groupings of this kind would at least include the 'Visegrad Four' (the Czech Republic, Hungary, Poland, and Slovakia), although they used to be only three as recently as the early 1990s. But beyond that core membership the boundaries are disputed. In a keynote address to the Hungarian Parliament on 30 October 2000 Dr Zbigniew Brzezinski spoke of fourteen central European states, of which he classified seven as functioning democracies, and seven as malfunctioning democracies. Between the Visegrad Four and the Brzezinski Fourteen there are various other possibilities. For example, the *Central European Political Science Review* lists seven affiliated associations—the Visegrad Four plus Austria, Croatia, and Slovenia—more or less approximately to the old Austro-Hungarian Empire. The European Union has identified ten 'Central and Eastern' candidate states for membership under the Helsinki enlargement process. That adds the three Baltic republics, Bulgaria, and Romania to the Visegrad Four plus Slovenia. But the outer boundaries remain fuzzy. Why, for example, Romania but not Moldova?

Why Slovenia but not Croatia? Subsequent developments in Serbia indicate that perhaps all the successor states of the former Yugoslavia may eventually require consideration. It has never been entirely clear where Central Europe comes to an end, either in the Balkans, or down the Danube. Perhaps the best demonstration of Central Europe's locational instability can be given by considering a single fixed point. When Kant promoted enlightenment from his chair at Konigsberg it seemed possible to exclude this city from Central Europe on the grounds that it was too western. Nowadays it is possible to exclude Kaliningrad on the grounds that it is too eastern. But, of course, Konigsberg and Kaliningrad are one and the same city.

In comparative analysis the contours and limits of any unit (or region) should be determined by the object of comparison. In this case our focus is on national processes of democratization. By this standard the Visegrad Four constitute an essential and exemplary core of the Central European region. But once we reach out beyond that core various alternative definitions of the region can be licensed, each with its own implications and biases. There is no single a priori correct strategy. Theorists who emphasize political cultural explanations may favour the Austro-Hungarian definition; whereas those most impressed by international conditionalities may settle for the EU's current list of candidate members. The key point about this admittedly arbitrary conception of contemporary Central Europe is that not all cases can be accorded an equal weighting. The Visegrad Four exemplify democratization in the Central European region to the extent that if they falsify a proposition then it must fail. Evidence from the other states may reinforce or qualify the overall picture, but it should only carry a secondary weighting.

There are several cross-regional comparisons that could be expected to highlight distinctive features of the Central European democratizations. But different pairings will emphasize different aspects of the regional experience, and some pairings will show up deficiencies whereas others will highlight strengths. So each choice of comparator requires explicit justification, and the conclusions drawn from any comparative analysis need to be duly qualified.

The three main candidates for a cross-regional comparison with Central Europe are (i) Southern Europe; (ii) Latin America; and (iii) the states emerging from the former Soviet Union. In principle the *Southern Europe* grouping normally refers to the three new democracies that joined the EU in the 1980s, although it could also include Italy, Malta, and even Cyprus and Turkey. In practice, however, the exemplar of Southern Europe is usually taken to be Spain. The underlying logic of this comparison is clear. It presents democratization, regional integration, and economic liberalization as fairly linear processes that are mutually linked and reasonably assured—particularly through the external guidance arising from EU membership. This comparison rests on an implicit 'stage theory', with Central Europe presumably located at an earlier point on an established trajectory.

Central Europeans are not necessarily so attracted to the implications of a comparison with *Latin America*. Here, too, we could distinguish between various images of democratization in the Latin American region. A very generic summary characterization of democratization in the Latin American region will suffice for this purpose. In general, and by comparison with Central Europe, democratization in Latin America has been proceeding fitfully and unevenly for about a generation. Over that period Latin America has been making incremental advances towards freedoms that are often uncoordinated and not securely on track. Over certain periods economic liberalization has advanced rapidly, while political democratization has been delayed. At other times and in other places the reverse sequence has been attempted. Even when the two processes advance in tandem they may lack credibility, given the manifold weakness of many state institutions, the extremes of social inequality, and the near-absence of citizenship in major segments of Latin American society, and the persistence of 'authoritarian enclaves'. Nevertheless for some purposes this cross regional comparison can also be instructive. Many of the flaws and uncertainties of the Latin American process are not unknown in Central Europe, they are simply less dramatic or less studied.

If Central Europe is compared with the *former* states of the *Soviet Union*, then of course the cards are stacked in favour of the former. Taking the Russian Federation as the core and exemplary instance of a former Soviet state, the relative failings and disappointments, as compared to the Visegrad Four, are self-evident in almost every area. Democratic institutions are not authoritative, civil society is disorganized and demoralized, economic liberalization has produced a miserable and criminalized market economy, state institutions are mostly decrepit, and most actors operate at least partially outside the ostensible 'rules of the game'. There is no need here to enter into details and qualifications. In broad terms the former Soviet Union states demonstrate to the Central Europeans what perhaps could have gone wrong, and what alternative outcomes they have been fortunate to avoid. Some analysts may still adhere to a version of the stage theory (Russia and the Ukraine will eventually build democracies similar to those of Central Europe), but if so they have to rely on a very long-run reasoning, laced with a great deal of more or less 'thoughtful wishing'. The most obvious alternative framework for this comparison—relying on 'virtuous' and 'vicious' circles—tells us that all countries in both regions are subject to at least two types of countervailing process. In the most successful cases (the Visegrad Four) the positive dynamics in favour of effective democratization tend to prevail, and progressively to dissipate contrary tendencies. In the least successful cases the opposite occurs. Not a few countries to the west of Russia are perhaps caught in an intermediate situation where either dynamic could still prevail.

So different definitions of 'Central Europe', and different strategies of cross-regional comparison, can be useful for highlighting different aspects of the changes that have been in process over the past decade. All may be relevant to some extent, certainly if democratization is understood (as it should be) as a long-term complex, dynamic, and open-ended process.

The overall argument of this section is that large cross-regional comparisons are a legitimate, and indeed for some research questions an indispensable, method of analysis. Democratization studies, involving long-term processes that are dynamic and open-ended, generate numerous research questions that can be usefully tackled by resort to this comparative method. Such cross-regional comparisons should, however, be undertaken with due methodological awareness, notably concerning the need to specify clearly the boundaries of the regions under consideration and the criteria of selection by which certain cases are held to be representative or exemplary. As with other strategies of enquiry this one should neither be fetishized (presented as *the* solution) nor demonized (ruled out of court on principle for sloppiness), but undertaken with care for appropriate levels of best practice (i.e. based on the realistic test of what others have already demonstrated to be possible) and with clarity about the scope and limitations of this particular method.

Paired Comparisons

The Rationale for 'Paired Comparisons': What they Can and Cannot Tell us

This section[6] considers the utility of 'paired' comparisons between just two cases of democratization. The next chapter presents a single case, also treated in a comparative manner. So we need to consider the logic of very 'small N' comparisons.

First, the size of the 'universe' or class under consideration will depend upon the analytical issues at stake. If the issue is the probability of durable democratization in developing countries, the relevant universe would include almost all Latin American republics and something like an equal number of other 'Third World' neo-democracies—about fifty in total. If the issue is, say, the contagion and demonstration effects arising from two 1970s democratizations on the Iberian peninsula (post-Franco and post-Salazar) the relevant universe would be all the twenty republics of Latin America (plus possibly Angola, Mozambique, and Timor). If the issue is the *type* of democratization likely to arise from liberalizing reforms within a long-standing civilian constitutional tradition of restricted or controlled electoral contestation, then the 'universe' is far smaller. In regard to this third analytical issue there are arguably only two clear cases for consideration: Colombia and Mexico.[7] At a stretch one might try to include Venezuela (although the restrictions on electoral contestation were looser), or Uruguay (although the 'long-standing civilian tradition' was broken by a decade of military authoritarian rule in the 1970s). So, one argument for the use of paired comparisons would be that for certain issues of general interest and significance (e.g. identifying *sub-types* of democratization) the relevant universe may consist of only two core cases (perhaps afforced by a few secondary examples that would not suffice to

---

[6] This methodological discussion was first written for a United Nations University research project and has also appeared in Manuel Antonio Garretón and Edward Newman (eds.), *Democracy in Latin America: (Re)Constructing Political Society* (Tokyo: United Nations University Press, 2002).

[7] As the number of eligible cases for comparison falls, the number of possible paired comparisons becomes more tractable. With fifty cases there are 1,225 theoretically possible pairings. With twenty cases this falls to 190 pairings. But with four cases only to six pairings are possible, with three only three, and of course two cases generate only a single pair.

establish conclusions on their own). Clearly this is not an argument for the use of paired comparisons to the exclusion of other comparative methods. It is merely an argument for allowing them to remain part of the tool-kit of the comparativists.

Second and more importantly, paired comparisons can be justified on the grounds that their main purpose is to deepen understanding of the two individual and unique processes under consideration, rather than to uncover universally applicable general truths. To say this need not be to abandon the quest for transferable knowledge. If, for example, we are able to specify more precisely what it is about the Mexican democratization process that sets it aside from (or for that matter confirms) standard models of democratization, such findings are of scholarly value on at least two counts. The Mexican reality is of sufficient significance both to Mexicans and to others influenced by her example for a fuller understanding of that one case to be worthwhile for itself. And whether Mexico confirms, defies, or modifies our pre-Mexican theorizations about democratization is of general importance for theory construction and confirmation. Appropriately paired comparisons can offer an incisive strategy for analysing the supposed uniqueness of particular national 'cases' or complex dynamic processes. Among other things, parity of esteem between cases is required when only two processes are being compared. Thus each country's apparent 'uniqueness' has to be given careful consideration (something which tends to be screened out by 'large N' surveys). Also, appropriately paired comparisons can provide yardsticks of external validation by which to evaluate theories or explanations generated from within just one national experience. And, when only two cases are being considered in depth, the classificatory categories and prefabricated theorizations of the general analyst can be subjected to more thorough critical scrutiny (and possible adjustment in the light of the evidence) than when either too many examples are processed at once, or when a single unique instance is considered and demands treatment as an 'exception'. Needless to say, it is just as possible that paired comparisons may reveal similarities, where the initial expectation would have been for difference, as difference even though all the standard explanatory values would have pointed to similarity. In a properly constructed paired comparison there should be no initial presumption which of these two alternatives will prevail. When social science generalists accuse the practitioners of paired comparisons of 'selection bias' through their choice of cases, they can be answered by the counter-accusation of 'interpretation bias' through the prefabricated choice of categories and predicted causal chains that structure most 'large N' studies. Once again, there is no single methodological 'right answer' to such debates. Best practice will depend upon the analytical question at issue. For most purposes large N studies will work better if designed with the lessons from paired comparisons in mind, and the best paired comparisons will be alert to the hypotheses generated by large N studies. Each has its own characteristic source of bias that can be offset through methodological self-awareness and intellectual pluralism.

In summary, therefore, paired comparisons cannot be expected to validate general covering laws, or to provide conclusive answers to most controversies concerning the analysis of each case taken singly. But paired comparisons can improve the precision of broader comparative analyses, for example by specifying sub-types and clarifying their scope and limitation; or by recalibrating general classificatory categories and interpretative schemes in accordance with feedback from two cases examined together. It is just as possible to guard against selection bias in paired comparisons as against interpretation bias in more general theorizing. Indeed the two should be used as checks against each other. Paired comparisons can also sharpen the insights derivable from single case studies, for example by providing guidance on the scope and applicability of externally generated categories and interpretations; or by providing well-specified comparators that should help the analyst of an individual case to identify appropriate counter-factuals, to isolate explanatory variables, and to generalize (or to resist generalizations) on the basis of in-depth case material.

Examples of Paired Comparisons

This subsection first compares Taiwan and Chile (both anti-communist and pro-market dictatorships which achieved export-led growth, thereby creating favourable conditions for a 'smooth' transition to democracy); then Taiwan and Mexico (both one-party regimes attempting to remain in office while supervising the installation of multi-party competition).[8] These are not the only features

---

[8] The first two pairings are taken from 'The Democratization of Taiwan: A Comparative Perspective', my chapter in Steve Tsang and Hung-mao Tien (eds.), *Democratization in Taiwan: Implications for China* (Basingstoke: Macmillan, 1999). Another interesting example of a paired comparison is Elizabeth J. Wood, *Forging Democracy from Below: Insurgent Transitions in South Africa and El Salvador* (Cambridge: Cambridge University Press, 2000) which contests élite-led theories and makes a case for an 'insurgent path' to democracy.

of the Taiwanese process that might be highlighted through 'paired' comparisons (for example, the theme of anti-communist military struggle unites Taiwan with South Korea). Nor are these the only possible comparisons relevant to the features highlighted here. After all, numerous ex-communists are also seeking to reconcile multi-party competition with self-perpetuation in office; and Franco's Spain also achieved considerable economic modernization before relinquishing its dictatorship. But the two Taiwan-based 'paired' comparisons presented here offer plausible prima-facie reality checks on the inferences that might be drawn from the Taiwanese experience, considered in isolation. In all the three countries involved in the Taiwan discussions, although it is still too early to be sure what the definitive results of these attempts will be, we have approximately a decade of experience to evaluate; and the contrast between the rules of the political game prevailing at the beginning and at the end of that period is sufficiently marked, and sufficiently similar, to authorize the language of 'regime change'. There then follows a paired comparison of Colombia and Mexico. A similar rationale applies to the two Mexico-based paired comparisons.

Both Chile and Taiwan experienced sustained economic dynamism during the last years of the dictatorial regime, carrying over into the first years of the democratic transition. Good economic performance has been linked to democratization through two main connections: sequencing, and the veto power of capital. According to these arguments, in order to construct a consolidated democracy in an initially poor country, it may first be necessary to rule by authoritarian means with strong and durable controls over labour, and unpopular measures to curb consumption and reward enterprise. Such controls may have to remain in place for a generation or longer, until they induce a self-sustaining system of productive efficiency. Only then is it safe to embark upon a controlled liberalization which may lead smoothly, and without economic dislocation, to an open and competitive political regime. If this 'sequencing' is correctly observed, then by the time the democratic transition takes place, the business community will have accumulated such organizational, material, and symbolic resources that the social 'power of capital' will ensure a continuation of growth-friendly policies and incentives, notwithstanding the emerging autonomy of the labour movement, or the effective enfranchisement of the entire adult population.

Both Chile and Taiwan can be cited as exemplars of these theses. In both the 'capitalist class' came to the brink of destruction before undergoing the drastic restructuring that subsequently generated so much entrpreneurial dynamism. Business and managerial elites were so threatened that they accepted a harsh regime of political tutelage as the only means of survival; they were also induced to seek expertise from the United States on an unusually intensive scale. In other countries, where such limiting conditions did not apply, it is by no means certain that authoritarian controls would produce such economic dynamism, or that economic success would pave the way for a 'smooth' democratization with the support of big business.

Both governments needed international recognition, and sought through export dynamism to overcome the revulsion deriving from their repressive origins. In both countries when the electorate was finally offered the opportunity to pass judgement on the legacy of authoritarian rule it clearly signalled the desire to protect and preserve the hard-won fruits of economic success, even if that meant condoning some of the harsh methods used to secure it. Hence until 2000 the KMT won successive re-elections, thus also preserving the business assets it had acquired; and although Pinochet was forced out of the presidency, his constitution and his 'binding laws' were not overturned, so that in effect the voters preserved the structure of property rights he had created.

Influential Chilean democrats dispute over-schematic versions of the 'sequencing' and 'veto power of capital' arguments, and the relevant counter-factuals should be examined with care in Taiwan as well. There is little dispute that harsh (indeed anti-democratic) measures were required in the 1970s if the private enterprise system was to be restored in Chile, but it is far more questionable how much of the Pinochet regime's overall record of repression was 'functional' from the standpoint of long-run economic performance. The large corporations that flourished under the later stages of authoritarian rule in the two countries were in general heavily sheltered by a favourable public policy environment which rendered them partially dependent on the preservation of a conservative political hegemony. They were not necessarily 'privately' owned. (The Chilean military benefited from state copper revenues, for example, and the KMT owned many enterprises through which it could offer sinecures to the old political class.) Indeed, the central legitimizing myth of the dictatorship was the claim that the restoration of democracy would involve a return to economic stagnation and insecurity. Since 1989 Chilean democrats have effectively demonstrated the falsity of this prediction. It should not be too readily assumed that either Chile or Taiwan would necessarily have achieved worse economic performance if they had democratized sooner.

Finally, notwithstanding some striking resemblances between Chile and Taiwan the differences also require careful attention. General Pinochet never led a political party, let alone one as formidable as General Chiang Kai Shek's KMT. He lost the only competitive election he ever contested. It was not until over a decade after the democratization of Taiwan that the KMT lost the presidency (in 2000), and even then the party retained its majority in the legislature. Chilean democrats went on to restore the constitutional democracy that had been their countrymen's source of pride for virtually the whole of the twentieth century (for more on this see Chapter 9). Chilean capitalists generally espoused a neo-liberal ideology which may have rendered them more autonomous from state control than most family-owned Taiwanese enterprises. Chilean labour organizations were viewed as potentially threatening, and were therefore weakened, whereas the KMT (like the PRI) favoured corporatist labour controls, and built up a large clientele of state employees. Whereas the Chinese Communist Party still looms with threatening force and massive national authority over the KMT-led democracy, the Chilean Communist Party never led more than a vulnerable minority movement, and is now relegated to near insignificance.

We now turn to a second 'paired comparison' between Taiwan and Mexico, considering the constraints under which party leaders and aspiring democrats must operate in the two countries. Although both had long-standing dominant party regimes, they also had very well established constitutional traditions, including periodic elections for public office which always involved a degree of candidate competition and responsiveness, even if the party outcomes were usually foregone conclusions. Thus in both countries the central issue of a 'transition' has been how to establish a clear-cut break with this authoritarian dominant party past, while at the same time preserving continuity of governmental institutions and established interests. Both the KMT and the PRI approached democratization as a source of legitimation through contested elections, without necessarily leading to the disrupted career patterns, public policy upheavals, and of retribution for past acts of fraud and repression that they and their backers feared could follow from loss of executive office. Yet in 2000 both parties were ousted from the executive as a result of genuine elections. This was the first time since the 1920s that either party had been out of office.

Prior to 2000 it was difficult to project a convincing image of democratization in either country, given the longevity of one-party rule and the 'apostolic succession' whereby new presidents emerged from within the ruling party. In the PRI the outgoing president and party chief traditionally 'points the finger' at his successor, and this *dedazo* is binding. Both Presidents Zedillo and Lee were nominated in this authoritarian manner. This is not just a question of electoral transparency (although prior to 1994 the Mexicans certainly undermined their own credibility by engaging in multiple electoral malpractices, and by rejecting the presence of international observers). After two or three generations of continuous one-party rule there will inevitably be an accumulation of official myths and cover-ups that demand re-examination before it is possible to establish any new consensus.

A 'smooth' but genuine transition implies that the same judicial system which administered martial law or which condoned PRI impunity is now to be trusted to uphold the rule of law. Similarly, the legislature which rubber-stamped authoritarian edicts must secure acceptance as an effective counterweight to the executive, despite probable continuities of personnel and operational procedures. (In Mexico the legislature was weakened by the no re-election rule, which blocked the emergence of a parliamentary career structure. In Taiwan, until 1990, parliament was also crippled by a different kind of no re-election rule.) Equally the television stations that broadcast official propaganda are now to be trusted with independent and, if necessary, critical reporting. (In Mexico it was virtually the same broadcasters who had covered up the 1988 electoral fraud that reported on the genuine results of 1994.) Finally, those who became rich and powerful under the shelter of the one-party regime can be expected not only to preserve their privileges, but to deploy their resources in order to defend their acquired interests under democratic conditions.

Despite these impediments a surprisingly smooth process of transition to opposition party victory has been engineered in both countries. In December 1994 President Zedillo became the first Mexican chief executive to take office with a credible democratic mandate, derived from more or less honest competitive elections. His party retained the majority in both houses of Congress (although this ended in July 1997), but without the strength to impose constitutional revisions against the resistance of the opposition parties. In 1997 an opposition mayor was elected to office in Mexico City. Similarly, in March 1996 President Lee secured a democratic mandate with roughly the same percentage of the popular vote, and under the same constitutional constraint. The KMT managed to retain its legislative majority in the 1998 elections but it finally lost its monopoly on the executive when the opposition won the presidential election in 2000. Three months later the PRI also lost the presidency (after seventy-one years in office). Both outgoing President Zedillo and outgoing President Lee had encountered substantial problems with their respective parties, however, neither of which were finding it easy to adapt to the institutional uncertainty of multi-party democracy and eventual loss of public office. Any paired comparison between these two experiences would highlight structural similarities between the two formerly dominant parties.

Nevertheless Taiwanese democracy can also be differentiated in major respects from that of Mexico. There is no equivalent to the Chiapas rebellion, or to the assassination of top party leaders, nor have past presidents been so wholly discredited by corruption scandals of the kind associated with the Salinas family. The gross social injustices that exclude large segments of the Mexican population from any substantive rights or guarantees have apparently to a large extent been overcome in Taiwan. President Lee was therefore able to invoke a degree of legitimate authority that was not available to his Mexican counterpart, who relied mainly on a reputation for sound economic management. However, there is also a huge shadow hanging over Taiwan's democratization which is not applicable to Mexico. This concerns the island's uncertain political status, and the ongoing competition with the communist-ruled mainland.

Two main factors differentiate Taiwan from Mexico. First, the KMT's uphill struggle for international recognition in competition with mainland China has furnished party leaders with an almost unanswerable justification for pre-emptive political reform from above: only by seizing the moral high ground of democratic legitimacy can the losing side in the Chinese civil war hope to stave off the verdict of 1949. Therefore the Taiwanese decision to initiate democratization in 1986 looks like an act of enlightened leadership from above, whereas the ruling party in Mexico seems to have been trying to fend off the evil day until it became too weak to continue resisting. Second, the KMT regime delivered an unbroken record of market-driven economic expansion and prosperity, benefits that should command an electoral reward in any open competition for votes. In contrast, notwithstanding President Zedillo's short-term record for economic success, the PRI's generation-long record of economic performance offered no comparable assurance of electoral gratitude.

The third paired comparison concerns 'democratization by reform' strategies in Colombia and Mexico.[9] Before democratizing

---

[9] This comparison is highly condensed from my chapter on 'Democratization through Reform' in Garretón and Newman (eds.), *Democracy in Latin America*. op cit.

reforms began both countries had well-established political 'regimes', in the sense that an elaborate set of formal and informal rules of the game structured political competition throughout each system; these rules were predictable and sustained over at least a generation; no single political actor was ever strong enough to break free from their constraints (although powerful groups and coalitions regularly sought to bend the rules in their favour, often with success). These were both 'civilian' regions in the sense that public offices rotated between elected officials who governed in accordance with legal forms and procedures, rather on the basis of military command; the police and the armed forces remained substantively subordinate to civil authority, and only retired military officials were allowed to compete for public office. These regions were 'constitutional' in the sense that the electoral calendar was reliably observed, and elected officials always stood down for their successors at the indicated moment (no consecutive re-election of the president was allowed in Colombia, no executive re-election and no immediate re-election of congressmen in Mexico). The Constitution provided for the existence of multiple parties, and the electoral process required acceptance of at least token forms of organized opposition. Yet these civilian constitutional regimes were far from fully democratic, at least in the sense that has come to prevail in contemporary discourse. The essential point is that in both Colombia and Mexico before the 1980s, although power circulated predictably and according to an impersonal system of rules, it derived from an elite pact to share the spoils of public office without excessive conflict. The voters may have endorsed this pact through their voluntary participation; they may even have induced adjustments to the balance of power within the elite as needed to maintain popular adhesion; and they were persistently called upon to ratify the elite circulation decisions negotiated prior to each election. But the electorate was not sovereign. It was not allowed to make choices independent of those already agreed upon by the rulers.

Since Colombia and Mexico both had long-established constitutional regimes they were governed by impersonal rules of the game which were quite stable, predictable, and routinized. The result was that the reforms adopted in Colombia and Mexico in the 1990s were rooted in an established matrix of rules and procedures, they were presented as adjustments to a functioning system that might require amendment, but that it was important to defend. The architects of these reforms presented them (and probably designed them) with a broader public interest objective in view. They would acknowledge that the existing system needed some retuning. They would debate (often quite publicly and at length) over the sources and degree of dysfunction they had encountered and over the relative merits of alternative remedies. Reform would not simply be decreed by a self-interested ruler. It would emerge through collective deliberation and negotiation. This would produce a menu of possible reforms, and even though in the end those in power might well impose the variant that suited their interests best, the alternatives were placed on the public agenda and might well be taken up later if the results of the first attempt proved disappointing. The basic dynamics of these two reforms involved official acknowledgement of the existence of some such legitimacy deficit, which—it was assumed—could be corrected by broadening the party system and improving the machinery of electoral representation.

From this characterization of the initial liberalizing reforms we can derive several consequences that differentiate this 'path' or 'sub-type' of democratization from the standard patterns identified in the early 'transitions' literature. There was far less scope for a polarizing division between 'hardliners' and 'softliners'; and much greater likelihood that most of the various strands of reformist would unite against the prospect of a destabilizing 'rupture'. Instead of a debate polarized between uncontrolled liberalization (leading to a 'democratic transition') and authoritarian regression, the major disagreements would concern alternative strategies, sequences, and timings of system-maintaining reform.

Implications

These three 'paired comparisons' illustrate the scope and utility of this particular method. It is one technique among several for coping with complexities of comparative democratization studies. It should not displace 'large N' or reporting unit type enquiries, nor comparisons across large regions, nor the study of single exemplary cases from a comparative perspective (Chapter 9 develops that option with reference to Chile). But it can complement all these, and can therefore help fill in the large gap we have identified between theories of democratization and really existing experiences. By asking similar questions, or seeking the analogies linking just *two* instances of democratization, it may be possible to formulate clear and instructive conclusions (middle-range generalizations rather than covering law regularities or estimates of probability) which attend to the 'thickness' or complexity and indeterminacy of the individual processes. This is an appropriate strategy for investigating *some* (though not *all*) of the dimensions of a given democratization process. For example, it may be particularly appropriate for investigating rather precisely chosen historical 'might have beens' (what if the Chilean junta had opted for a fuller return to democracy when it was in a position of strength as the KMT in Taiwan did in the mid-1980s, for example?). Other equally important issues about democratization (e.g. the use of parliamentary institutions) may require a broader survey of examples.

If we view democratization as a very long-term process with no single final, clear-cut end point, then every purported 'model' or success story merits comparative scrutiny, and appropriately paired comparisons should have much to offer here. A provisional balance sheet might indicate a favourable outcome in one country as opposed to another, but that verdict would always depend on how the successful case subsequently performed, and on how the less successful responded to their experiences of relative failure. So the 'paired comparison' method is unlikely to validate a single 'right answer' to the question how to democratize. Much would depend upon contextual judgements about what was possible and appropriate in different settings, and in view of contrasting social perceptions and understandings. Alternative paths would have to receive equal consideration, and the elusiveness of outcomes would have to be acknowledged. The next chapter investigates this elusiveness and open-endedness through a more detailed (but still comparative) examination of the 'exemplary' Chilean case.

9

An Exemplary Case: Chile

> The outcome (of redemocratization) is often an incomplete
> democracy, a regime basically democratic, but riddled with
> inherited authoritarian enclaves; non-democratic institutions,
> unresolved human rights problems, and social actors not fully
> willing to play by democratic rules.
>
> (Manuel Antonio Garretón)

An Exemplary Case

This chapter[1] is a case study of the democratization of Chile, viewed
as an exemplary case, that is, one which is not only of importance in
itself but is also instructive for comparativists with no special commitment to this particular instance. The big issues contested in
Chile—popular front; revolution in liberty; peaceful road to socialism; free-market authoritarianism; pacted transition; international
legal liability for human rights violations—tend to be exemplary
issues. Whichever side prevails, the outcome is meaningful and
salient at the international level. Of course, Chileans usually battle
over local stakes and parochial issues. They mostly choose their
sides, adopt their strategies, and interpret their results in accordance with highly specific, mostly domestic, realities that are far
removed from the great abstract principles of global controversy.
But these routines of normal politics acquire greater coherence and
deeper significance when they can be structured according to more
universal principles. Experience suggests that, perhaps for reasons
of geography or political culture, politically aware Chileans have
learnt through repeated episodes of intense engagement that this
overarching and exemplary dimension of their debates makes a
difference to the outcome. It mobilizes additional resources from

---

[1] A longer version of this chapter has been previously published (in Spanish only)
in Amparo Menéndez Carrión (ed.), *La caja de Pandora* (Santiago: Planeta, 1999).

without; it solidifies domestic commitments to each side; it raises both the tone and the stakes in contention; it turns pragmatic and incremental politics ('normal' politics) into issues of principle and system ('foundational' politics). It therefore renders Chilean politics both more noble and demanding, and also more intractable and potentially irreconcilable.

To achieve full democratization, and to be recognized internationally as exemplary in that respect, is no doubt a noble and demanding objective. But the higher the objective the greater the strain. It would be less stressful if democratization were conceived of as an incremental process of pragmatic accommodations, trade offs, and agreements to differ, with the emphasis on the routine and the normal, rather than the exemplary and the foundational. But on this second view, Chilean democratization would face a distinctive handicap. Most Chilean actors would feel diminished if their activities were only of local interest. The sense of national identity is strongly developed, and Chileans are taught to pride themselves in the exemplary significance of their country's politics. In fact, as indicated in Chapter 2, democratization always contains both a foundational and transformative component (most apparent during the 'transition' phase), and a routinizing and dedramatizing component (increasingly pre-eminent as the new regime becomes routinized). But in the Chilean case the 'pacted' nature of the transition signified an effort to limit the internal risks and uncertainties of a debate over foundational issues (these were side-stepped by the agreement to work within the constraints set by the 1980 authoritarian constitution). To offset these domestic limits on full democratization it became all the more important to secure international recognition for the Chilean democratization process as an exemplary achievement. So the 1999 arrest in London of General Pinochet touched a particularly raw nerve.

What Chileans actually saw themselves as undertaking was a *re*democratization (i.e. largely reverting to the well-tried and fully internalized political conventions of the pre-coup period, with some prudential lessons added on) rather than designing a new set of political institutions. To a large extent their democratization involved the reinstatement of an old civilian political class which had been suspended (often exiled), but not destroyed. If anything these returning democratic actors were more cautious and defensive than before, and were less disposed to open space for non-traditional forms of participation or political mobilization. One could even suggest that the civilian architects of Chile's re-democratization were so eager to restore as much as possible of a known system of inter-party bargaining and conciliation that they tried to skip the risky 'transition' phase altogether, and to move directly from authoritarian rule to a pre-set and rather rigid formula of multi-party accommodation. Pragmatic and incremental politics quickly displaced work on the underlying issues of principle and system which had proved so divisive in the past. For this very reason, however, it was more vital than ever for Chile to project an international image as an exemplary instance of full democratization. The recognition and approval this would generate from abroad would help to compensate for the compromises, postponements, and suppressions of doubt that were required at home.

In this book, processes of democratization are viewed as complex long-term, dynamic, and open-ended. They include some important elements that can be more or less objectively measured, or at least empirically verified. For example, the electoral process in Chile can be assessed on various indicators and compared with similar processes in other recently democratizing countries. There will always be some margin of error in such comparisons, but the main conclusions are fairly clear and checkable by any analyst. Electoral fraud is difficult and rare, the turnout is usually high, geographical coverage is usually even, and so forth. Corruption is not perceived to be anything like as severe as in most neo-democracies. (See Annex Table 3). By testing such components of democratization in this way, standards of comparative analysis may be refined and upgraded. Questions that in other countries may become distorted by partisan polemics can be removed from the area of power struggle and converted into elements of consensus and social solidarity.

However, not all the components of a democratization process can be technified in this way. There remains a considerable range of more elusive elements that are critical to any overall comparative evaluation of the progress of democratization, but that cannot be so easily pinned down by standardized indicators of performance. For example, the subordination of the armed forces to legitimately constituted civil authority is obviously a key component of democratization. There are some readily observable indicators of this, but they are partial and incomplete. In Chile both the unrevised 1980 Constitution, and the 'transitional' agreements of 1989 formally consecrate a degree of military non-subordination that has also been more subjectively demonstrated by the personal career and truculent outlook of General Pinochet and his associates. As a consequence, over its first decade the Chilean transition has patently fallen short of most comparators in this key area. But objective measurement of the scale and significance of this shortfall is another matter. In this area there is no avoiding the need for a close contextual reading of a wide range of often quite subjective sources. Different analysts may quite legitimately arrive at sharply contrasting judgements on the basis of the same evidence. Alternative interpretations attempt to cover the same evidence working from opposed first principles. Perhaps these differences will eventually be arbitrated through experience (although even that remains to be seen). In any case a key element in alternative judgements will be some assessment of how military leaders can be expected to behave in certain hypothetical situations that might arise in the future. However hard the analyst tries to restrict judgement to the available evidence, there is an inherently counter-factual (or even speculative) component to such interpretations. Yet if Chile's democratization is to be seriously compared with that of other countries, it is impossible to omit this theme, or to avoid the problems of subjective interpretation that it raises. The question is not just how military leaders *say* they might act in various circumstances, but also how far civilian politicians are willing to test such assertions, and how judgements about the quality of that civil–military interaction reshape political attitudes and relationships more generally. Similar issues arise in other key areas, such as the justice system, or state–business relations.

Another example concerns the ending of the military regime. Since the pre-democratic regime controlled the levers of power, why would it ever have acted against its interest by taking decisions which might lead to its own demise? One possible answer is that authoritarian rulers are so cut off from accurate neutral information about what their subjects think and desire that they are structurally prone to strategic miscalculation. This might help to explain how Pinochet came to organize a plebiscite that would unite the opposition and force his ousting from the presidency.

It has been conjectured that when outgoing authoritarians calculate that they will lose the ensuing democratic election, they then resort to various forms of 'power sharing' which have the effect of constraining subsequent scope for democratic alternation. This sounds plausible, but it rests on judgements about the relevant cases which seem to grossly underestimate the role of authoritarian miscalculation in decision-making. Of course, at some point even the most blinkered authoritarian discovers his mistake and may then attempt to rig the ensuing electoral structure. But if the discovery is made too late, or the rigging is done in too blatant a manner, the effect may be the opposite of that intended. The real point is to determine how far anti-democratic forms of power sharing were adopted as well-informed strategies for self-preservation, and how far they were shaped by other more normative or contingent factors.

This introduces an element of teleology into the discussion, but of course we must recognize the danger of that. Chapter 10 will discuss the general issues arising from such an approach, and will defend the inclusion of a teleological stand in discussions on democratization. But it is all too tempting to reason backwards from the desired or imagined end (in this case 'democratic consolidation') to the supposedly necessary or justified means. In reality there is more than one starting-point, more than one possible route, and there is a good deal of path dependence. The supposed relationship between means and end is in fact highly uncertain or contingent. (Indeed, if it were not, the mechanisms we could identify might as well be used by those aiming to block democratic consolidation as by those aiming to bring it about.) So for all these reasons, although it may be necessary to recognize the presence of teleological elements in many accounts of democratization, it is also vital to build up strong defences against the excessive enthusiasm it can inspire. Such defences include insisting on constantly rechecking the evidence and the logic of the argument, and on the existence of plausible 'paths not taken' counterfactually. As we saw in Chapter 8, paired comparisons can be extremely useful for highlighting the concrete reality of alternative paths, processes, and outcomes.

A further check on teleological enthusiasm can be derived from the thought that democratization is a form of regime change, and all varieties of new regime, however 'representative and legitimate', also involve construction of a new system of domination, with its supporting myths and selective reinterpretations of the past. In the cases that concern us, if a durable and coherent regime emerges it will not only be a form of political representation, but also a system of property rights and a hierarchy of social power relations that are bound to be in important respects inegalitarian and exclusionary. This leads on to debates about 'substantive' versus 'formal' democracy, the need for a strong 'civil society', the hope that in the long run a democratic franchise will spawn socially ameliorative pressures for reform—in short, the whole debate about the 'quality' rather than factual existence of a democratic regime.

This also fits with a view of democratization which acknowledges its normative (in Alex Wilde's terms, 'expressive') dimensions, and which acknowledges the importance of political leadership and of the discursive process of persuasion and resocialization. It is within that context that we can now turn to a discussion of the behaviour of political actors in a democratization process.

Viewed from a comparative perspective, the initial questions to ask about political behaviour in any specific democratization process are as follows. Who are the relevant political actors? Where do they come from? How is their political authority constituted? What norms or conventions (whether inherited or improvised) are likely to shape their interaction? To what extent is a democratic transition likely either to redistribute opportunities between them, or to reshape these modes of interaction? These are all rather formidable questions. A good place to begin is with some reflections on the utility of 'the political class' as a construct.

'The political class' is a staple of French political analysis, but is little used by Anglo-Saxons who prefer the precision of 'political institutions'. The difference may arise from the fact that, although French institutions have been subject to periodic breakdown and replacement, analysts have been aware of underlying continuities arising from the persistence of various informed structures of political recruitment, socialization, and reproduction. Clearly the French experience is more pertinent than the Anglo-Saxon for analysing regime change in Latin America. However, identifying the scope and limitations of a 'political class' is harder than explicating overt institutional forms and procedures. In Chile there is a distinct and continuous category of activists associated with the long-standing party system and the authority of the legislature. However, its limitations also require emphasis. Links with other *fuerzas vivas* such as the business elite, the media, and the military are not strong. Even within the 'political class' there has always been room for the periodic eruption of 'anti-political challengers (technocrats, anti-party populists, anti-system revolutionaries). Despite the continuity and sophistication of the Chilean political class, its centrality in society is contested (the displacement of Congress to Valparaiso and the insertion of unelected lifetime senators is symptomatic of this), and its fortunes fluctuate considerably over the generations. Like the French 'classe politique' resilience comes at the price of adapting to a wide variety of ideological and power relationships. Nevertheless, at least by most Latin American standards, Chile has developed an unusually resourceful, coherent, and effective political class.

A Case of Redemocratization

In the case of Chile, comparative analysis has already indicated that we are dealing with a strong example of *re*democratization.

That is to say, prior to the 1973 coup Chile had already established an unusually well-developed and sophisticated system of party competition, and of constitutional rule. Although the Pinochet regime lasted for seventeen years, and produced far-reaching changes in the economic and social system of the country, the pre-existing political class survived sufficiently intact both in its personnel and in its operating procedures to offer the prospect of a *restoration* of long-established and collectively remembered democratic procedures. In practice, of course, this restoration was highly approximate. The passage of time, the change of generations, the desire to learn from past failures, and the changed balance of power in society, were all factors precluding any direct return to the *status quo ante*, quite apart from the 'binding laws' (*leyes amarres*) and constitutional impediments bequeathed by the outgoing authoritarian rulers as their condition for accepting a peaceful transfer of public office. In any case, the remembered past of pre-1973 Chile was far from consensual. In so far as a restoration was envisaged, it was the restoration of a selectively reconstructed past, of a democratic Chile as it perhaps could and should have been but not as it had actually existed.

But for all these qualifications, the comparative perspective enables us to highlight the strong significance of the restorative component of Chilean democratization, at least when contrasted with almost all other processes of this kind. The contrast with countries lacking any previous experience of competitive elections under constitutional rule is the most straightforward to establish. In this case all the questions about political behaviour posed at the outset of this section would have to be answered in a different way. With no ready-formed and pre-tested cadre of democratic politicians to summon back from exile or internal retreat, a wide array of unscripted political actors would presumably present themselves for audition (to use the metaphor developed in Chapter 2)—priests and poets, strike leaders, broadcasters, and tycoons. Some might enjoy the backing of substantial organizations, others would seem to come from nowhere. In any case, even the best supported would lack the specialized backing of an experienced party familiar with the vicissitudes of electoral competition. If these anti-authoritarian sources of political recruitment proved too shallow, then the space opened up for democratic political brokerage would be filled by operators defecting from the authoritarian power structure as it is dismantled.

Either way the operating procedures that these innovators bring with them are unlikely to be those of a seasoned class of democratic

politicians. This is not to claim that such newcomers are necessarily *worse* democrats than the old hands, only that their behaviour is
likely to be *different*. It could be more experimental, perhaps in
some cases more inspiring, but also more risky and prone to unnec-
essary misjudgements. In general terms one should expect that a
first-time attempt at democratization is more likely to misfire, to
falter, and to require subsequent rectification. On the positive side,
however, such an attempt is also more likely to bring in a wide array
of previously excluded or non-participating political actors. By contrast, a strong *re*democratization (as in Chile) is more likely to be
dominated by the desire to avoid risks, to limit experimentation,
and to screen the behaviour of any new entrants until they conform
to the strong system of constraints and mutual understandings
already developed by the established political class.

Even within the more restrictive category of *re*democratization,
the Chilean case seems unusually constrained. In Peru, for example, the parties and politicians who were excluded from power by
the military in 1968 returned to compete for, and indeed win access
to, public office a decade later. So this was also a *re*democratization,
but of a less controlled variety. The enfranchisement of illiterates
and other measures of popular mobilization (land reform, unioniza-
tion, etc.) under the military regime meant that the old parties
found themselves contending with newer challengers on their left,
and social confrontation became a more prominent feature of political competition. In due course the old political class and its institutions fell into ever greater discredit, despite redemocratization,
and after his 1992 closure of Congress and *auto-golpe* President
Fujimori was able to establish a form of personal rule founded on a
repudiation of all its legacies. When, in 2000, his personalist regime
also failed, the remnants of old political class obtained yet another
opportunity to rehabilitate itself, although again its purchase on
the popular imagination may still be precarious. Chilean democrats
correctly believe their society to be very different from that of Peru,
but even so the potential vulnerability of their own political class is
underscored by this comparison.

In Spain (a comparison with more appeal in Chile) the parties
that came to the fore after the death of Franco tended to appeal to
a pre-Civil War baseline that supposedly anchored their identities
and even helped define their core orientations. Yet in practice the
forty years of Francoism had broken these continuities in a way that
seventeen years of Pinochet did not. Spain and Portugal can still
both be analysed from the standpoint of *re*democratization, but not
in the clear sense that applies to Chile. Perhaps only Uruguay offers

a comparably strong experience. (Indeed, the Uruguayan redemo-cratization was a more complete restoration of the old order than that of Chile.)

Some superficial indicators of Chilean political continuity attract little attention within the country, yet they are striking from a comparative perspective. Most obviously there is President Eduardo Frei Montalvo (1964–70) and his son President Eduardo Frei (1994–2000), both leaders of the same Christian Democratic Party. Still at the top leadership level, President Patricio Aylwin (1990–4) was a key figure in the same party in 1973, and played almost as prominent a role in the ending of the earlier constitutional order as in the restoration of the current one. These are not isolated examples—consider Foreign Ministers Valdés (father and son) or Communist Party leader Gladys Marín, and so on. There are also striking continuities of personnel at lower levels in the party system, in the media, and in the state apparatus. Naturally there is also rotation and new entry into the 'political class' (notably among the parties of the right, now in opposition) but perhaps no more than would have been inevitable even without any interruption to the constitutional order. On the left, the phenomenon of exile has affected patterns of political recruitment but to some extent this may have reinforced continuity, rather than breaking them. Party voting patterns and partisan allegiances also displayed marked evidence of continuity.

But if the *identity* of key political actors in the Chilean (re)democratization process is heavily constrained, can the same be said of the political *behaviour* of these actors? In one sense the styles of political interaction prevailing before 1973 and after 1990 could be described as diametrically opposed. But at a deeper level there is an important source of linkage—actors conscious of the continuity of their respective identities renew interactions with each other under the constraints given by their shared past experiences of mismanaging a constitutional regime. An abstract or game-theoretical model of bargaining might capture some broad features of the logic that has guided the parties of the *Concertación* since their alliance began in the late 1980s, but the durability and intensity of the bonds linking them can hardly be explicated without reference to their memories of what happened previously when 'they' allowed inter-party competition to escalate without limits. Such memories are central to any understanding of the behaviour of actors under conditions of intense polarization, and the 'theatrical' effects and pedagogical consequences of political violence. These hidden realities need to be disinterred if we are to understand what Alex Wilde

has recently labelled the 'conspiracy of consensus' that characterized Chilean politics in the 1990s.[2] In addition, they enable us to
deepen our grasp of the complex relationship between the interests
of political actors and the democratic values they also invoke, and
that must at least to some extent constrain their behaviour.

In a stable and consensual democratic society it may make sense
to analyse the party preferences of voters by analogy with the pur-
chasing strategies of consumers in a supermarket. But in Chile a
surface appearance of individualized consumer sovereignty over-
lays memories of intense polarization, with one side viewed as
destructive supermarket looters and the other as selfish hoarders.
More generally, during the 'breakdown' phase of an authoritarian
regime, society is typically much more insecure and polarized—
spectator excitement in the closing stages of a close-fought soccer
match may provide a better analogy than the atomized utility-
seeking of the supermarket customer. Of course highly structured
rationality is evident both in the supermarket and in the soccer
match —but the resulting interactions may be very different. In the
second, more polarized, situation individuals have little scope for
privacy or neutrality. The pressure to participate, and to take sides,
can be overwhelming. (Victor Jara's couplet 'Ud no es nada, ni
chicha ni limonada' well conveyed this climate of forced choice in
Chile at one such critical moment.) Leaders of rival political projects (like captains of soccer teams) may be selected and rewarded
for their capacity to mobilize ever broader and more intense expressions of mass support as the polarization proceeds. As recently as
the 1980s, this was the climate in which *poblaciones* protested
against the Pinochet regime—or indeed Soweto turned out against
apartheid.

But just as every soccer match comes to an end, so every process
of political mobilization and polarization reaches a point of culmi-
nation, after which the distribution of gains and losses begins to
emerge, and some demobilization occurs. For political leaders
engaged in processes of regime breakdown and transition, successful strategy requires multiple skills. Strong mobilization ability
may be needed to outmanœuvre and overawe opponents as polarization intensifies. But it is also necessary to stand outside one's
own partisanship, and to judge the alternatives open to one's antag-
onist. Mutual signalling and confidence-building between the rival

[2] Alex Wilde provides an extensive listing of recent Chilean works on this topic
in his excellent 'Irruptions of Memory: Expressive Politics in Chile's Transition to
Democracy', *Journal of Latin American Studies*, 31/2 (May 1999), 473–4.

sides may need to be cultivated even as the passions of conflict esca-late. It is also crucial correctly to judge the timing of the shift from confrontation to cooperation, and to find a manner of presentation that maintains group cohesion and minimizes the extent of opposi-tion to demobilization. Even after the distribution of gains and losses has been negotiated, it may be necessary to maintain a cer-tain capacity for remobilization in order to ensure that the result-ing settlement is implemented on favourable terms. In terms of the soccer analogy the object is not just to win the match, but also to persuade the losers that they were fairly beaten, to preserve their willingness to participate in the next cycle, and to prevent hotheads from invading the pitch and beating up the players.

If we concentrate on the short-term rationality of individual actors it may seem as though they are obeying only one unqualified imperative: for example, to maximize their side's lead in goals over their opponents. But on a longer and more holistic view even the most rowdy and polarized of soccer matches involves the joint enact-ment of a shared normative framework. No doubt we can postulate the theoretical alternative of a strictly Hobbesian state of nature, but nothing of this sort existed even at the worst moments of Pinochet's Chile or indeed, reverting to our paired comparisons, in the darkest days of apartheid. Not only in Chile, but even in South Africa, it was because the rival camps shared so much common his-tory and discourse, and even to some extent held joint aspirations, that their division took the form of highly structured and collective polarization between competing (but also communicating) projects, rather than an atomized war of all against all. Consider the shared discursive fields provided by Christianity, constitutionalism, and the wish to assume a respected place in the international family of nations. This is not to belittle the normative divide separating the democratic project from its alternatives, but merely to insist that at the various 'critical junctures' when political actors defined their interests and selected their strategies they were always operating within a normative framework that could permit *both* polarization *and* constructive interactionism.

Of course they were also operating within a context of intense power inequalities, physical insecurities, and fundamental dis-agreements about goals. It is hardly possible to capture the major features of either individual or collective decision-making in such conditions merely by a priori deduction from the postulates of util-ity maximization. It would, for example, make no sense to try to compress the choices about imprisonment that have been made by such central and strategic democratic leaders as Nelson Mandela and Aung San Suu Kyi within the narrow confines of the 'prisoners' dilemma' debate. Not even the calculations of the Chilean DINA chief, General Manuel Contreras (eventually jailed for the criminal acts conducted under his authority) can be adequately illuminated by such an artificial and impoverished construct. What is missing here (and in so many other reductionist applications of choice theory) is adequate recognition of the tacit normative assumptions within which political prisoner and jailer both operate. In this battle of wills the power at stake concerns not so much the brute fact of who will be locked up by whom, as the persuasive and interpretative field within which the act of imprisonment will be judged as legitimate or oppressive.[3]

Within such a context the rationality of violence deserves far more careful consideration than it has so far received in democratization studies. At times of intense political polarization there is both an instrumental and a discursive content to political violence. In so far as it can be used to secure constructive political results, it must be highly controlled, precisely targeted, and elaborately justified. These are very demanding requirements, and in practice resort to such 'rational discursive' violence characteristically opens the way to much more undiscriminating, counterproductive, and self-damaging sequences of reactions. Nevertheless, the historical record contains some troubling and analytically intractable material. If ETA had not assassinated Franco's chosen successor it is far from clear that the Spanish transition would have followed such a smoothly negotiated path. It is at least arguable that the Zapatista assault on New Year's Day 1994 played an indispensable, and on balance positive, part in destabilizing Mexico's 'perfect dictatorship'. Finally, and critically for our case study, would the Chilean party elites have come together in such a strong and binding democratic pact, if it had not been for several years of near insurrection in *poblaciones* on the margins of Santiago, followed by the 'great fear' that was triggered by a nearly successful assassination attempt on the dictator, and the revenge killings it would have precipitated?[4]

---

[3] How can one expect to construct an adequate theory of politics on the microfoundations provided by the prisoners' dilemma, which by assumption precludes consideration of the legitimacy of constituted authority and the justice of its procedures?

[4] These are all controversial hypotheses derived from counter-factual reasoning. As matters of fact they are generally unprovable, but as questions of interpretation and belief they raise central issues of democratic legitimation.

The Weight of History

Such reflections on collective memory point to the more general significance of the 'weight of history' as a critical explanatory consideration. Chileans may have suppressed memories of polarization, but they also share strong memories based on long-standing experience, of how to work a competitive multi-party electoral system with universal suffrage, an effective division of powers, and alternation in office between programmatically differentiated party elites. The restoration of a mildly modified version of these past practices was something that both the political class and public opinion more broadly could easily understand and readily internalize. The guiding and stabilizing role of past experience was manifest in the reappearance of the same families, parties, and even similar electoral configurations as before. In such a context the task of explaining the progression of stages from breakdown through transition to near consolidation is greatly simplified. If the authoritarian regime was to be displaced, there already existed a tacit social consensus on the main outlines of the system that could be expected to take its place. This 'social construction of reality' could therefore proceed teleologically, with intervening steps or stages heavily conditioned by the anticipated outcome. But clearly there can only be *re*democratizations in countries that at some earlier period established a democratic regime for the first time. And just as clearly an increasing proportion of the present wave of democratic transitions involves countries which lack the firm memories and clear precedents found in Chile, Uruguay, and a few other examples. In some cases the 'weight of history' may be completely adverse to democratic experimentation. The Dominican Republic and Venezuela are often cited as Latin American examples of this condition. In both cases the absence of helpful antecedents seems to have contributed to an erratic path, in which the initial transition to democracy was not stabilized, and a further decade of coercive politics was required before the relevant elites found a way to design mutually reassuring rules of the democratic game. Such examples suggest that an adverse history may increase the learning costs and prolong uncertainty about the logic and sequences of the transition process, even if the eventual outcomes prove to be a conventional democracy.

In a few cases the restoration of past democratic political practices may be an overwhelmingly dominant theme, and in certain others the repudiation of a wholly undemocratic past may be root and branch, but in many (probably a majority) of instances the reality lies in between. In such cases it should be possible to rescue some positive precedents and some useful legacies from the past, but they are fragmentary, insufficient, and ill-adapted to current use. Therefore the process of transition involves an elaborate exercise in selective reappropriation and adaptation of past legacies, combined with some entirely new political inventions, perhaps borrowed from abroad or deduced from theoretical reasoning. There is now a substantial body of literature on such processes of pact-making and institutional design, but it may pay too much attention to the abstract logic of the rule-making exercise, and give insufficient recognition to the discursive task of winning consent. Here the 'invention of tradition', and the accommodation of idiosyncratic memories and dislikes, may be more crucial for the long-term success of the enterprise than a formal or strictly rational-legal approach.

When a transition to democracy was still an isolated and unfamiliar experience, national historical memories may have been an almost irreplaceable source of orientation. But now that there are so many parallel occurrences there is more scope for demonstration effects, selective transfer of experience, and internationally supported learning processes. For example, the Chilean plebiscite entered into the consciousness of political activists in South Africa and elsewhere, just as the release of Nelson Mandela affected perceptions all round the world of the durability of racial injustice. Chapter 2 argued that democratization frequently involves episodes of high drama in which moral themes of universal significance are acted out. From this standpoint there could be a particular interest in comparing the apparently quite dissimilar experiences of Chile and South Africa, on the grounds that they constitute two recent high points in a global debate over the possibilities of freedom and justice. One could also point to certain easily overlooked more specific elements of interaction. For example, as late as November 1989 the Chilean dictatorship and the apartheid regime were charged with collusion by the UN General Assembly.[5] Shortly thereafter the success of Chile's negotiated transition produced a direct impact on the strategic calculations of at least some players in the ensuing South African process (the Goldstone Commission exemplifies this). These types of interaction between successive

---

[5] A resolution of 22 No. 1989 deplored 'the action of Chile, which has become an important outlet for the sale of South Africa's military hardware in contravention of the Security Council's arms embargo' (B. Boutros-Gali, 1994, 415).

democratization processes have played a significant role in altering perceptions of what is possible.

But neither national memories nor international examples can provide more than background factors within which the transition drama must be played out by self-directing actors. Following the argument presented in Chapter 2 such actors are engaged in processes of persuasion where much depends on their ability to invoke narrative imagery that is suitably tailored to their audiences; and where the plot must be allowed to unfold according to an extended discursive logic. Some key political strategists may *think* that since they know the eventual outcome of the transition sequence it would be best to proceed there immediately, skipping all the messy and emotional intervening stages. That seems to have been an assumption underlying the strategy of some in the Concertación. But even if the end *is* preordained the participants must still be instructed, educated, persuaded, and socialized into their new condition. All that takes time. There are also contrasting logics to the succeeding acts of the democratization drama. Unless these sequences are enacted and experienced, the emerging new political regime will lack an adequate base of support and understanding in the society at large.

Schematically, then, the logic of the 'breakdown' phase requires that the authoritarian coalition loses its cohesion, while the anti-dictatorial opposition also re-evaluates assumptions about the implacability of the regime, and begins to discriminate between the die-hards and those with whom compromise is possible. It is not possible to assert a priori what will cause an authoritarian coalition to disintegrate, without first characterizing its initial composition and sources of cohesion. In Chile the problem of Pinochet's succession was a major point of weakness that was absent for example in South Africa (in South Africa, of course, the discredit of racial supremacist ideology was a source of vulnerability not present in Chile). What one can note in general is the dominant group's progressive loss of belief in its inherent right to rule. As that conviction spreads, the need to develop some alternative justification for the maintenance of power creates deepening divisions between those in office, and opens the way for dialogue with convergent elements of the opposition. Typically such changes start slowly (almost imperceptibly) and then gather speed. It is not necessarily impossible for an authoritarian elite to regain control and check the process, but unless this reassertion of the established order is very prompt and effective it soon becomes much harder and more costly.

The transition phase reflects a different distribution of power and so obeys a distinctive logic. Although the intransigents on both sides may still harbour hopes of a comeback, and may still exercise some veto power, the initiative has passed to those in government and opposition prepared to demonstrate a capacity to collaborate in the creation of a different regime. In these conditions the government needs the tacit endorsement of the moderate opposition, and vice versa. Outcomes are now determined as the product of interactions between these former antagonists, and can no longer be dictated unilaterally.[6] Again, it takes time, and requires theatrical demonstrations of this new reality, before the wider communities involved can be persuaded of its permanence, and can be reconciled to the (often disappointing) practical implications. A priori there is no logical necessity for the process to unfold in this way, yet by inductive reasoning it has been found possible to formulate in advance a relatively specific set of expectations which are in fact than fulfilled in future cases.

If this stage of 'transition' is to be followed by progress towards what the standard literature refers to as the 'consolidation' of a democratic regime, then the logic of political behaviour will have to change once again. Debates over 'foundational' issues would have to be replaced by incremental choices concerning routine questions of public policy. 'Die-hards' or figureheads from the authoritarian regime, who had to be marginalized and outmanœuvred in the transition phase, may now be readmitted to the routines of political competition which constitute a reproof to their former beliefs. 'Rules of the game' become routinized, political mobilization declines, and the focus of political life shifts to dense institutional agencies populated by professional managers and powerbrokers.

As a heuristic device this threefold classification of 'stages' in a democratization process no doubt retains some value. But it is far from providing a rigorously specified or logically compelling analysis, applicable to all cases. Certainly if we try to situate the Chilean experience within this framework we immediately encounter its limitations. Despite the personalization of presidential power, the Pinochet regime never 'broke down'. On the contrary, it proved resilient enough to force a reluctant opposition to accept the terms

---

[6] Some suggest that in periods of crisis or regime transition there is more scope for conscious acts of political creativity than in normal times, because habitual and structural constraints are lifted. But Michael Dobry, *Sociologie des Crises Politiques* (Paris: Presses de la Fondation Nationale des Sciences Politiques, 1992), 79, denounces this as a 'heroic illusion' and argues that structural determinants on choice do not typically diminish in crises.

of its far from democratic constitution (which had been far from legitimately ratified by a lopsided plebiscite in 1980). President Pinochet even came within reach of securing a popular vote extending his personalized rule from 1989 to 1997 (there were 3.1 million votes in favour, compared to almost 4 million against, on a turnout of over 95 per cent). In order to secure a peaceful transfer of office to civilian rule the opposition had to acquiesce to a series of restrictive 'rules of the game' which entrenched the veto power of the heirs to the outgoing regime. These so-called 'authoritarian enclaves' remain substantially in place a full decade later, despite repeated efforts by the governing Concertación to dismantle them. The 1980 Constitution remains largely unreformed in its anti-democratic provisions. Beyond this level of institutional formality, most supporters of the dictatorship still consider it to have been justified in its essential policy, and the armed forces, in particular, remain not only impenitent but almost threateningly so. Appeals for reconciliation and tolerance still tend to be rebuffed. By some standards, therefore, Chile has hardly yet entered the 'transition' stage of democratization. Some key 'foundational' issues are not only unresolved, but have at times even tended to be written out of the agenda of public debate. Yet, in other respects institutional life has become routinized, political mobilization has become rare and marginal, and some kind of rather stable 'rules of the game' have taken on an aura of permanence. *Some* kind of regime may have been more or less 'consolidated', albeit not a strictly and fully democratic regime.[7]

This contrast between the 'standard' stages of democratization and the distinctive course of regime change in Chile presents us with something of a paradox. Even accepting that the threefold classification is only a heuristic device, and not a binding theory, we are still left with the question whether Chilean deviation from that

[7] Thus Garretón has formulated the apparently paradoxical suggestion that in Chile 'consolidation' has preceded full 'transition'. By this he means that Chile's redemocratization has produced a consolidated but hybrid (or incomplete) democratic regime. He generalizes that when transitions 'occur within the institutional framework of the authoritarian regime, with one of the opposition's main problems being how to work from within this framework in order to change it and achieve democratic institutions (then) the outcome, not surprisingly, if often incomplete democracy, a regime basically democratic by riddled with inherited authoritarian enclaves: nondemocratic institutions, unresolved human rights problems and social actors not fully willing to play by democratic rules'. Manuel Antonio Garretón, 'Redemocratization in Chile', *Journal of Democracy*, 6/1 (Jan. 1995), 147. He concludes that for Chile to become fully democratic it would still need to 'confront and tame . . . such problems of transition as do exist' (p. 159).

model counts as an exception to it, or a confirmation that the regime change in Chile is not a 'real' democratization. Neither of these alternative conclusions is very attractive.

The standpoint of this chapter is to indicate several possible lines of escape from this dilemma. First, if we view democratization as a very long-term process with no preordained unitary outcome, then we can simply recognize the existence of the paradox, and allow more time for it to be resolved. Second, if we consider that one of the most distinctive features of the Chilean regime change was the desire of the old political class to 'skip stages' and bypass the rules and uncertainties associated with any real transition, then we can say that the outcome so far is precisely the kind of hybrid regime one might expect from such a deceptively smooth and controlled strategy. Third, the Chilean experience would seem to support the view that a wholehearted process of democratization must involve more than a mere recalibration of the interests of already established power contenders. Viewed comparatively, and from a long-term perspective, it must also involve some redefinition of identities, to incorporate distinctively democratic procedural and substantive values.

An End to 'Guardianship'?

The present political order is founded on the substantially authoritarian and questionably legitimate constitution of 1980, as modified by the agreements and plebiscites of 1989. The prevailing constitution entrenches the veto power of nominated senators, the National Security Council, and the immovability of the military high command. In his message to Congress of 21 May 1999 President Frei declared that the time had passed when the country could combine an open economy with a democracy limited in this way, and that the country's full development would require full democracy. He proposed a plebiscite to reform the constitution and remove various obstacles that be identified to the full exercise of popular sovereignty. But no such plebiscite has been held, since the entrenched minority retains its capacity under the existing institutional rules to veto democratic reforms.

But even if all the reforms proposed by President Frei were to be implemented in full, would that be the end of the Chilean process of democratization? Historical and comparative analysis suggests that this would be too hasty an inference. Those who feel that their interests are protected by the continuation of the existing anti-democratic procedures would need to change their outlook and learn to pursue their interests solely within the limits prescribed by a constitutional system based on full popular sovereignty. Chilean historical experience suggests that such a change in basic orientation would not be either easy or quick. This chapter has sought to underscore that point by drawing attention to the need for an extended period of public deliberation and resocialization in order to embed a new democratic consensus. It has argued that in the specific case of Chile the outgoing authoritarian elites withdrew in such good order, and the returning political class was so eager for a smooth and uncontested transfer of power, that this essential period of public reflection and dramatic re-education was heavily curtailed and even in some key respects (acknowledging responsibility for human rights abuses) suppressed. A decade later the consequences of that omission still hang over the Chilean process of democratization and contribute to its peculiar unevenness. The 'expressive' and symbolic' aspects of democratization have been neglected, with the result that democratic politics remain constrained 'in an arrested state', to use Alex Wilde's formulation.[8] If so, among the distinguishing features of Chilean democratization one should highlight its non-conformity to conventional expectations of a three-stage progression (breakdown, transition, consolidation) and the probability that a process which always requires at least a generation for its completion may, in this case, either take considerably longer or eventually turn out substantially differently from the standard hypothetical pattern. Here too, as with the earlier points listed in this conclusion, all judgements will inevitably contain some degree of subjectivity, but they can be made more specific and impersonal by informed use of appropriately selected international comparisons.

What President Frei referred to as a 'limited democracy' could also be analysed in terms of the classical concept of the 'guardian' state or, to use Weberian language, in terms of 'legal domination'. The Chilean experience highlights the theoretical issues at stake in these terminological debates and democratization processes. The concept of guardianship has an extremely long and distinguished pedigree, and contains many variants. The version most visibly present in contemporary Chile can be traced to imperial Austrian roots, and associated with the doctrines of Friedrich Hayek, whose work was explicitly invoked by the authors of the 1980 Constitution. In this context a few lines on the broad principles will suffice. The key

---

[8] 'Irruptions of Memory', 475.

assumption is that there exists a permanent set of collective interests which antedate popular sovereignty and which provide the preconditions for civilized coexistence and personal autonomy, without which democracy would be self-destructive or worthless. Different versions of guardianship specify these permanent interests in different ways—national security, the rule of law, the sanctity of contract, etc. The key theoretical point is that, under unlimited popular sovereignty, the citizenry would be free to destroy the very prerequisites of their own freedom. Ordinary people cannot be assumed to anticipate and resist such destruction. Therefore, even under a competitive electoral system, their sovereignty should be restricted to those spheres of choice compatible with the preservation of the prior and unchangeable collective interests. Hence some form of 'guardianship' is required whereby democratic encroachment on these reserve domains can be precluded. For example, as discussed in Chapter 6, above, the guardians might be economic specialists entrenched in a central bank which was insulated from partisan pressures, and which had the single and exclusive responsibility for ensuring the stability of the monetary system. Or they might be military specialists, similarly charged with preserving internal peace regardless of demotic politics. Or they could be legal experts sheltered from party politics within a self-contained supreme court responsible for interpreting the Constitution and providing an ultimate court of appeal. Or they could be senators appointed for life to represent one or other of these supposedly supra-political categories of guardianship, and to counter-balance the shortsightedness of their directly elected colleagues in the upper house. In all cases, their main duty would be to disregard the temporary preferences of one or other electoral majority and to attend steadfastly to the specific and permanent interests of the collectivity which they, by training and selection, could interpret more reliably than the people at large.

Within the Chilean setting, the Popular Unity government of 1970–3 provided an important sector of society with an intense exposure to the case for such 'guardianship'. Hyper-inflation, looming civil war, the disregard of legal and constitutional precepts, and the absence of a moderating authority in the legislature could all be attributed to the irresponsibility of an unconstrained and badly led electorate. This is not the place to debate whether that diagnosis of the Allende experiment is correct. All we need to note is that it seemed convincing to those who overthrew his government, and therefore it guided their reasoning about how future episodes of popular sovereignty would need to be constrained. This basic theory of guardianship continues to enjoy substantial support, particularly among strategic sectors within the Chilean legal, military, and business elites, to this day.

This theory of guardianship may be made clearer if re-expressed in the language of Weberian realism. In this version all modern societies have to contend with the 'ethical irrationality of the world' (that is, there is no longer any over-riding moral unity derived from a single religious certainty). It is therefore necessary to develop some form of legitimate domination derived from self-interest which can provide an orderly structure of social choices, and can rule out (as illegitimate) those moral imperatives whose consequences would destroy social coexistence. Such legitimate domination will take a legal and bureaucratic form in the modern state (which is, famously, a territorial entity with a monopoly on the legitimate use of violence). For our purposes the key question about this legitimacy is whether the consent of the citizenry provides its foundation (popular sovereignty) or whether it is some prior source of legitimacy which demands such consent. Weber's attitude to democracy may have evolved as German nationalism and militarism met defeat at the end of the First World War, and he became involved in efforts to draft a Constitution for the Weimar republic. But it seems clear that the notion of domination (derived from Roman law) essentially grounded authority on conquest, and only subsequently (and conditionally) on consent.

These theoretical considerations provide us with some further elements for situating the Chilean experience of democratization in its comparative context. The authority of the 1980 Constitution was grounded on the physical defeat of the pre-1973 civilian government. During the 1980s Chilean democrats demanded that government should be based on popular consent, and in that they were in tune both with Chile's traditional self-image of its politics, and with the international aspirations of most Chilean opinion-formers. But the 1980 Constitution was not repudiated or overthrown. Instead it secured reluctant consent from the great bulk of the electorate, and it proved capable of accommodating substantial change (including the restoration of the old political class) and of progressively extending the domain of popular consent. In origin, however, it remained an instrument of domination, and those origins continued to carry with them substantial practical biases and institutional distortions which limited the scope of popular sovereignty.

Chile's democratization process is not unique in this regard. The Mexican revolutions imposed the 1917 Constitution as an act of domination, and Mexican rulers proceeded to interpret it in a heavily biased manner for the next eighty years, notwithstanding the elements of popular sovereignty that it also invoked. Only very recently has the balance begun to shift from domination to freely given democratic consent, and even now that shift in emphasis is far from absolute or secure. President Fujimori's *auto-golpe* of 1992 was essentially an act of domination which aimed to supersede his prior (and limited) constitutional legitimacy based on consent. President Chávez of Venezuela may also be displaying comparable tendencies when he refers to a 'Bolivarian Revolution'. What these examples suggest is that a state of ambiguity between an authority derived from imposition and an authority derived from popular consent may persist over an extended period; and that there is no guarantee that in the long run the second principle will necessarily supersede or outweigh the first. (In France such alternatives have persisted over two centuries, with 1848 superseded by 1851, 1945 by 1958, and so on. Gaullism was a fusion of guardianship and popular sovereignty strands of legitimacy.) Chile's democratization process needs to be evaluated with these theoretical and comparative cautions in mind.

As worldwide interest in the Pinochet case illustrates, Chile's way of answering these partially analytic but partially moral questions is viewed as of significance for democracy in general, and not just for the national variant thereof. To that extent the Chilean elite's conviction that what they can achieve in their country is of international rather than merely local importance may be grounded in reality. But what is of universal significance is not the specific fate of one individual ruler, or the short-term victory of one side or another in a specific legal battle. For, as this chapter has repeatedly argued, there is no single cut-off point or final outcome signalling that democratization is now complete. Various different outcomes of the Pinochet case can therefore be accommodated within the longer term sweep of a democratization process. What matters about the Pinochet case is the way it is assimilated by all the rival forces in Chilean society. What matters is whether it serves to foster a more tolerant and consensual pattern of political interactions between the contending forces, whether it helps to overcome legacies of mutual suspicion and distrust, and to affirm shared democratic values. The verdict is still open on these issues, and a protracted process of public deliberation would be required before they could be resolved. It will not happen without effort, or without democratic leadership; but both theory and comparative experience suggest that it can happen. Chile *can* be resocialized away from the guardian state and towards a more secure and broad-based form of popular sovereignty. That *would* fix Chile's place in the comparative study of democratization processes.

The implication is not that Chilean democratization is permanently blocked. It is only that the process is far from complete, that much still depends on future efforts and choices, and that the eventual outcome is in no way predetermined by what has taken place so far. In this respect the state of Chilean democracy is not very different in essence from that of most other new democracies. The differences are of timing, balance, and context, and these are certainly important. But in fundamental normative terms the issue is the same as elsewhere: can an incomplete and imperfect process be extended and deepened?

This chapter has pointed to certain distinguishing characteristics of the Chilean political class—its long-standing identification with a complex and well-elaborated constitutional tradition; its strong continuities of personnel and recruitment structure (notwithstanding the dictatorship); its shared political memories (some of them traumatic); its strong desire (indeed need) for international recognition and approval, especially from the leading Western democracies; its post-1990 cohesion around an essentially restorational project; and so forth. No doubt these are all relative, qualitative, and indeed debatable propositions. To establish them it is necessary to deploy historical judgement, to scan a broad range of sources of evidence (some objective and easily accessible, others much more intangible), and at times to invoke controlled counter-factual analysis. (Why did the Concertación not break down after Aylwin's presidential term? What has held it together, even when the Christian Democrats found themselves heavily outvoted by the Socialists in the June 1999 open primaries, and so the Concertación passed the Chilean presidency to Socialist Ricardo Lagos after the November 1999 presidential elections?)

Unless such structural and contextual characteristics of a particular country are specified and integrated into the analysis of its democratization process, the real and distinctive forces at work in that particular case are liable to be misrepresented or even omitted. This applies both to the dynamics of actor behaviour, and to the subjectivities of collective understanding around which any given political experience will be structured. Abstracting from such complexities may produce some neat theories, but they are unlikely to work as rounded explanations of long-term political evolution or regime change.

A rounded evaluation of Chilean democracy needs to take a long-term view, and to identify the most important national specificities which differentiate this process from others in its class. Since every country is specific in a multitude of ways, we need some method for identifying the most salient and relevant national peculiarities. This chapter has drawn from three main methods: theoretical reflection, structured comparison, and historical inquiry. All three can be combined, and each should serve as both a stimulus and check on the other two. This approach privileges such specificities as the *re*democratization aspect of Chile's experience, and such peculiarities as distinguish its political class, and its view of Chile's place in the world. Chile's democratization, like all such processes, should be viewed as very long-term, open-ended, and subject to continuous debate, revision, and even to 'dialectical' lurches. Viewed from this perspective it would be mistaken to adopt any predetermined or foreshortened time frame, and argue that—for example—if Chile's constitutional system has persisted for at least a decade than the democratization process must be complete. On the contrary, Chile experienced over thirty years of 'parliamentary republic' after 1891, and over forty years of electoral competition under constitutional rule after 1931, without in either case finally completing or perfecting its democratic regime. So there can be no preordained closure or quick cut-off point to such processes, which always contain tensions and the potential for deviation. At best such tensions can only be controlled through deliberation, dialogue, and the promotion of tolerance.

10

On Theory and Experience in Democratization Studies

> Our account of this science will be adequate if it achieves such
> clarity as the subject matter allows.
>
> (Aristotle)

Previous chapters have presented a succession of definitions,
metaphors, models, normative constructs, and theoretical traditions that can help organize our thinking about contemporary
processes of democratization. If theory-building means only the construction of tightly defined covering law type predictive theories,
then this exercise has generated almost nothing that can be 'tested'
against the evidence. If looser probabilistic claims are counted as
theory then some provisional judgements become possible, but their
predictive power remains quite low. After all, although comparative
democratization studies were already well advanced by the end of
the 1980s, almost all political scientists were caught by surprise
when the great majority of communist regimes underwent mostly
peaceful and almost simultaneous transitions to what may at least
provisionally be labelled 'democracy' in the 1990s. Some eminent
scholars had even explicitly predicted that this would not come
about.[1] Looking ahead from the standpoint of 2001, existing scholarship provides only limited guidance on the parallel question of
whether or not democratization is predictable in the Islamic world.
This is not to decry rigorous predictive theorizing in those domains
where it is feasible, but only to note that most of our subject-matter
is not of that kind.

Nevertheless we have generated a considerable range of categories, concepts, and hypotheses that are intended to assist thinking

---

[1] Notably, in 'Will More Countries Become Democratic?', *Political Science
Quarterly*, 99/2 (Summer 1984), Samuel Huntington specifically stated that 'the
likelihood of democratic development in Eastern Europe is virtually nil' (p. 217),
although in other respects this was a judicious and balanced article.

about comparative processes of democratization. This volume has concentrated attention on interpretations that revolve around the conception of democratization as a complex, dynamic, long-term, and open-ended process. If that is indeed the nature of our subject-matter, then the type of theory-building and hypothesis-testing that would be possible and appropriate ('adequate' in Aristotle's terminology) would be interpretative rather than demonstrative. This does not mean that any interpretation is as good as any other. On the contrary, generating a good interpretation, like writing a good history, involves satisfying exacting requirements of argument, evidence, and exposition. Even the best of historical interpretations invite subsequent and successive reinterpretations. While it may be possible definitely to eliminate errors and misconceptions, the historian or the interpretavist should not expect final closure. In place of the dichotomy between proposition and evidence one should expect an ongoing dialogue between interpretation and experience. At any rate in the specific field of comparative democratization studies, if the object of study is indeed complex, dynamic, long-term, and open-ended then, as old processes unfold and new experiences arise established, interpretations are likely to be repeatedly challenged and even destabilized. But given the practical necessity (and the moral desirability) of developing well-founded interpretations of what is possible when democratization gets under way, scholars should not shirk this interpretative dialogue between theory and experience, just because of the unattainability of closure.

On Teleology

It may reasonably be objected that to classify democratization as complex dynamic, long-term, and open-ended is to redirect scholarship not just from a demonstrative to an interpretative method of reasoning, but also to a teleological mode of interpretation. Although the eventual outcome may be distant and open-ended, does not this conception imply that we should reason back from that assumed outcome to the processes required to bring it into existence? Part of the appeal of the strong form of predictive theory in the social sciences is precisely as a defence against the alternative of a strong form of teleological reasoning, in which the analyst starts from some subjectively predetermined certainty about the eventual outcome ('the inevitable triumph of socialism', for example) and is therefore able to disregard contrary evidence. Just as the subject-matter of democratization does not allow much scope to strong versions of predictive theory, so also it cannot endorse teleology of this strong kind. Both the theory and the experiences we have reviewed in this volume clash with any a priori assumptions of a single path or necessary outcome, or indeed of irreversible advance. Such 'end of history' type convergences on liberal democracy will always be hostage to the unexpected, and whenever they seem most plausible they will attract most resistance. However, not all forms of teleological interpretation should be subsumed under the strongest and least defensible variant. If we are to endorse interpretative theory construction and to compare long-term open-ended processes, some aspects of a teleological perspective must be entertained.

In fact, both at the individual and the collective level, the social choices we make at present are only intelligible in terms of the meanings we assume they will have in the future. The social futures we envisage are never purely objective and given in advance. Above all when we are dealing with collective political arrangements there is no way to avoid engaging in exercises of the collective imagination (including 'thoughtful wishing') about what lies ahead. Thus, the democratically elected leaders of various post-communist states in Central Europe may not know precisely when their countries will be admitted to the European Union, or on what terms, or even what probability to attach to a setback or veto. But despite these uncertainties a great deal of their political energies may be devoted to preparing for a hypothetical desired future entry to the EU (or to NATO). Interpretations of this type of future-oriented political behaviour cannot be reduced to mere estimates of statistical probabilities. Present behaviour is controlled by the subjectively assessed *meaning and desirability* of an anticipated future, and not solely by its objective likelihood. For example, the eventual admission of Poland to the EU is not just a legal transaction to be evaluated on a calculus of objective interest. It is also a change of identity, an affirmation of values, a recasting of collective perceptions about the parameters of future political life. All this can be perceived and understood well before it happens and independently of its chance of occurring. This example shows how teleological projects can reshape currently existing political arrangements and how visions of the future (which may or may not turn out to be well-founded) can control behaviour in the present. (Other current examples include the prospective Free Trade Area of the Americas, or even the hypothetical reunification of the two Koreas.) Bearing such examples in mind it may not be so unreasonable to view long-term open-ended processes of democratization as teleological projects of transformation which have the capacity to alter current realities especially in incompletely formed new democracies. Under the spell of a collectively imagined eventual democracy the citizens of defective 'really existing' new democracies may sometimes be willing to endure their current disappointments encouraged by the belief that at some point the promises of their regime will be more fully realized.

An interpretative approach to democratization has to take into account the fact that such faith in democracy, viewed as a teleological project, may play a significant role in driving forward such processes. And yet standard teleological explanations are at variance with this volume's stress on open-endedness. In Chapter 1 we presented democratization as a process that is necessarily subject to reinterpretation and revision by the society in question. Since the citizenry retains the power to reconsider and modify their democratic practices in the light of reflection and experience, democratization must therefore be an open-ended process. Is there any sense in which an open-ended process can also be understood as a teleological project? The following analogy may be helpful here.

The building of a democracy may be compared with the building of a city. (Likewise redemocratization may be compared to urban reconstruction after a natural disaster). Only individual agents can build a city, and to undertake such a sustained effort they must doubtless be allowed to pursue their own self-interests, and to act rationally (that is, to seek efficient connections between their means and ends). However, no adequate account of the construction of Paris, or of the rebuilding of London after the Great Fire, could be derived solely from these rational action postulates. They merely constitute necessary background conditions for works of human creativity that require a much more fully elaborated explanation. To build a great city (or a great democracy) requires co-ordinated and purposive collective action over various generations. The separate components of such overall action may each have their own distinctive rhythms and rationalities, but they also require a definite degree of co-ordination in accordance with some over-arching conception of the eventual totality. Thus, for example, each road will somehow fit in with the overall transport network of the city. Each building will relate to the built environment as a whole. Any great city constrains the development of these various component elements. Any democracy worth the name can be expected to exert similar pressures on those actors enmeshed within it to adjust their interactions in the light of this over-arching political framework. The resulting city (or political regime) remains always open-ended and subject to redesign. Therefore the steps required to bring it about are open to continual adjustment and modification, but always in the light of the common enterprise and the resulting shared vision of a future direction. In such cases debate over a 'shared vision' will often involve something much more controversial and precise than just some vaguely imagined future. It will involve quite specific measures of advance planning on behalf of an organized community. But, of course, such plans are never finally completed, and are subject to permanent renewal. Every individual city develops within its own distinctive constraints and potentialities. So there is not just one single ideal model applicable to all processes of city-building at all times and in all places. In addition, outcomes take generations to construct and meanwhile involve permanent renegotiation of expectations and intentions about the planned or imagined future. Outcomes are also continually adapted in the light of experience.

Generalizing from this analogy between city-building and democratization, when a complex and relatively open-ended outcome is collectively both imagined and desired, the resulting process of social construction needs to be analysed from at least two alternative perspectives. From the standpoint of the actors intending to create, let us say, a more united Europe, or a stronger rule of law (or even a 'consolidated democracy') collective action involves rational planning, foresight, and co-ordination. But the desired outcome is also an imagined future with its own structure and properties that will constrain and discipline today's actors if and when it comes into existence. It is a potential social fact to which they will collectively have to adjust. It is both their chosen creation and a prospective system of control over them.

In the case of democratization processes this volume has highlighted the diversity of forms that a prospective democracy might take, the alternative routes for getting there, and the always provisional nature of democratic outcomes (subject to further deliberation and potential change in light of future democratic decisions). Nevertheless, despite all these elements of open-endedness, we have also presented democratization as a constraining process. The constraints include resocialization (Chapter 2); the strengthening of civility (Chapter 3); a self-restraining state (Chapter 4); limits on the power of money (Chapter 5); the delicate balancing of legitimacy and authority in the realm of monetary policy (Chapter 6); and the requirements of public security (Chapter 7). All these components of democratization can be viewed from the standpoint of present-day actors as the acceptance of self-limitations in exchange for the benefits of a desired future order. But they can also be viewed from the standpoint of that hypothetical future order as the constitutive elements of a process of democratization. In this sense, there may be a 'teleological' strand to our version of democratization, notwithstanding its open-endedness and its dependence on citizen consent. This strand concerns the ways in which the requirements of any prospective democratic order may constrain the possibilities for present action. There are two key objections to any teleological explanation that seeks to account for outcomes in terms of human intentions. These are the prevalence of unforeseen consequences, or unintended 'side effects'; and the instability of collective intentions. (For example, the intention to protect human rights may be very widespread and deeply felt in a period when gross violations are prevalent, but it may dissolve in conditions where good human rights performance can be taken for granted, and other priorities—such as collective security—come to seem more pressing.) This volume's stress on democratization as a complex dynamic and long-term process therefore precludes endorsement of any strongly teleological explanation (for example, of democracy as an end of history, or a utopian closure). Instead the account of democracy developed in Chapter 1 envisages a deliberative process that would allow for adjustments in the light of unintended consequences or shifts in collective priorities (i.e. democracy as an 'error-correction' mechanism). In a democracy the problems of unintended consequencies and temporally unstable collective intentions are tackled through periodic competitive elections that confirm or modify the prevailing policy mandate in the light of new developments.[2] If democracy is viewed in this way as 'floating but anchored' then democratization could be both open-ended and still guided by some overall sense of direction. It would indeed be driven by a collectively imagined future of progression towards a more rule-based, participatory, and consensual form of self-government.

The theory and experiences reviewed in this volume open up a wide range of possibilities concerning advance and retreat, and concerning variations in the content of prospective democratization processes. For example, against the theory that resocialization is a vital component of democratic transitions (Chapter 2), experience indicates there can be regime changes where the 'rules of the game' are comprehensively overhauled, while the key players are not exposed to social pressures to adjust, and public opinion is not alerted to the logic of the new procedures. Similarly, against the theory that some minimum of security for the median citizen is a

[2] Susan Stokes, *Mandates and Democracy* (Cambridge: Cambridge University Press, 2001) brings out the complications.

virtual prerequisite for democratization viewed more broadly, (Chapter 7), we can identify a substantial number of ostensibly democratic regimes that are close to falling below any plausible minimum threshold in this area. Similarly, if theory asserts that democracy requires a certain infrastructure of accountability, or a 'rule of law' system with at least some general penetration in the society (Chapter 4); or some balance to the exercise of unbridled money power through the markets (Chapter 5); or at least *some* political authority over the conduct of monetary or economic policy (Chapter 6); or a certain level of administrative coherence and coordination; then in any of these areas experience reveals a scope for regression or deviation quite as extensive as the possibilities for cumulative advance towards full democratization. Likewise, if national income levels, historical traditions, religious or cultural specificities, or ethnic divisions make any difference to either the course or the content of democratization processes (understood as complex, long-term, and dynamic undertakings) then the range of contemporary national experiences are scattered so widely across this matrix that the fit between theoretical expectations and observable experiences is likely to be both loose and unstable. While narrowly defined indicators of regime type have been systematically calibrated and assessed, such findings provide only partial and provisional insights from the standpoint adopted here, since this volume takes a much broader and more qualitative view of the relevant 'outcomes', and also assumes that the processes under examination are very long-term and frequently non-linear.[3]

On Overlapping Processes

But if we regard democratization as a complex, long-term, dynamic, and open-ended process geared to the realization of a set of shared values and objectives, then we need to recognize that other processes of comparable character may be under way at the same time. For example, nation-building can be analysed in a parallel manner. Contrary to the theory that this process must be completed before democratization can begin, comparative experience indicates that several variants of overlap are also possible. Democratization can begin when nation-building is under way but not complete.

[3] For a parallel interpretation see Jonathan Hartlynn, 'Contemporary Latin American Democracy and Consolidation: Unexpected Patterns, Re-elaborated Concepts, Multiple Components', in Joseph Tulchin (ed.), *Global Governance and Social Inequity* (Washington, DC: Wilson Center Press, 2001).

Democratization and nation-building can proceed in tandem. Or, indeed, democratization can begin before nation-building has started (East Timor, for example). The only theoretical combination lacking an empirical counterpart is the case when democratization is completed before nation-building has begun. None of this should surprise us, once it is recognized that *both* democratization and nation-building are best understood as long-term, open-ended, and potentially reversible processes. Another counterpart process would be the establishment of a market economy. This can clearly precede democratization, or accompany it. But is it possible for democratization to be completed before a transition to market has begun? According to a strong current in liberal theory, the security of private property is a prerequisite for individual freedom, which is in turn an essential component of any full system of democracy. A socialist tradition has long contested this view, in which case it might at least theoretically be possible for a socialized economy (let us say today's Cuba) to achieve full democratization without constructing a market economy. For our purposes it is only necessary to note that so far there are no experiences of this kind. However, any theorist who asserts that this combination is necessarily impossible risks encountering another surprise like those that have dislocated similar contentions in the past. The short, sharp, inevitable, one-way route to the market postulated in the 1990s could well prove to be another over-ambitious theory awaiting falsification through experience. In addition to nation-building and marketization there are also various other long-term dynamic processes that might, in principle, run in parallel with democratization. Perhaps the establishment of an 'ever closer' European Union should be included here, or the construction of an integrated world market.

If democratization is a long-term process then the forces that drive it forward at one stage may not operate in the same way, or with the same degree of intensity, at later stages. Alternative temporal patterns of democratization require consideration. In *some* cases a quick step change from authoritarian rule to full democracy *may* indeed be possible. (The redemocratization of Uruguay after a decade of harsh military rule seems to exemplify this pattern.) A process of linear advance steadily sustained over a decade or a generation may also be possible (for example, in response to a stable and compelling structure of external inducements, such as prospective membership of the European Union). But experience indicates that *many other* temporal possibilities exist. There can be sudden advances, followed by long periods of stagnation or even reversal. There can be protracted periods of reluctant and partial reform, followed by a perhaps unexpectedly complete and abrupt breakthrough (Mexico after the electoral defeat of the PRI is possibly in this camp). There are also possibilities of decline or reversal, as noted in the discussions of Colombia and Sri Lanka below. At the theoretical level, it may be worth revisiting the classical literature on cyclical patterns in the history of democracy.[4] What is indicated by both theory and experience is that when democratization is viewed as a long-term process, the range of alternative temporal possibilities becomes extensive.

Just as there are various different rhythms of change possible in a democratization process, so too with the counterpart processes that may overlap, or compete with, democratization in the bid for popular support. Thus nation-building has sometimes been achieved abruptly; at other times, as a linear advance, and also more erratically. The same is true of marketization. Experience suggests that there is no one necessary and inevitable line of advance or period to completion in any of these processes. But if so, there is an important analytical inference to be drawn. Much recent scholarly literature has attempted to specify the 'right sequence' linking two parallel processes (such as economic and political liberalization, for example). But there may not be any one generally applicable correct sequence, if the two processes in question are themselves of variable temporality. On the contrary, to the extent that in a particular setting both of the ongoing processes are complex and open-ended, then it follows that both possess the potential for mutual adjustment and accommodation to make them more compatible. But equally, the same characteristics also carry the potential for friction and for spiralling into mutual incompatibility. In either case our approach would argue against any mechanistic conclusion about the inevitability of conflict, and equally against any assumption of necessary compatibility. In the abstract this indeterminacy could apply whether the two processes were undertaken simultaneously or sequentially. To the extent that both processes are also complex and long-term, the way each is phased

---

[4] Polybius, *The Rise of the Roman Empire* (Harmondsworth: Penguin edn., 1979). Book VI, paras. 8 and 9, outline the 'law of nature according to which constitutions change, are transformed, and finally revert to their original form. Anyone who has a clear grasp of this process might perhaps go wrong, when he speaks of the future of a state, in his forecast of the time it will take for the process of change to take place, but so long as his judgement is not distorted by animosity or envy he will very seldom be mistaken as to the stage of growth or decline which a given community has reached, or as to the form into which it will change.' (pp. 309–10) For a contemporary discussion see Philippe C. Schmitter and Javier Santiso, 'Three Temporal Dimensions to the Consolidation of Democracy', *International Political Science Review*, 19/1 (1999).

and configured should also permit variation, stretching, delay, or acceleration to alter their prospects of mutual accommodation. In any particular episode all plausible counter-factuals need to be sympathetically considered (e.g. if Chile had democratized ten years earlier, would the resulting regime have been less economically efficient?) The idea that necessary laws of sequencing can be extracted from the static comparison of a limited number of not entirely uniform cases is a denial of these open-ended potentialities and rests on an inappropriately rigid ('billiard ball') model of causation.

It is also necessary to recognize the possibility that democratization could coincide with various other equally broad-based processes of comparable complexity that could turn out to be at least partially incompatible with democracy-building. For example, Chile's 'peaceful road to socialism' of the 1970s (and similar projects envisaged by, for example, the Communist Party of Italy) attempted to combine at least some aspects of democratization with state capture of the 'commanding heights' of the economy. The Zionist attempt to create a national homeland for the Jewish people has sought to reconcile democratization, nation-building, and an exclusivist project of political and cultural renaissance which (with the benefit of hindsight) may turn out to be incompatible with the universalistic foundations of democracy. The Islamic Republic of Iran is also attempting to undertake a long-term process with a clearly democratizing content, but it aims at the same time to consolidate a theocratic system which may prove irreconcilable with democracy. The Republic of South Africa is trying to democratize and at the same time seeking to overcome the socio-economic legacy of apartheid, an enterprise which could well prove at least partially inconsistent with 'institutional ized uncertainty' about the outcome of elections, and in tension with democratic demands for the protection of minority rights.

In synthesis, then, comparative experience indicates that processes of democratization as characterized in this volume, frequently overlap with, and may sometimes even clash with, other counterpart processes of similar scope and durability. As mentioned in chapter one some of the earlier literature portrayed democratization as a cut-and-dried one step shift to a new equilibrium. This idea was accompanied by catchy slogans such as 'the end of history', 'consolidation', and 'the only game in town'. However, an overview of the entire spectrum of available experiences, taking into account such phenomena as the incidence of political corruption (Chapter 5) or the perceived absence of citizen security (Chapter 7), indicates that democratization processes are often more protracted and troubled than this language would suggest. Prior and rival commitments (e.g.

to an exclusivist group identity, or to an intolerant style of political organization) often provide sources of resistance to democratization that may not only persist but even intensify once a regime change gets under way. The losers from democratization may feel cornered and become determined to obstruct, particularly if the 'value' component of democracy is downgraded as the experience unfolds, while the supporters and beneficiaries of the process will not necessarily maintain the same level of commitment over time, once it seems that their most pressing objectives have been secured. Indeed, in theoretical terms, if democratization is viewed as a protracted and open-ended process then the source of its momentum becomes a key issue. Institutional design can perhaps create incentives to 'lock in' desired patterns of behaviour, and to exclude some forms of opposition, but this will only work in the long run if accompanied by some more active and deliberate sources of reinforcement. Otherwise the new procedures will become taken for granted and may be allowed to degenerate, while collective disillusion with the gulf between democratic promises and lived realities will open space for alternative projects to capture the popular imagination. If democratization as a long-run process is to be sustained this must at least partially be driven by some degree of normative commitment. Democratic aspirations and values are required to keep such processes on track, and to insulate them from the siren songs of alternative projects. The worldwide diffusion of democracy over the past generation suggests that such aspirations may now be widely lodged in the individual and collective imaginations of much of humanity. But even if this is so they are not the only aspirations in contention, and the protracted steps required to turn aspirations of this type into reality are very diverse, and much easier in some settings than in others.

On Narrative Construction

Given these characteristics of our subject-matter, the need to incorporate an element of 'soft' teleology into the analysis, and the limited insights that are to be expected from standardized 'reporting unit' exercises in comparative politics, the merits of the structured historical narrative deserve restatement. This is sometimes dismissed as 'mere story-telling', but Flyvbjerg makes a good case when he reverses the argument: 'Knowledge at the beginner's level consists precisely in the reduced formulas which characterize theories while true expertise is based on the ability to discriminate between situations, with all their nuances of difference, without distilling them into formulas or standard cases.'[5] Collingwood elaborated on this argument from the standpoint of the methodologically self-conscious historian. His position was that 'narrative intelligibility is established not only by explanatory judgements, but also by judgements of significance, the latter requiring the historian to take up a retrospective standpoint. It is to a considerable extent from such a standpoint that selection into a narrative is made'.[6] On this view, instead of seeking to understand large historical processes such as democratization by procedures aimed at suppressing all elements of subjectivity and perspective on the part of the analyst, and all nuance and complexity in the object of analysis, the narrative approach requires the conscious and trained deployment of all these resources.

The best, and perhaps the only, way to grasp the dynamics of a long-term open-ended process is through narrative construction. But for that purpose the analyst must have a standpoint, a method for fitting developments into a coherent account, and a way of telling the story which necessarily includes some elements of judgement, interpretation, and indeed preference. For example, any narrative we might construct concerning the democratization of South Africa would have to include some standpoint on the question of apartheid. But this is not to say that the story must be told in a didactic or one-sided way. Far from it, to tell the story well requires sufficient breadth of judgement and awareness of nuance and complexity to accommodate its richness and its moral ambiguities.

If this is true of narrative construction in general, it is especially true when applied to contemporary processes of democratization, both because without a standpoint the observer would be disqualified from grasping the story or explaining the action, and because since these are still open-ended processes the narrative must reflect the ambiguities and leave open the possibility of alternative resolutions. The long-term nature of many of these processes also underscores the need to adopt a narrative structure. For example, the contours and dilemmas of democratization in contemporary Chile (Chapter 9) are barely intelligible in the absence of some familiarity with the history of the Allende government and the Pinochet coup. Both the biographies of the key individuals and the outlooks of the collective actors are heavily influenced by their experiences and memories of past conflicts. In a similar manner, even the most

---

[5] B. Flyvbjerg, *Making Social Science Matter* (Cambridge: CUP, 1001), 84–5.

[6] Dray's summary of Collingwood on narrative in William H. Dray, *History as Re-Enactment: R. G. Collingwood's History of Ideas* (Oxford: OUP, 1998), 314.

'consolidated' of post-communist democracies—say Hungary or Poland—turn out on closer inspection to be almost obsessively pre-occupied with earlier historical legacies. Unless the analyst has a familiarity with these antecedents, and a standpoint from which to evaluate them, she will be poorly placed to sum up the current distribution of political forces, let alone to assess the chances of the existing democracy staying on track. In the absence of trained analysts capable of making such narrative judgements in a judicious and comparative manner, these judgements will be made in some other way, because the collective demand for them ensures some kind of supply, however deficient it may be.

Narrative construction should therefore be celebrated rather than disdained as mere 'story-telling'. But while it is an indispensable skill when reconstructing individual processes of democratization it is equally important to know how to generalize. Of course historical narratives do not have to be confined to single cases. It is perfectly possible to narrate the parallel emergence of democracies in a succession of post-communist countries in Central Europe, for example, using the shared periodization and trajectories as the common features of all cases, and then introducing variety to the extent that, for example, Hungary and the Poland compete with each other in claims to regional leadership, or Slovakia appears to deviate from the dominant pattern of advance. Thus narrative construction can accompany and enrich generalization, rather than exclude it. Indeed, Chapters 8 and 9 have illustrated several strategies of enquiry that combine both approaches: 'paired' comparisons, comparisons across large regions, and analytical induction (e.g. generalization from an exemplary or paradigmatic case). Equally, much theory-building is at least implicitly historical, as when theorists of institutional design hypothesize that at a critical conjuncture it would have been possible either to adopt a presidential or a parliamentary system; either a first-past-the-post or a proportional representation mode of election; and so forth. Such general arguments are distilled from highly specific historical experiences, and rest on rather precise assumptions (e.g. about which choices were unconstrained, and which counter-factual outcomes warrant systematic attention), assumptions that cannot be arbitrary but must be grounded in an at least implicit narrative framework.

Indeed, some of the most productive theoretical generalizations, metaphors, and heuristic models in the field of democratization studies can be enhanced and more productively exploited by making explicit its unstated referents. For example, Dankwart Rustow's pioneering article proposing a 'dynamic model' of democratic transitions was partially inspired by his extensive knowledge of Turkish politics. Viewing pre-1970 Turkey as one of his exemplary cases helps to clarify the scope and merits of his theory while alerting the user to its implicit assumptions (e.g. concerning state formation) which may not be of universal applicability.[7] Similarly, students of post-communist democratizations have drawn attention to the inappropriateness of some of the assumptions of previous theorizing about democratization derived exclusively from consideration of the demise of anti-communist authoritarian regimes. In a like manner, current and future attempts to establish democracy in jurisdictions such as Bosnia and East Timor extend the domain of enquiry to what may roughly be characterized as international protectorates. This is not a state of affairs contemplated by much pre-existing theorization so in the future, as in the past, our stock of generalizations is likely to require substantial adjustment as unanticipated narratives unfold.

If democratization is an adaptive and discursive process of social construction, then in principle it can be modified to fit with, say, market liberalization, or indeed with Islamicization. More precisely each process can be modified to diminish friction with the other. But why might such modifications be undertaken? Those who wanted to restore democracy in Chile might do so because unless they could harmonize their project with the requirements of a market economy they would not have enough support to sustain a viable democratic regime. Similarly in a society where the popular desire for Islamicization is strong, any viable process of democratization may require innovations in the area of religious policy. Likewise, any future democratization of Cuba may require adaptations that take into account the distinctive beliefs and aspirations that may emerge in a post-Castro setting. Generalizing from these disparate examples, for the normative claims of democracy to engage the collective

---

[7] Baogang He re-evaluates Rustow's 'theory of sequence' in the light of thirty years of additional experiences, including fifteen post-1970 cases in which democratizing states were challenged by the secession question. Clearly, new evidence has falsified the over-ambitious generalization that democratization must be preceded by resolution of the national identity question, a generalization strongly influenced by the Turkish case. Baogang He traces the flaw in the theory to Rustow's neglect of the political management of the national identity question. In cases such as Spain and Taiwan, democratic processes appear to have assisted in the management of previously intractable national identity problems, and this has spawned a counter-theory. However, in much of Africa and Central Asia, democratic procedures have failed to address such problems, so that scholars working with this material find Rustow's insights still relevant. See Baogang He, 'The National Identity Problem and Rustow's "Theory of Sequence"', *Government and Opposition*, 36/1 (winter 2001).

imagination at a particular time and place, it may well be necessary to attend to other equally supported counterpart projects of social transformation. For this reason, rather than envisioning a single uniform and final end-state as the necessary outcome of all democratization processes, it may be better to think in terms of a range of relatively open-ended democratic outcomes, each of which would be 'viable' (rather than 'consolidated') in a particular context.

Such references to specific contexts, and particular times and places, remind us that the dominant unit of analysis in democratization studies has always been the nation-state. Whether the issue under consideration is citizenship, institutional design, or the control of monetary policy, most theorizing takes the state as the background datum. Yet, of course, states come in many shapes and sizes, and indeed vary greatly in their autonomy and effectiveness. The Freedom House annual surveys include some democratizations in territories that are not strictly speaking sovereign states at all (Bosnia, East Timor, Taiwan, etc.). Others might be classified as 'failed states'. At any rate in practice, some national cases are of particular significance, not just because of their inherent importance but because of the general analytical issues they illuminate. There follows a selection of critical topics and exemplary cases selected to demonstrate the two-way interaction between theoretical considerations and specific national (or regional) experiences. Most of these examples raise doubts about the permanence and centrality of the state in theories of democratization, as well as each challenging standard assumptions on a more specific front.

'Stateness': Indonesia and Nigeria

Three years ago both Indonesia and Nigeria embarked upon transitions to democracy. This was an unprecedented development in Indonesia, and a third attempt in Nigeria. In both cases the experience so far has been fraught with difficulties, including some large-scale violence at the regional level, and severe problems in establishing a new balance between federal and state levels of political authority, and between the executive, the legislature, the courts, and the armed forces. Nevertheless in both countries democratization remains in place, at least for now. These are both demographically weighty oil-dependent developing countries with large Muslim electorates, and both face severe regional imbalances. If they can be successfully democratized this will have major implications for the politics of their respective regions, and for democratization as a worldwide project. Whichever way they turn out, the lessons for democratization studies in general will have to be carefully pondered.

In the absence of consent concerning the boundaries and regional configurations of a state it is difficult to establish democratic institutions across its territory. The electorate, the legal system, taxation, and the projection of citizenship rights all require a pre-established unified field within which they can operate on something like a homogeneous basis. If we think in terms of theatrical metaphor concerning transitions propounded in Chapter 2, the drama of democratization presupposes an already constituted single audience. Schematically, then, this generates the proposition that state formation must precede democratization. The recent experiences of both Indonesia and Nigeria have a strong bearing on this question of 'stateness'.

For historical and geographical reasons, both Indonesia and Nigeria have seemed vulnerable to territorial fragmentation, and indeed disintegration. Biafra attempted to secede from Nigeria in the late 1960s, and East Timor was forcefully incorporated into Indonesia in 1975, only securing its emancipation in 1999. The armed forces of the two countries became politically decisive, in part because of their role in holding these fissiparous territories together. This was not just a case of suppressing secession in one isolated location. The departure of Biafra would have left the rest of Nigeria out of equilibrium, and it was feared that the withdrawal from East Timor would fuel separatist demands in other parts of the Indonesian archipelago.

But, as the post-independence histories of Indonesia and Nigeria make clear, neither democratization nor state formation invariably conforms to a system of binary coding. These are both long-term, complex, and potentially contested dynamic processes. There can be no assurance that state formation will be terminated before democratization must begin. Indeed, the legacy of authoritarian and personalist rule in these two countries lends some support to the opposite proposition, namely that it is only through the creation of a workable democratic regime that the otherwise unresolvable problems of uncompleted state formation may be overcome. (The third possibility, of course, is that neither centralization imposed by force nor voluntary cooperation induced by constitutional agreement will suffice to resolve problems of state formation that are destined to recur and destabilize *all* variants of political regime.)

The Indonesian and Nigerian cases may bring this topic back to greater prominence in forthcoming academic debates on democratization. If so, they will not be raising questions that are either new or esoteric. Instead they will be reviving classical debates that are of universal significance. These two cases provide particularly sharp tests of rival contentions. How they develop may clarify our understanding of the relationship between 'stateness' and 'democracy' in general.

Size and Democracy: the Insularity of Small Island States

A classical theme in democratic theory was the idea that democracy could only work in small units—the Greek city-state, the Swiss canton, etc. The success of the United States of America was a spectacular demonstration that under some conditions this restriction (which reflected republican ideals and a preference for direct rather than representative democracy) could be overcome. By the end of the twentieth century the Freedom House listing of new democracies included such populous nations as Bangladesh, Brazil, Indonesia, and Mexico with 100 million plus inhabitants. But it also included a much larger number of countries with less than a million inhabitants, many of them islands. Small island states often possess quite a few of the characteristics that used to be regarded as favourable for democracy—a strong sense of community, direct access to political leaders who would be expected to have close familiarity with local conditions, etc. However, small island states are also by definition highly insular, in the sense that their populations feel a strong sense of difference between themselves and outsiders; they may overvalue local knowledge and the importance of local concerns; and they may distrust or resist pressures from outside, and may not find itself easy to view themselves in a comparative setting. This insularity of small island states may serve to reinforce democracy where it has become internalized as a local value (e.g. in Barbados, and more general in the Anglophone Caribbean). But equally it may impede or destablize democratization where this is associated with the imposition of inappropriate external standards. In June 2000 two significant Pacific island democracies (Fiji and the Solomon Islands, with populations of 800,000 and 400,000 respectively) were overthrown by armed coups. Efforts by Australia, New Zealand, and the EU to intercede and assist with the restoration of democracy encountered these problems of insularity. It might be thought that small compact societies heavily dependent on external economic support would be much more promising than the demographic giants as exemplars of democratization, especially where the Anglo-Saxon colonial legacy was supportive, but these recent developments raise new doubts about postulated associations linking size and democracy, and cast a shadow over many of the other small islands in the Freedom House list. Insularity may be a different impediment to democratization from gigantism, but it is not necessarily more tractable.

Time Horizons and 'Consolidation': Colombia and Sri Lanka

In 1969, both Colombia and Sri Lanka were candidates in the original Dahlian list of twenty-six 'polyarchies' (although in the event Colombia was relegated to the status of a 'near polyarchy' and Ceylon to the still lower rank of a 'competitive regime). Both have held regular competitive elections and maintained a constitutional division of powers ever since then. Compared to the 120 electoral democracies identified by Freedom House in June 2000 (Annex Tables 1 and 2), these are among the more durable, resilient, and securely entrenched of democratic regimes. Yet both have been wracked by violent civil insurgencies almost throughout their forty-year histories of unbroken institutional continuity, and at this writing both regimes are closer to military debacle at the hands of their challengers than ever before. Far from being 'the only game in town', the game of electoral competition appears increasingly like a side show as compared to the real struggle for political power, which is being waged through warfare. At least a tenth of the national territory is outside official control ('beyond the pale', as the English used to say of Ireland) and the loyalties of many more localities are an object of continuous contestation. Recent developments such as President Pastrana's failed peace initiative, and President Kumaratunga's failed attempt to secure a military victory, have highlighted the fact that apparently durable polyarchies, and even 'consolidated' democracies, can undergo progressive regression towards political deadlock and indeed social anarchy. These experiences underscore the key argument of Chapter 1, that democratization processes need to be viewed as very long-term, open-ended, and indeed potentially reversible. The prevalent assumption in the academic literature has been that once a transition has occurred in any given country it is postulated that the persistence of this regime over time will lead to its progressive 'consolidation'. If polyarchical rules define the terms of access to public office and of influence over public policy, then in due course all those political actors who seek office or wish to exert influence will be constrained to pursue their objectives within the said rules. The electoral calendar will shape the timetable horizons of all power contenders, and the consolidation of the regime will extend the time horizon of all citizens into a predictable sequence of electoral decisions. The political horizon will thereby be extended into the indefinite future.

However, recent elections in Colombia and Sri Lanka have done nothing to settle the vital political issues confronting electors in those two countries, and there is no confidence that future elections will offer them any better prospects. As the FARC, the Tigers, and the other non-electoral power contenders grow stronger, there are ever fewer benefits available to those who try to live within the rules of the constitutional system, and the risks of so doing continue to escalate. Chapter 7 discussed the huge gulf between an official democratic discourse of citizenship, on the one hand, and the lived reality of acute personal insecurity that can be found in various new democracies. Both Colombia and Sri Lanka present very disturbing evidence of where this can lead to, if taken to extremes. The inhabitants of the contested zones face possible expulsion from their homes and workplaces at the shortest notice. Young men from across the entire territory face impressment into military or guerrilla service as the conflict requires, and all other aspects of public policy are held hostage to the exigencies of the armed struggle. Thus the time horizons of most citizens have been foreshortened to the limit.

Thus far the literature on democratization has tended to treat these two countries as 'deviant cases', and has tried to focus on the respects in which they are likely to correspond to normal experience once the exceptional circumstances of armed conflict have been resolved. But it is by no means clear that they are either so deviant or so transient as has been assumed to date, and this is one area where recent developments—both methodological and prospective—could soon force a reappraisal. At the methodological level the main challenges are likely to concern the assumptions (i) that 'whole countries' should constitute the essential unit of analysis, and (ii) that the binary coding of national regimes by the year is an adequate procedure of categorization. On a more theoretical level these cases raise significant doubts about the proposition that democratization typically stabilizes and extends the time horizons of all players and that regime consolidation necessarily socializes all players into observing the rules of 'the only game in town'. Recent developments in Colombia and Sri Lanka also point to the need for more clarity about the notions of 'regression/breakdown' and 'decay' as they apply to formally democratic regimes.

Democracy and War: South Asian Experiences

Another classical discussion in the literature on democratization revolves around the proposition that democracies do not got to war with one another. Although this theory has distinguished antecedents, a plausible argument, and has been briefly supported by extensive empirical work, it remains vulnerable to two related difficulties. The first is that, once at war, countries may not conduct their political arrangements in a particularly democratic manner. In the light of the defects revealed by war, the pre-war status of the political regimes as democracy may be brought into question. If, as we have argued in chapter one, the designation of any country as a democracy involves a certain degree of interpretation and social construction then the fact that an apparently democratic regime resorts to war with an apparently democratic neighbour may itself constitute major grounds for reinterpretation of the status of one, or the other, or both. Various illustrations of this can be quoted from recent Latin American history, but here we shall consider the evidence from South Asia. Bangladesh, India, and Sri Lanka would all seem to fall within electoralist definitions of what should count as a democracy. Yet in the late 1980s India became temporarily entangled in the violent conflicts of Sri Lanka (the Tamil minority on the island enjoyed some sympathy from a much larger Tamil constituency in the subcontinent, to the alarm of the Sinhala majority). What started as an attempt by the larger democracy to assist reconciliation in a troubled neighbour soon turned into a potential threat to regime stability on both sides of the Jaffna straits. In a similar vein, the Indian army played a critical role in the liberation and democratization of Bangladesh in 1971. That raised fears of domination by Delhi, which tend to turn elections in Bangladesh into irreconcilable struggles. The interaction between broadly democratic India and only intermittently and superficially democratic Pakistan is much more fraught. In summary the interdependencies between these three democracies of very unequal size and contested national profiles may not function either to avoid wars or to promote democratization. It is equally possible to envisage the long-term dynamics as working towards a virtuous circle or a downward spiral. The interactions are complex, open-ended, and potentially unsettling, both to established theory and to hoped for democracies. Second, if this is so then even highly compelling statistical evidence that in the past democracies did not fight each other would not serve to generate reliable predictions about the future, least of all if the number of weak and potentially clashing new democracies continues to rise.

'Pays Légal et Pays Réel': Mexico

Recent and prospective developments in Mexico promise to breathe new life into the debate between those who privilege the logic of institutional design at the 'formal' level, and those who consider that the most important requirement for well-functioning democratic institutions is not that they should be perfected as textual propositions, but that they should be accepted and internalized as appropriate procedures for decision-making by the society at large. French political discourse is impregnated with the distinction between the 'pays légal' and the 'pays réel', which dates back at least to the Napoleonic period of institutional rationalization, and this contrast is conspicuous in Mexico as well.

The Mexican Constitution of 1917 was about as modern and rational a foundation for a liberal democracy as it was possible to find at that time, and it has been updated regularly (and for the most part sensibly) ever since. The 1978 law on political parties and political organizations was more eccentric, but it too contained sound design principles and they too have been revised and perfected more recently. The 1996 Federal Electoral Law is also close to a model of its kind, and it provides sound assurances both concerning the integrity of the electoral court and the equitable financing of contending political parties. No doubt more could still be done to improve the formal design of Mexico's democratic institutions, but not much more. So the principal remaining question is whether the actually existing political forces at large in the society will prove reliable and skilful in working within the formal institutions that they inherit. There are three main forces to consider—the long-ruling party which had become accustomed to enjoying informal privileges and advantages after seventy odd years of uninterrupted ascendancy; the conservative challengers who come from a Catholic moral tradition of resistance to revolutionary statism, and who have in recent years grown in strength and self-confidence, while diluting their doctrinal purity; and a centre-left opposition that appeals to many traditionalists from the ruling party, while offering the prospect of alternation and a clear out of the technocracy. All these three forces, in their different and contrasting ways, have become adjusted to the strong informal conventions that have qualified and distorted the ostensible rules of the political game. There is probably no need for further innovations in institutional design. But it would be a huge innovation if the contenders for power learn to conduct their interactions in accordance with the logic of these formal institutions.

So recent and prospective developments in Mexican politics will merit the closest attention by scholars of democratization. They seem likely to provide something approaching a laboratory experiment to test the rival claims of the institutional design school, and their critics from the 'public sphere' line of interpretation.

Geopolitics: EU Enlargement and China

East Germany could not long remain under communist rule, once Poland the Czech Republic became multi-party democracies. Paraguay was hard pressed to perpetuate the ascendancy of the Colorado Party after all its neighbours adopted competitive elections. But geopolitics is an unfashionable branch of political science, and isolated examples of this kind have not been fully incorporated into the mainstream of democratization studies. However, the December 1999 decision of the Helsinki Summit to open negotiations with twelve (and ultimately thirteen) southern and eastern 'new democracies' over accession to the EU could force this type of analysis more to the centre of our attention. In a parallel process, the growing national self-confidence of a still Communist Party-ruled People's Republic of China has already precluded the establishment of full democracy in Hong Kong, a major economic power which fulfilled all the prerequisites suggested by 'modernization' theory. A larger test now looms over whether mainland China's geopolitical weight will also suffice to reabsorb Taiwan, and thus preclude permanent democratization there as well. The background to this issue was presented in Chapter 8.

There is a substantial literature about the enlargement of the EU, including its democratizing potential and also rather more scattered but nevertheless useful literature on the democratization of Hong Kong and Taiwan, taking into account their relations with mainland China. But the more comparative and theoretical issues arising from such cases tend to be discussed in terms of 'transnationalism', 'conditionality', and the growth of 'international civil society', rather than from a geopolitical perspective.[8] Yet when we consider world history over the twentieth century it is apparent that all the major geopolitical conflicts—First World War, Second World War, and cold war—were couched in terms of democracy versus its enemies and in each case the self-styled democratic alliance prevailed. This suggests that the claim to democratic legitimacy may be a powerful factor in international struggles for ascendancy, perhaps because it both motivates allies and supporters and reassures enemies that the consequences of defeat need not be intolerable.

Viewed from this standpoint, the EU's commitment to extend its frontiers almost to St Petersburg, Lvov, and ultimately to near Damascus, must be understood as a heroic geopolitical initiative, and not merely a low-key succession of technical negotiations. Similarly, Beijing's successful reincorporation of Hong Kong, and its clear determination to achieve eventual reunification with Taiwan without abandoning its current political regime, must be understood as a second geopolitical initiative of 'world historical' significance. Both of these projects are very long-term, and their eventual outcomes are still uncertain. In both cases the desired outcome would be to consolidate a new force in world politics with sufficient economic, demographic, and territorial weight to alter the overall balance of power in its favour. A successful EU composed of twenty-eight or thirty democratic states, all solving their problems through peaceful cooperation and legal integration (and even converging their sovereignties in an 'ever closer union'), would be a historical accomplishment that would end centuries of internecine conflict in Europe and might help to restore the old continent to the centre of world affairs. It would also counterbalance the recent unipolar ascendancy of the USA, and through partnership with Washington would reinforce the pre-eminence of liberal democracy as the template for political modernity. Equally, of course, a failure by the EU to deliver on this promise after raising such expectations would constitute a major defeat for liberal democracy as a global practice, and not just as a regional experiment. Similarly, a reunified China under Communist Party leadership would close the book on a century of external impositions and a half-century of latent civil war, restoring a united China to the position of influence merited both by its demography and its economic potential. But this Beijing project

---

[8] A useful recent compilation which exemplifies this trend is Jean Grugel (ed.), *Democracy without Borders: Transnationalisation and Conditionality in New Democracies* (London: Routledge, 1999).

is at least as long-term and uncertain as that of the Helsinki summit. Moreover, Taiwan will deploy the moral authority of liberal
democracy as a major weapon in its struggle to resist adverse incor-
poration. Not only does the democratic status of Taiwan elicit international support that would never have flowed to the KMT alone;
the example of the Taiwanese regime both threatens Communist
supremacy on the mainland, and offers reassurance to those
tempted to break with one-party dominance. In both cases the
geopolitical stakes are distinctly high, and the outcome is uncertain. In both cases the success (or failure) of current processes of
democratization is a critical component of a broader struggle for
geopolitical ascendancy.

Democratic 'Developmental States': South Korea and Taiwan

Recent developments in East Asia reopen the debate about the
'sequencing' of economic growth strategies and decisions to democratize. One school of thought (especially influential in the early
1990s) asserted that a certain type of developmentally oriented
authoritarian rule ought not to be viewed too critically by those
committed to democracy. Growth-promoting authoritarian regimes
such as Franco's Spain, Chiang Kai Shek's Taiwan, or the Park and
Chun regimes in South Korea, might all be good for democracy in
the long run. By providing discipline and security during a period of
vulnerability they could deliver the kind of sustained economic and
social transformations that modernization theorists had postulated
as requisites for successful democratization. In such circumstances
a period of unfettered authoritarian rule might be considered an
indispensable precursor to its eventual negation. This argument
always rested on two subsidiary propositions, neither of which were
straightforward to establish. The *first* was that in the absence of a
strong authoritarian regime no sustained economic take-off would
occur. The *second* was that, once it *had* occurred, (i) the authors of
this success would not be able or willing to block the 'institutional
uncertainty' of competitive elections, and (ii) the vested interests
created by their regimes would feel secure enough to provide economic continuity during the process of regime change. The so-called
'East Asian financial crisis' of 1997/8 cast these arguments in a new
light, not least in South Korea, where the case would be made that
a successful response to the economic crisis required a degree of
institutional legitimacy, and a capacity for the peaceful renewal of

political leadership and correction of failed policies, that could only be delivered under democratic auspices. In fact the election to the presidency of long-standing democratic campaigner and opposition candidate Kim Dae Jung turned out to be the decisive event that established a bottom to the collapse of economic confidence in Korea, and that paved the way to a subsequent (and so far rather remarkable) recovery. Recent Korean experience therefore suggests that the 'sequencing' analysis may have been flawed. In particular it invites further examination of the assumption that an earlier establishment of democratic governance in this setting would necessarily have diminished the country's long-term potential for accelerated development. It also directs attention to the negative legacies of authoritarian rule both as impediments to economic rationality, and as potential obstacles to full democratization.

This has provided a striking case study, which has proceeded in parallel with a scholarly debate about the desirability and scope for combining 'democracy' and 'developmentalism' into a 'democratic developmental state'. This is not a narrowly East Asian debate, since Chile, for example, can be analysed within the same parameters. Gordon White's posthumously published initial survey of the field balanced well-founded grounds for scepticism (democratic developmental states were, he thought, likely to be 'rare birds') with some persuasive arguments of the 'thoughtful wishing' variety about how important it would be for democratization as a whole if some successes of this kind could be recorded, and some preliminary specifications of the conditions that might favour this alternative not only in East Asia but more generally.[9] His hypothetical list of potential candidates included Chile, South Africa, Hungary, and Taiwan, to illustrate the point that all geographical areas might contain exemplars. He also argued that 'the evolution of a democratic developmental state requires a prolonged process of political and institutional *tâtonnement* or "groping" which involves trial and error, reversals and advances . . . (they) are only likely to emerge in pieces, rather than as a systemic whole' (p. 46). Admittedly, this proposed academic innovation has yet to develop a convincing body of supporting theory and evidence. Even the paradigmatic cases of Korea and Taiwan are as yet inconclusive, and open to alternative interpretations. If democracy and development are to become mutually supportive, but in a piecemeal manner, this raises doubts about whether the main analytical focus should be on 'the state' (a hierarchical and

---

[9] Mark Robinson and Gordon White (eds.), *The Democratic Developmental State: Political and Institutional Design* (Oxford: OUP, 1998), ch. 1.

centralizing institution) rather than on more local and socially embedded forms of convergence. Nevertheless, the combination of the South Korean (and to a less extent the Taiwanese) transformations into developmentally effective democratic regimes with the awakening of a scholarly interest in such possibilities at a more abstract level, opens the way to more sustained work on this understudied corner of our subfield.

Civil Society and Democratic Norms: Brazil and India

Neither Brazil nor India figures among Gordon White's hypothetical list of democratic developmental states, although he does concede that 'certain states *within* India, might qualify. Similar claims might be made on behalf of certain states within Brazil. However, great extremes of regional diversity and social inequality within a given state do not necessarily justify disaggregating it into component parts, or attibuting democratic characteristics only to certain locations or social sites and not to others. On the contrary, as for example John Markoff has indicated in his wide-ranging survey of the social history of democracy, democratic and undemocratic practices frequently exist side by side, with democratization generated by the *interaction* between established elites and social movement challengers, each invoking their own versions of democratic claims. As the product of such 'dialectical' interactions, the geographical location and institutional content of democracy are not fixed. Hence pioneering experiments are by no means confined to the wealthiest or most powerful of countries or regions.[10] This view of democratization as a creative product of dissatisfaction and competitive emulation would suggest that vast and internally differentiated societies such as Brazil and India could be particularly creative forcing grounds for democratic innovation. From this standpoint the key ingredients would have to include not only size and diversity, but also an institutional framework capable of providing enough stability for alternative overarching experiments to be undertaken, and enough common values for their lessons to seem communicable from one location to another.

Brazil and India both sustain stable federalized authority structures which make it possible for self-styled Marxist parties to govern in huge urban agglomerations such as Calcutta and São Paulo,

[10] John Markoff, *Waves of Democracy: Social Movements and Political Change* (Pine Forge Press, 1996), ch. 5.

(or indeed in whole states such as West Bengal, Kerala, and Rio Grande do Sul) at the same time that much more conservative elites have the opportunity to demonstrate their alternative versions of democratic governance, for example in the Punjab, or in Salvador and the state of Bahia. These are both examples of political competition and social emulation *within* a unified political system which nevertheless contains a multiplicity of sub-units or separate cells, each commanding sufficient resources and political authority to make them semi-autonomous polities in their own right.

Such examples raise important issues for the comparative study of democratization. It is also debatable whether the accession to national office of the BJP has damaged Indian democracy—at least to the extent initially anticipated. In each case it could be argued that feedback from what may loosely be termed 'civil society', and the permissions/restraints arising from socially embedded norms and expectations have steered these new governments towards similar styles of governance to those displayed by their predecessors. Obviously party competition for electoral favour also strengthens the tendency to converge on politics acceptable to the 'median voter'. The existence of regional strongholds also means that neither 'ins' nor 'outs' are fully excluded from the exercise of public authority. These stabilizing features of federalism only work, however, when supported by societal reinforcements (which seem absent in Nigeria, for example). Recent developments in these continent-countries indicate the importance of attending to the uneven emergence of supportive forms of civil society and democratic norms, as much as to the centralized and rational design of institutional solutions.

'Globalization' and Democratization: the IMF, the WTO, the World Bank

The comparative study of democratization can hardly continue to focus on the self-contained national political system as its exclusive unit of analysis, at a time when, as discussed in Chapter 6, so much leverage over economic issues is clearly shifting away from the Ministries of Economics and budgetary committees of individual countries, and when intergovernmental cooperation between democracies is leading to an evident pooling of sovereignty in multiple arenas, legal, regulatory, and indeed on many more strictly political questions. One area of globalization where recent developments may be prompting a quite focused extension of the literature on democratization concerns the changing roles and political profiles of such key international economic institutions as the IMF, the World Bank, and the World Trade Organization.[11] In their origins, these were all ostensibly 'technical' bodies, and they still have charters and governance structures which limit their areas of responsibility and proscribe them from intrusion into the so-called 'domestic politics' of member states. In practice, however, the ending of the cold war led to a rapid expansion of their geographical coverage, and to the acquisition of a range of additional responsibilities going beyond their original mandates and taking them into much more highly sensitive and indeed politicized areas of policy-making.

Perhaps the most extreme example has been the role the IMF acquired in supervising the overall direction of economic transformation in post-Soviet Russia and the Ukraine. It even seemed at times that the Fund had become so closely identified with, for example, the Yeltsin administration's policies that an electoral victory for the main parties of the opposition might have constituted a more or less direct rebuff to the directors of the Fund. In a similar manner, the World Bank has become identified with a so-called 'no party' democracy in Uganda, and there is every prospect that the WTO will find itself intimately embroiled in the politics of economic reform in mainland China, now that the decision is imminent to admit the PRC to that body.

In all these cases, it is clear that the international organization in question is not acting solely according to its own procedural logic. On the contrary, leading Western powers tend to set the main policy guidelines, and hope to pursue their national policy objectives through the intermediation of these agencies. But when the results prove unsatisfactory to Western (and therefore international) opinion, for example because of gross corruption or flagrant violations of human rights in the target countries, then it is the international organization that must cope with the recriminations rather than its lead country governors or directors. Indeed, recent debates within the US Congress have tended to produce a weakening of support for these 'global' institutions, as they are blamed for the consequences of policies assigned to them by Western governments. This somewhat

---

[11] e.g. David Held, *Democracy and the Global Order: From the Modern State to Cosmopolitan Governance* (Cambridge: Polity, 1995), but also more specialized contributions such as Gregory H. Fox and Brad R. Roth (eds.), *Democratic Governance and International Law*; or Thomas Carothers, *Aiding Democracy Abroad: The Learning Curve* (Washington, DC: Carnegie Endowment, 1999); or Leslie Elliott Armijo (ed.), *Financial Globalization and Democracy in Emerging Markets* (Basingstoke: Macmillan, 1999).

unexpected and counter-intuitive consequence of involving such agencies in initiatives which incorporate highly questionable assumptions about democracy promotion may well require more systematic and sustained attention from students of democratization over the next few years.

The Politics of Memory: Chile

The arrest in London in October 1998 of self-appointed Senator for Life Augusto Pinochet provides a vivid example of how an unforeseen political development can reopen the debate about a central issue of democratization that most of the academic community had viewed as near to closure. As we saw in Chapter 9, the key 'actors' in the Chilean democratization had agreed to a clear set of 'rules of the game' which reflected the real distribution of power between them. They had made a clear distinction between the decision-making procedures by which they would all abide, and substantive policy outcomes over which they might continue to disagree. The procedures included what some termed 'authoritarian enclaves' left over from the imposed Constitution of 1980. But it had been democratically ratified in the plebiscite of 1988, and the ensuing institutional arrangements were open to revision by an agreed constitutional procedure (albeit one designed to obstruct democratizing innovations). Chilean politics were exceptionally well institutionalized, and this settlement seemed 'consolidated'. It rested on a 'rule of law' authority rather than just on some moral claim to legitimacy. The law provided a clear separation between the impunity for anti-democratic acts committed in the past, and the high standard of legal liability to be required of all Chileans once democracy had been installed. Past battles were not to be reopened, in the interests of present and future political coexistence. Some democratization scholars even held up the Chilean example as a model to be learnt from more generally. Those who dissented from this view might be dismissed as moralists, or nostalgists for a discredited past.

Since October 1998 the Pinochet case has taken several unexpected turns, and it would still be premature to assess the final outcome and its impact on Chile's democratization. However, it is already clear that Pinochet-related innovations have disturbed preexisting assumptions about the relationship between collective memories of past human rights violations and the solidity of ensuing democratic institutional arrangements. An emerging corpus of international moral and legal norms concerning gross violations of human rights has proved strong enough to destabilize the expedient pact through which Chile had redemocratized, with protected enclaves and guarantees of impunity.

If even in well-institutionalized Chile such a pragmatic deal cannot be made to last beyond a decade, future authoritarian rulers considering exit will be considerably less likely to risk following Pinochet's example. Chilean political culture values the rule of law and the observance of international liberal standards of good practice more highly than is the case in most new democracies (certainly than in most of Latin America, Africa, and Asia). Yet even in Chile it has never been a foregone conclusion that international legal norms would prevail in this area. If we understand 'democratization' as a broad and long-term process of convergence around such norms and values the recent 'eruption of memory' (Alex Wilde's telling phrase) in contemporary Chile indicates that such processes are likely to be long and painful, even where the standard criteria of democratic 'consolidation' are apparently satisfied. The Haider issue in Austria confirms that, thus conceived, democratization is a virtually permanent project under construction, not a closed book. Current comparative work in this area[12] challenges the assumption of a sharp caesura between pre-democratic legacies and post-transition political dynamics. Both legal scholarship and human rights analysis point to the necessity of incorporating a moral dimension into our understanding of democratization processes. That leaves open various questions. *What* kind of moral considerations can properly be included? *Whose* judgements or interpretations qualify for consideration? *Which* judicial or other investigative procedures can be considered authoritative from a democratic standpoint? Such questions, both moral and analytical, have been raised anew by the Pinochet case.

Conclusion

This volume has drawn attention to the diversity of ongoing democratization processes, and has argued that they are best understood in a holistic manner, and as long-term, open-ended undertakings, guided by ideas and values as well as calculations of self-interest.

---

[12] See Alexandra Barahona de Brito, Carmen González-Enríquez, and Paloma Aguilar (eds.), *The Politics of Memory: Transitional Justice in Democratizing Societies* (Oxford: Oxford University Press, 2001).

Mainstream social science tends to be sceptical about explanations couched in terms of normative commitment. Yet it would be hard to explain the rapid diffusion of the market economy, both as an institutional system and as a system of beliefs, without including some consideration of the aspirations and values that have driven it forward, and have sustained it at times of adversity. If this applies to the spread of the market, then it also deserves consideration in the case of democratization. Such normative commitment can be embedded in solid structures of interest and organization, and therefore should not be excluded from explanatory analysis as mere exhortation. In the case of democratization, all the established powers in the post-cold war international system regard themselves as democracies, and undertake active policies intended to promote democratization elsewhere. Although this is sometimes criticized as a manifestation of 'Western imperialism', the comparative evidence is clear that in a surprisingly wide range of countries and regions reached by such democratic conditionality and demonstration effects, both elite and popular opinion can be energized by this kind of normative vision. Since democracy implies the dissemination of responsibilities, it invites participation and deliberation from broad new constituencies. The underlying demand for democratic participation comes not solely from those who were excluded under authoritarian rule; factions within the old authoritarian coalition may be quite as interested in opening the system; and all may be motivated by international influences as well as by domestic interests. The desire to participate can generate democratizing aspirations that extend beyond the boundaries of any single nation, and that may drive cumulative long-term change even in the face of intervening disappointments and distortions. In the absence of some understanding of this dimension of normative commitments democratization would be difficult to explain.

A key conclusion that could be drawn from the confrontations between theory and experience that have run through this volume is that whatever general knowledge we accumulate requires iterative checking and adjustment in the course of feedback from an ongoing series of uncontrolled practical experiments. Far from precluding knowledge accumulation this procedure may enrich it, and may generate useful knowledge that can be applied to specific cases. But on this account the method of knowledge accumulation would be essentially like that of a lawyer developing expertise out of case material. No doubt legal reasoning involves the establishment of causal linkages where possible, but it also focuses on the intentions and responsibilities of actors. For example, in specific areas like citizen security, the feedback from case-study research underscores the gulf between democratic theory and official discourse, on the one hand, and citizen perceptions of the real predicament they face, on the other (Chapter 7). Citizens attribute responsibility for insecurity, rather than merely tracing impersonal causes. Useful knowledge can most certainly be accumulated in this area, knowledge that is not only of use for specific countries but also valuable for the understanding of democratization processes more generally. Such knowledge can combine the detailed assembly of various types of empirical evidence with broad-ranging theory, and can be geared to quite precise public policy prescriptions. In this area, as in others also covered in this volume, useful knowledge accumulation is clearly attainable. The resulting knowledge may not be as *certain* (i.e. unqualified and universal) as some might wish, but it can be presented with a high degree of confidence as compared to what otherwise would be available, just as an experienced and well-trained lawyer can make a much stronger case than an amateur or a novice.

Whether the observer views democratization with trained eye of a professional lawyer, the dispassionate gaze of an impersonal scientist, the committed look of a political activist, or the sceptical outlook of a veteran journalist, the object under examination resists any definitive portrayal. The explanation for this developed in this volume is that contemporary processes of democratization are best seen as a long-term, open-ended exercises in social construction.

From this perspective, durable democracies can be regarded as regimes that have slowly evolved under pressure from their citizens, and that have therefore been adapted both to the structural realities and to the social expectations of the societies in which they have become established. If so, then what counts as a durable democratic outcome will be shaped by a continuous process of electoral feedback and citizen deliberation. This would permit, and indeed require, a substantial range of variations between different democratic regimes over space and time. Evidently (as discussed in Chapter 1) the range of variation must remain within certain limits, but too much reliance cannot be placed on a priori or stipulative definitions (e.g. where a disembodied authority asserts the necessary and sufficient conditions for a consolidated democracy, without fully attending to what those who must live under that regime would say). The normative, value-laden, even idealistic elements of what people believe a democracy can and should be integral to the meaning of the term (i.e. it is what Sartori labelled a 'deontological' concept). But, if so, then all 'really existing' democracies will be permanently open to objection that in some respects they fall short of the ideal. That would make democracy a radical and potentially destabilizing aspiration, and means that democratization remains to some extent a permanently open-ended process.

These considerations would apply to all really existing democracies, old as well as new, durable as well as perishable. But the focus of this volume has been on contemporary experiences of democratization in new, or relatively new, democracies. Under such conditions the outcomes are particularly likely to be incomplete, and perhaps elusive. We can now recapitulate the main reasons for this that have been identified in successive chapters of this book. In the early, or transition, phase of a democratization the 'theatrical' process of resocializing the public to a new political system may have been performed well, or badly (Chapter 2); existing or emerging patterns of 'civil society' are not necessarily particularly 'civil' or fully congruent with the universalistic logic of political citizenship (Chapter 3); systems of institutional design and political accountability may be flawed, or—even if reflecting best practice as recommended by the experts—ill-adapted considering the social context (Chapter 4); there may be inadequate counterweights to the corrosive expansion of money power in the political process (Chapter 5); those charged with exercising monetary authority may do so without popular consent, or inadequate checks on their conduct (Chapter 6); citizen insecurity may sap public confidence in the democratic regime (Chapter 7). In addition, this chapter has drawn attention to a theme underlying all these possibilities and recurring in many of the diverse national experiences considered here. The degree of 'stateness' existing in many (even most) new democracies may fall far short of what is required by standard democratic discourse and assumed in most democratization theory. Indeed it could be that far from constituting a precondition for a transition to democracy as used to be believed, contemporary democratizations may constitute the best available hope for state-building. But even this inversion of conventional ideas of sequencing, like its predecessor, is likely to be tested and destabilized as further experiences unfold.

The essential point about contemporary democratizations is that they have resisted any unified and definitive portrayal, and seem likely to continue to do so. But if this is the truth about our object of study, it need not be a source of discouragement. Despite the prospect that democratizations will continue to throw up further surprises, and so to destabilize parsimonious analyses, with an appropriate method and approach it should remain possible to generate 'useful knowledge' about the subject. This refers for example to knowledge concerned with understanding and perhaps even diminishing the separation between theory and experience; and also to knowledge about how ongoing democracies can adapt and respond to new stresses and unfolding challenges (for example, forced migration or environmental degradation). It is probably just as well if democratization is, as postulated here, a long-term complex, dynamic, and open-ended process, since many of the policy challenges that lie ahead share the same characteristics, and differ from the tasks for which previous models of democracy were designed. Diversity, adaptability, and deliberation are all troublesome characteristics that tend to get screened out of the more rigorous variants of social science theorizing. But they are also characteristics that can flourish in a context of democratization and that help account for its resilience, and also its normative appeal.

Annex

TABLE 1. *Dahl's Polyachies and Near-Polyarchies, c.1969*

Fully Inclusive Polyarchies

Australia	Iceland	Netherlands
Austria	India	New Zealand
Belgium	Ireland	Norway
Canada	Israel	Philippines
Costa Rica	Italy	Sweden
Denmark	Jamaica	Trinidad & Tobago
Fed. Republic of Germany	Japan	United Kingdom
Finland	Lebanon	Uruguay
France	Luxembourg	

Special Cases: Electoral Restrictions

Chile	Switzerland	USA

Near Polyarchies

Colombia	Dominican Republic	Turkey
Cyprus	Malaysia	Venezuela

Source: Robert A. Dahl, *Polyarchy: Participation and Opposition* (New Haven, Conn.: Yale University Press, 1971).

TABLE 2. *Electoral Democracies in 2000*

Albania		El Salvador	(free)	Macedonia	(free)	Russia	
Andorra	(free)	Estonia	(free)	Madagascar	(free)	St Kitts & Nevis	(free)
Argentina	(free)	Finland	(free)	Malawi	(free)	St Lucia	(free)
Armenia		Georgia		Malti		St Vincent & Grenadines	(free)
Australia	(free)	Germany	(free)	Malta	(free)	Samon	(free)
Austria	(free)	Ghana	(free)	Marshall Islands		San Marino	(free)
Bahamas	(free)	Greece	(free)	Mauritius	(free)	Sao Tome & Principé	(free)
Bangladesh		Grenada	(free)	Mexico	(free)	Senegal	(free)
Barbados	(free)	Guatemala		Micronesia		Seychelles	(free)
Belgium	(free)	Guinea-Bissan		Moldova		Sierra Leone	(free)
Belize	(free)	Guyana	(free)	Monaco	(free)	Slovakia	(free)
Benin	(free)	Haiti		Mongolia		Slovenia	(free)
Bolivia	(free)	Honduras		Mozambique		Solomon Islands	
Botswana	(free)	Hungary	(free)	Namibia	(free)	South Africa	(free)
Brazil		Iceland	(free)	Naseru	(free)	Spain	(free)
Bulgaria	(free)	India	(free)	Nepal	(free)	Sri Lanka	
Canada	(free)	Indonesia	(free)	Netherlands	(free)	Suriname	(free)
Cape Verde		Ireland	(free)	New Zealand	(free)	Sweden	(free)
Central Africa Rep.		Israel		Nicaragua	(free)	Switzerland	(free)
Chile	(free)	Italy	(free)	Niger	(free)	Taiwan Republic of China	(free)
Colombia		Jamaica	(free)	Nigeria	(free)	Thailand	(free)
Costa Rica	(free)	Japan	(free)	Norway	(free)	Trinidad & Tobago	(free)
Croatia	(free)	Kiribati	(free)	Palau	(free)	Turkey	(free)
Cyprus(Greek)	(free)	Korea, South	(free)	Panama	(free)	Tuvalu	(free)
Czech Rep.	(free)	Latvia	(free)	Papua New Guinea	(free)	Ukraine	(free)
Denmark	(free)	Liberia		Paraguay		United Kingdom	(free)
Djibouti		Liechtenstein	(free)	Philippines	(free)	Uruguay	(free)
Dominica	(free)	Lithuania	(free)	Poland	(free)	Vanuatu	(free)
Dominican Rep.	(free)	Luxembourg	(free)	Portugal	(free)	Venezuela	(free)
Ecuador				Romania	(free)		

Source: Freedom House, *Freedom in the World (2000–2001)* (New York: Freedom House, 2001). 192 jurisdictions were rated in 2000, of which 120 were classified as 'electoral democracies', and 85 were classified as 'free electoral democracies'.

TABLE 3. *Corruption Perception Index Scores: 52 'New Democracies'*

	2001 Ranking	Annual Scores (1–10 Rating)			
		2001	2000	1997	1995
Chile	18=	7.5	7.4	6.1	7.9
Spain	22	7.0	7.0	—	—
Portugal	25	6.3	6.4	7.0	5.6
Botswana	26	6.0	6.0	—	—
Taiwan	27	5.9	5.5	—	—
Estonia	28	5.6	5.7	—	—
Italy	29	5.5	4.6	5.0	—
Namibia	30	5.4	5.4	—	—
Hungary	31	5.3	5.2	5.2	4.1
Trinidad	31=	5.3	—	—	—
Slovenia	34	5.2	5.5	—	—
Uruguay	35	5.1	—	—	—
Lithuania	38=	4.8	4.1	—	—
South Africa	38=	4.8	5.0	5.0	5.6
Costa Rica	40=	4.5	5.4	6.5	—
Mauritius	40=	4.5	4.7	—	—
Greece	42	4.2	4.9	—	—
South Korea	42=	4.2	4.0	4.3	4.3
Peru	44=	4.1	4.4	—	—
Poland	44=	4.1	4.1	5.1	—
Brazil	46	4.0	3.9	3.6	2.7
Bulgaria	47=	3.9	3.5	—	—
Croatia	47=	3.9	3.7	—	—
Czech Republic	47=	3.9	4.3	5.2	—
Colombia	50	3.8	3.2	2.2	3.4
Mexico	51=	3.7	3.3	2.7	3.2
Panama	51=	3.7	—	—	—
Slovak Republic	51=	3.7	3.5	—	—
El Salvador	44=	3.6	4.1	—	—
Turkey	54=	3.6	3.8	3.2	4.1
Argentina	57=	3.5	3.5	2.8	3.2
Ghana	59=	3.4	3.5	—	—
Latvia	59=	3.4	3.4	—	—
Malawi	61=	3.2	4.1	—	—
Thailand	61=	3.2	3.2	3.1	2.8
Dominican Rep.	63=	3.1	—	—	—

TABLE 3. (*cont.*)

	2001 Ranking	Annual Scores (1–10 Rating)			
		2001	2000	1997	1995
Moldova	63=	3.1	2.6	—	—
Guatemala	65=	2.9	—	—	—
Philippines	65=	2.9	2.8	3.1	2.8
Senegal	65=	2.9	3.5	—	—
Romania	69=	2.8	2.9	3.4	—
Venezuela	69=	2.8	2.7	2.8	2.7
Honduras	71=	2.7	—	—	—
India	71=	2.7	2.8	2.8	—
Nicaragua	77=	2.4	—	—	—
Ecuador	79=	2.3	2.6	—	—
Russia	79=	2.3	2.1	2.3	—
Ukraine	88=	2.1	1.5	—	—
Bolivia	84=	2.0	2.7	2.1	—
Indonesia	88=	1.9	1.7	—	—
Nigeria	90	1.0	1.2	—	—
Bangladesh	91	0.4	—	—	—

Source: Transparency International.

BIBLIOGRAPHY

Aguilar Rivera, José Antonio, *En Pos de la Quimera: Reflexiones sobre el Experimento Constitucional Atlàntico* (Mexico City: Fondo de Cultura Económica, 2000).

Aiker, Hayward, *Rediscoveries and Reformulations: Humanistic Methodologies for International Studies* (Cambridge: Cambridge University Press, 1996).

Arendt, Hannah, *The Origins of Totalitarianism* (2nd end. London: Allen & Unwin, 1958).

——*On Revolution* (London: Faber & Faber, 1964).

Arias, Enrique Desmond, and Davis, Corinne M., 'The Role of Criminals in Crime Management and Dispute Resolution: Understanding Drug Traffickers' Control in Rio's *Favelas*' (paper delivered to the Latin American Studies Association, Washington, DC, Sept. 2001).

Aristotle, *Ethics* (Harmondsworth: Penguin, 1976 edn.).

——*The Politics* (Harmondsworth: Penguin, 1981 edn.).

Armijo, Leslie Elliott (ed.), *Financial Globalization and Democracy in Emerging Markets* (Basingstoke: Macmillan, 1999).

Ayers, Robert, *Crime and Violence as Development Issues in Latin America and the Caribbean* (Washington, DC: World Bank, 1998).

Barahona de Brito, Alexandra, González-Enríquez, Carmen, and Aguilar, Paloma (eds.), *The Politics of Memory: Transitional Justice in Democratizing Societies* (Oxford: Oxford University Press, 2001).

Barro, Robert, 'Inflationary Finance under Discretion and Rules', *Canadian Journal of Economics*, 16 (1983).

Becker, David, 'Latin America: Beyond "Democratic Consolidation"', *Journal of Democracy*, 10/2 (summer 1999).

Beetham, David (ed.), *Defining and Measuring Democracy* (London: Sage, 1994).

Bobbio, Norberto, *Liberalismo e democracia* (São Paulo: Editora Brasiliense, 1988).

——*Democracy and Dictatorship: The Nature and Limits of State power* (Minneapolis: University of Minnesota Press, 1989).

——*Estudos sobre Hegel: Direito, sociedade civil, estado* (São Paulo: Editora Brasiliense, 1989).

Boutros-Gali, Boutros (New York: United Nations, 1994).

Boylan, Delia, 'Democratization and Institutional Change in Mexico: The Logic of Partial Insulation', *Comparative Political Studies*, 34/1 (Feb. 2001).

Burki, Shahid Javed, and Perry, Guillermo, E. (eds.), *Beyond the Washington Consensus: Institutions Matter* (Washington, DC: World Bank, 1998).

Burns, Arthur, F., *Reflections of an Economic Policy-Maker: Speeches and Congressional Statements: 1969–1978* (Washington, DC: American Enterprise Institute, 1978).

Caldeira, Tesesa, *City of Walls: Crime, Segregation and Citizenship in Sao Paulo* (Berkeley, Calif.: University of California Press, 2000).

Camps, Victoria, and Giner, Salvador, *Manual de civismo* (Barcelona: Editorial Ariel, 1998).

Capie, Forrest, Goodhart, Charles, Fisher, Stanley, and Schnadt, Norbert (eds.), *The Future of Central Banking: The Tercentenary Symposium of the Bank of England* (Cambridge: Cambridge University Press, 1994).

Canovan, Margaret, *Hannah Arendt: A Reinterpretation of her Political Thought* (Cambridge: Cambridge University Press, 1992).

Carothers, Thomas, *Aiding Democracy Abroad: The Learning Curve* (Washington, DC: Carnegie Endowment, 1999).

Carrillo Flores, Fernando (ed.), *Democracia en Déficit: Gobernabilidad y Desarrollo en América Latina y el Caribe* (Washington, DC: Inter-American Development Bank, 2001).

Chevigny, P., *Edge of the Knife: Police Violence in the Americas* (New York: The New Press, 1995).

Cohen, Jean L., and Arato, Andrew, *Civil Society and Political Theory* (London: MIT Press, 1992).

Collier, D., and Adcock, R., 'Democracy and Dichotomies: A Pragmatic Approach to Choices about Concepts', *Annual Review of Political Science*, 2 (1999).

——and Levitsky, S., 'Democracy with Adjectives: Conceptual Innovation in Comparative Research', *World Politics*, 49/4 (1997).

——and Mahoney, J., 'Insights and Pitfalls: Selection Bias in Quantitative Research', *World Politics*, 49/1 (Oct. 1996).

Collingwood, R. G., *The New Leviathan: On Man, Society, Civilization and Barbarism* (rev. edn. Oxford: Oxford University Press, 1992).

Cornelius, Wayne, Eisenstadt, Todd, A., and Hindley, Jane (eds.), *Subnational Politics and Democratization in Mexico* (San Diego: Center for US–Mexico Studies, University of California, 1999).

Crabtree, John, and Whitehead, Laurence (eds.), *Toward Democratic Viability: The Bolivian Experience* (Basingstoke: Palgrave, 2001).

Dahl, Robert, *Polyarchy: Participation and Opposition* (New Haven, Conn.: Yale University, 1971).

——*Democracy and its Critics* (New Haven, Conn.: Yale University Press, 1989).

——*On Democracy* (New Haven, Conn.: Yale University Press, 1999).

Dalton, Bronwen, 'The Social Construction of Corruption in South Korea' (D.Phil. dissertation, Oxford University, 2000).

Darwin, Charles, *The Origin of Species* (New York: Mentor Edition, The New American Library, 1958; 1st publ. 1859).

Das, D., and Marenin, O. (eds.), *Challenges of Policing Democracies: A World Perspective* (Reading: Gordon & Breach, 2000).

Dealy, Glenn, C., *The Public Man: An Interpretation of Latin American and Other Catholic Countries* (Amherst, MA: Massachusetts University Press, 1977).

Diamond, Larry, *Developing Democracy: Toward Consolidation* (Baltimore: Johns Hopkins University Press, 1999).

——Plattner, Marc E., Chu, Yun-han, and Tien, Hung-mao (eds.), *Consolidating the Third Wave Democracies* (Baltimore: Johns Hopkins University Press, 1997).

Di Palma, Guiseppe, *To Craft Democracies: An Essay on Democratic Transition* (Berkeley: University of California Press, 1990).

Dobry, Michel, *Sociologie des crises politiques* (Paris: Presses de la Fondation Nationale des Sciences Politiques, 1992).

Dominguez, Jorge, 'The Caribbean Question: Why has Liberal Democracy (Surprisingly) Flourished?', in Jorge Dominguez, Robert Pastor, and Delisle Worrell (eds.), *Democracy in the Caribbean* (Baltimore: Johns Hopkins University Press, 1993).

Dray, William H., *History as Re-Enactment: R. G. Collingwood's Idea of History* (Oxford: Oxford University Press, 1995).

Dryzek, John, *Discursive Democracy* (Oxford: Oxford University Press, 2000).

Dunn, John (ed.), *Democracy: The Unfinished Journey: 508 B.C. to A.D. 1993* (Oxford: Oxford University Press, 1992).

Eckstein, Harry, 'Case Study and Theory in Political Science', in Fred I. Greenstein, and Nelson W. Polsby (eds.), *Handbook of Political Science* (London: Addison-Wesley, 1975).

Eliot, George, *Felix Holt: The Radical* (Harmondsworth: Penguin, 1972; 1st publ. 1866).

Ellis, Joseph T. *American Sphinx: The Character of Thomas Jefferson* (New York: Vintage, 1998).

Escalante, Gonzalbo, *Ciudadanos imaginarios* (Mexico City: El Colegio de México, 1992).

Fainzylber, P. *et al.*, *Determinants of the Crime Rate in Latin America and the World: An Empirical Assessment* (Wasington, DC: World Bank, 1998).

Fierlbeck, Katherine, 'Fetishizing Civil Society', paper delivered at the Canadian Political Science Association conference, June 1996.

Fine, Robert, and Rai, Shirin (eds.), *Civil Society: Democratic Perspectives* (London: Frank Cass, 1997).

Flyvbjerg, Bent, *Making Social Science Matter: Why Social Inquiry Fails, and How it can Succeed Again* (Cambridge: Cambridge University Press, 2001).

Foucault, Michel, 'Foucault et la Question du Libéralisme' *Horizons-Documents-Le Monde / Le Siècle, Paris* (Olsen, 2000).

Fox, Gregory H., and Roth, Brad R. (eds.), *Democratic Governance and International Law* (Cambridge: Cambridge University Press, 2000).

Fukuyama, Francis, *Trust: The Social Virtues and the Creation of Prosperity* (New York: Simon & Schuster, 1995).

Freeden, Michael, 'Political Concepts and Ideological Morphology', *Journal of Political Philosophy*, 2/2 (1994).

Freeden, Michael, *Ideologies and Political Theory: A Conceptual Approach* (Oxford: Oxford University Press, 1996).

Freedom House, *Freedom in the World, 2000–2001* (New York: Freedom House, 2001).

Fruhling, H., and Tulchin, J. (eds.), *Crime and Violence in Latin America: Citizen Security, Democracy, and the State* (Washington, DC: Woodrow Wilson Center Press, 2001).

Gallie, W. B., 'Essentially Contested Concepts', *Proceedings of the Aristotelian Society*, 56 (1956).

Gárreton, Manuel Antonio, 'Redemocratization in Chile', *Journal of Democracy*, 6/1 (Jan. 1995).

——and Newman, Edward (eds.), *Democracy in Latin America: (Re)Constructing Political Society* (Tokyo: United Nations University Press, forthcoming, 2002).

Gay, Robert, *Popular Democracy and Political Organizations in Rio de Janeiro* (Philadelphia: Temple University Press, 1994).

Geertz, Clifford, *Negara: The Theatre State in Nineteenth Century Bali* (Princeton, NJ: Princeton University Press, 1980).

Gellner, Ernest, *Relativism and the Social Sciences* (Cambridge: Cambridge University Press, 1895).

——*Conditions of Liberty: Civil Society and its Rivals* (London: Allen Lane, the Penguin Press, 1994).

Gerhardt, Michael J., *The Federal Press* (Princeton: Princeton University Press, 1996).

Giliomee, Hermann, and Simkins, Charles (eds.), *The Awkward Embrace: One Party Domination and Democracy* (Amsterdam: Harwood, 1999).

Goldthorpe, John, 'Current Issues in Comparative Macrosociology: A Debate on Methodological Issues', *Comparative Social Research*, 16 (1997).

Goodin, Robert E., 'Keeping Political Time: The Rhythms of Democracy', *International Political Science Review*, 19/1 (Jan. 1998).

——and Klingemann, Hans-Dietrich, *A New Handbook of Political Science* (Oxford: Oxford University Press, 1996).

Gould, S. J., 'Fulfilling the Sandrels of World and Mind', in J. Selzer (ed.), *Understanding Scientific Prose* (Madison: University of Wisconsin Press, 2000).

Greskovits, Béla, *The Political Economy of Protest and Patience: East European and Latin American Transformations Compared* (Budapest: Central European University Press, 1998).

Gross Siqueira Cunha, Luciana, 'Access to Justice and Judicial Assistance in Brazil', paper delivered to the Latin American Studies Association in Washington, DC, Sept. 2001.

Grugel, Jean (ed.), *Democracy without Borders: Transnationalisation and Conditionality in New Democracies* (London: Routledge, 1999).

——*Democratization: A Critical Introduction* (Basingstoke: Palgrave, 2001).

Gunther, Richard, Diamandourous, Nikiforos, and Pühle, Hans-Jurgen, *The Politics of Democratic Consolidation: Southern Europe in Comparative Perspective* (Baltimore: Johns Hopkins University Press, 1995).

Habermas, Jürgen, *Strukturwandel der Öffentlichkeit* (Frankfurt: Suhrkamp, 1993).

Hadenius, Axel, *Institutions and Democratic Citizenship* (Oxford: Oxford University Press, 2001).

Hall, John (ed.), *Civil Society: Theory, History, and Comparison* (Cambridge: Polity Press, 1995).

Hamilton, Alexander, Madison, James, and Jay, John, *The Federalist, or the New Constitution* (London: Everyman Editions, J. M. Dent, 1911; 1st publ. 1787–8).

Hampshire, Stuart, *Justice as Conflict* (Princeton: Princeton University, 2000).

Harré, Rom, and Krausz, Michael, *Varieties of Relativism* (Oxford: Blackwell, 1995).

Hartlynn, Jonathan, 'Contemporary Latin American Democracy and Consolidation: Unexpected Patterns, Re-elaborated Concepts, Multiple Components', in Joseph Tulchin (ed.), *Global Governance and Social Inequity* (Washington, DC: Wilson Center Press, 2001).

Havel, Václav, Klaus, Václav, and Pithart, Petr, 'Rival Visions', *Journal of Democracy*, 7/1 (Jan. 1996).

He, Baogang, 'The National Identity Problem and Rustow's "Theory of Sequence"', *Government and Opposition*, 36/1 (winter 2001).

Hegel, G. W. F., *Hegel's Philosophy of Right* (Oxford: Oxford University Press, 1942; tr. T. M. Knox; 1st publ. in German in 1821).

Held, David, *Democracy and the Global Order: From the Modern State to Cosmopolitan Governance* (Cambridge: Polity Press, 1995).

——*Models of Democracy* (2nd edn. Cambridge: Polity Press, 1996).

Hirst, Paul, *Associative Democracy: New Forms of Economic and Social Governance* (Cambridge: Polity Press, 1994).

Hodess, Robin, *Global Corruption Report 2001* (Berlin: Transparency International, 2001).

Holm, T. T., and Eide, E. B. (eds.), *Peacebuilding and Police Reform* (Ilford: Frank Cass & Co., 2000).

Howell, Jude, and Pearce, Jenny, *Civil Society and Development: A Critical Exploration* (Boulder, Co.: Lynne Reiner, 2001).

Human Rights Watch, *Police Brutality in Urban Brazil* (New Human Rights Watch, York: 1997).

Huntington, Samuel P., 'Will More Countries Become Democratic?, *Political Science Quarterly*, 99/2 (summer 1984).

——*The Third Wave: Democratization in the Late Twentieth Century* (Norman: University of Oklahoma Press, 1991).

——*The Clash of Civilizations and the Remaking of World Order* (New Simon & Schuster, York: 1996).

Ibn Khaldun, Wali, *The Mugaddimah* (London: Routledge & Kegan Paul, 1958, 3 vols; tr. F. Rosenthal from a 14th-cent. Arabic text).

Inder Singh, Anita, *Democracy, Ethnic Diversity, and Security in Post-Communist Europe* (London: Praeger, 2001).

Inoguchi, Takashi, Newman, Edward, and Keane, John, *The Changing Nature of Democracy* (Tokyo: United National University Press, 1998).

Jaeger, Werner, *Paideia: The Ideals of Greek Culture* (Oxford: Blackwell, 1954).

Jelin, Elizabeth, and Hershberg, Eric (eds.), *Constructing Democracy: Human Rights, Citizenship and Society in Latin America* (Boulder, CO: Westview, 1996).

Jonas, Susanne, *Of Centaurs and Doves: Guatemala's Peace Process* (Boulder, Colo.: Westview Press, 2000).

Kádár, András (ed.), *Police in Transition* (Budapest: Central European University Press, 2001).

Kaufmann, Daniel, 'Civil Liberties and Accountability for "Good Governance" and Anti-Corruption', paper delivered at the Carter Center, Atlanta, conference on 'Challenges to Democracy in the Americas', 16–18 Oct. 2000.

Kertzer, David, I., *Ritual, Politics and Power* (New Haven, Conn.: Yale University Press, 1984).

Key, Vernon, O., *Politics, Parties and Pressure Groups* (Ithaca, NY: Cornell University Press, 1964).

King, Gary, Keohane, Robert O., and Verba, Sidney, *Designing Social Enquiry: Scientific Inference in Qualitative Research* (Princeton: Princeton University Press, 1994).

Kohi, Atul, *Democracy and Discontent* (Cambridge: Cambridge University Press, 1995).

Kong, Tat Yan, *The Politics of Economic Reform in South Korea: A Fragile Miracle* (London: Routledge, 2000).

Konstan, David, *Greek Comedy and Ideology* (New York: Oxford University Press, 1995).

Kydland, Finn, and Prescott, Edward S., 'Rules rather than Discretion: The Inconsistency of Optimal Plans', *Journal of Political Economy*, 85/3 (June 1977).

Lagos, Marta, 'Between Stability and Crisis in Latin America', *Journal of Democracy*, 12/1 (Jan. 2001).

Lijphart, Arend, *Patterns of Democracy: government Forms and Performance in Thirty-six Countries* (New Haven: Yale University Press, 1999).

——and Waisman, Carlos H. (eds.), *Institutional Design in New Democracies: Eastern Europe and Latin America* (Boulder, Colo.: Westview, 1996).

Linz, Juan J., and Stepan, Alfred, *Problems of Democratic Transition and Consolidation: Southern Europe, South America and Post-Communist Europe* (Baltimore: Johns Hopkins University Press, 1996).

Lukes, Steven, *Emile Durkheim* (Harmondsworth: Penguin, 1973).

McCormick, John P., 'Machiavellian Democracy: Controlling Elites with Ferocious Populism', *American Political Science Review*, 95/2 (June 2001).

Mahoney, James, and Rueschemeyer, Dietrich (eds.), *Comparative–Historical Analysis* (Cambridge; Cambridge University Press, 2002).

Mainwaring, Scott, and Welna, Christopher (eds.), *Democratic Accountability in Latin America* (Oxford: Oxford University Press, 2002).

Manin, Bernard, Przeworski, Adam, and Stokes, Susan (eds.), *Democracy, Accountability, and Representation* (New York: Cambridge University Press, 1999).

Maravall, José María, *Regimes, Politics and Markets: Democratization and Economic Change in Southern and Eastern Europe* (Toronto: University of Toronto Press, 1973).

Markoff, John, *Waves of Democracy: Social Movement and Political Change* (Lakewood, Ohio: Pine Forge Press, 1995).

Maxfield, Sylvia, *Gatekeepers of Growth: The International Political Economy of Central Banking in Developing Countries* (Princeton: Princeton University Press, 1997).

Méndez, Juan E., O'Donnell, Guillermo, and Pinheiro, Paulo Sergio (eds.), *The (Un)Rule of Law and the Underprivileged in Latin America* (South Bend, Ind.: Notre Dave University Press, 1999).

Ménendez Carrión, Amparo (ed.), *La caja de Pandora* (Santiago: Planeta, 1999).

Merzer, Martin, *The Miami Herald Report: Democracy Held Hostage* (New St Martin's Press, York: 2001).

Mill, John Stuart, 'A System of Logic' (1843), in *Collected Works*, vii, ed. J. M. Robson (Toronto: University of Toronto Press, 1973).

——*Considerations on Representative Government* (1861, repr. London: Everyman's Library, 1910).

Mirowski, Philip (ed.), *Natural Images in Economic Thought* (Cambridge: Cambridge University Press, 1994).

Moggridge, D. E., *Keynes* 3rd edn. (Toronto: University of Toronto, 1993).

Moser, Caroline, and McLlwaine, Cathy, *Violence in Post-Conflict Context: Urban Poor Perceptions from Guatemala* (Washington, DC: World Bank, 2001).

Munck, Gerardo L., *Game Theory and Comparative Politics: Theoretical and Methodological Perspectives* (Cambridge: Cambridge University Press, forthcoming).

Neely, Mark E., jun., *The Fate of Liberty: Abraham Lincoln and Civil Liberties* (New Oxford University Press, York: 1991).

Nel, F., and Bezuidenhout, J. (eds.), *Policing and Human Rights* (Cape Town: Juta & Co., 1997).

Newey, Glen, 'Philosophy, Politics and Contestability' *Journal of Political Ideologies*, 6/3 (Oct. 2001).

Newton, Kenneth, 'Trust, Social Capital, Civil Society and Democracy', *International Political Science Review*, 22/2 (2001).

Norris, Pippa (ed.), *Critical Citizens: Global Support for Democratic Government* (Oxford: Oxford University Press, 1999).

Nussbaum, Martha C., *Love's Knowledge: Essays on Philosophy and Literature* (Oxford: Oxford University Press, 1990).

O'Donnell, Guillermo, 'On the State, Democratization and Some Conceptual Problems', *World Development*, 21/8 (Aug. 1993).

O'Donnell, Guillermo, Schmitter, Philippe, and Whitehead, Laurence (eds.), *Transitions from Authoritarian Rule: Prospects for Democracy*, 4 vols. (Baltimore: Johns Hopkins University Press, 1986).

Offe, Claus, 'Capitalism by Democratic Design? Democratic Theory Facing the Triple Transition in East Central Europe', *Social Research*, 58/4 (1991).

Olson, Mancur, 'Dictatorship, Democracy, and Development', *American Political Science Review*, 87 (1993).

Olvera, Alberto J., 'Sociedad Civil, Esfera Pública y Gobernabilidad', paper delivered at the Latin American Studies Association, Washington, DC, Sept. 2001.

Peters, Guy B., *Comparative Politics: Theory and Methods* (Basingstoke: Macmillan, 1998).

Pocock, J. G. A. *The Machiavellian Moment: Florentine Political Thought and the Atlantic Republican Tradition* (Princeton: Princeton University Press, 1975).

Polybius, *The Rise of the Roman Empire* (Harmondsworth: Penguin, 1979; trans. of a text written in Greek around 145 BC).

Popkin, Margaret, *Peace without Justice: Obstacles to Building the Rule of Law in El Salvador* (University Park, Penn.: Pennsylvania University Press, 2000).

Popper, Karl, *The Poverty of Historicism* (London: Routledge & Kegan Paul, 1986).

Posada, Eduardo (ed.), *Party Finances in Europe and Latin America* (London: Institute of Latin American Studies, London University, 1998).

Potocki, Jan, *The Manuscript Found in Saragossa* (Harmondsworth: Penguin English trans., 1995; originally publ. in Paris, 1813).

Prillaman, W. C., *The Judiciary and Democratic Decay in Latin America; Declining Confidence in the Rule of Law* (Westport, Conn.: Praeger, 2000).

Przeworski, Adam, *Democracy and the Market: Political and Economic Reforms in Eastern Europe and Latin America* (Cambridge: Cambridge University Press, 1991).

——and Limongi, Fernando, 'Democracy and Development', in Axel Hadenius (ed.), *Democracy's Victory and Crisis* (Cambridge: Cambridge University Press, 1997).

Pufendorf, Samuel, *On the Duty of Man and Citizen According to Natural Law* (Cambridge: Cambridge University Press, 1991; trans. of a text publ. in Latin in Germany in 1673).

Putnam, Robert D., *Bowling Alone: The Collapse and Revival of American Community* (New York: Simon & Schuster, 2000).

Pye, L., and Pye, M., *Asian Power and Politics: The Cultural Dimensions of Authority* (Cambridge, Mass: Belknap Press, 1985).

Rawls, John, *Political Liberalism* (New York: Columbia University Press, 1993).

Robinson, Mark, and White, Gordon, *The Democratic Developmental State: Political and Institutional Design* (Oxford: Oxford University Press, 1998).

Rueschemeyer, Dietrich, Stephens, Evelyn, and Stephens, John D., *Capitalist Development and Democracy* (Cambridge: Polity Press, 1992).

Rule, James B., *Theory and Progress in Social Science* (Cambridge: Cambridge University Press, 1997).

Rustow, Dankwart, 'Transitions to Democracy: Toward a Dynamic Model', *Comparative Politics*, 2/3 (1970).

Santiso, Javier, 'Théorie des choix rationnels et temporalités des transitions démocratiques', *L'Année sociologique*, 47/2 (1997).

——'Pasado de unos y futuro de otros: Analisis de las democratizaciones Mexicana y Chilena', *Foro Internacional*, 39/2–3 (Apr.–Sept. 1999).

Sarmiento, Domingo F., *Facundo, or Civilisation and Barbarism* (Harmondsworth: Penguin, 1998 edn., 1st publ. in Spanish in 1845).

Sartori, Giovanni, *Democratic Theory* (Detroit: Wayne State University Press, 1962).

——*The Theory of Democracy Revisited* (Chatham, NJ: Chatham House Publishers, 1987).

——*Comparative Constitutional Engineering: An Enquiry into Structures, Incentives and Outcomes* (Basingstoke: Macmillan, 1994).

Schedler, Andreas (ed.), *The Self-Restraining State: Power and Accountability in New Democracies* (Boulder, Colo.: Lynne Rienner, 1999).

——'Measuring Democratic Consolidation', *Studies in International and Comparative Development*, 36/1 (spring 2001).

——and Santiso, Javier, 'Democracy and Time: An Invitation', *International Political Science Review*, 19/1 (1998).

Schmitter, Philippe, 'On Civil Society and the Consolidation of Democracy: Ten Propositions' (mimeo, Stanford Dept. of Political Science, 1995).

—— and Karl, Terry Lynn, 'What Democracy is . . . And is Not', in Larry Diamond and Marc F. Plattner (eds.), *The Global Resurgence of Democracy* (Baltimore: Johns Hopkins University Press, 1993).

——and Santiso, Javier, 'Three Temporal Dimensions to the Consolidation of Democracy', *International Political Science Review*, 19/1 (1999).

Schumpeter, Joseph, *Capitalism, Socialism, and Democracy* (London: Allen & Unwin, 1st publ. 1943).

Segerstråle, Ullica, *Defenders of the Truth: The Sociobiology Debate* (Oxford: Oxford University Press, 2000).

Sen, Amartya, *Development as Freedom* (New York: Knopf, 1999).

Shapiro, Ian, and Hacker-Cordon, C. (eds.), *Democracy's Edges* (Cambridge: Cambridge University Press, 1999).

Shue, Henry, *Basic Rights: Subsistence, Affluence, and US Foreign Policy* (Princeton: Princeton University Press, second edition, 1996).

Silva, Ari de Abreu, 'Processos institucioniais de adminstração de conflitos: O impeachment presidencial', paper delivered at the first annual meeting of the Brazilian Association of Political Scientists, Rio de Janeiro, Dec. 1998.

Skinner, Quentin, *Reason and Rhetoric in the Philosophy of Hobbes* (Cambridge: Cambridge University Press, 1996).

Smith, Adam, *The Wealth of Nations* (London: Methuen, 1961; text 1st publ. in 1776).

Stepan, Alfred, *Arguing Comparative Politics* (Oxford: Oxford University Press, 2001).

Storing, H. J. (ed.), *The Complete Anti-Federalist* (Chicago: Chicago University Press, 1981).

Tarrow, Sidney, 'Making Social Science Work across Space and Time: A Critical Reflection on Robert Putnam's *Making Democracy Work*', *American Political Science Review*, 90 (1996).

Taylor, Charles, *Hegel* (Cambridge: Cambridge University Press, 1975).

Thucydides, *History of the Peloponnesian War* (Harmondsworth: Penguin, 1972 edn.).

Tocqueville, Alexis de, *Democracy in America* (New York: Vintage, 1945; 1st publ. 1838).

Topolski, Jerry, 'Methodological Foundations of Comparative Studies of Large Regions of the World', *Estudios Latinoamericanos*, 14/1 (Polish Academy of Sciences, 1992).

Transparency International, *Global Corruption Report 2001* (Berlin: Transparency International, 2001).

Tsang, Steve, and Tien, Hung-mao (eds.), *Democratization in Taiwan: Implications for China* (Basingstoke: Macmillan, 1999).

Tulchin, Joseph S., and Espach, Ralph H. (eds.), *Combating Corruption in Latin America* (Washington, DC: Woodrow Wilson Center Press, 2000).

Ullica Segerstråle, *Defenders of the Truth: The Sociology Debate* (Oxford: Oxford University Press, 2000).

United Nations Development Programme/Pittsburgh University, *Auditoria de al Democracia* (San Salvador: UNDP, 2000).

United States Senate Permanent Sub-Committee on Investigations, November 9 1999, Hearing on Private Banking and Money Laundering (Washington, DC).

van Gunsteren, Herman, 'Accountability: Governing by Looking Back', paper presented to the International Political Science Association conference in Quebec City, Aug. 2000.

Vanhanen, Tatu, *Prospects of Democracy: A Study of 172 Countries* (London: Routledge, 1997).

Veja, São Paulo, 7 Feb. 2001 (special report 'Somos todos reféns').

Vilas, Carlos M., 'Prospects for Democratization in a Post-Revolutionary Setting: Central America', *Journal of Latin American Studies*, 28/2 (May 1996).

Von Wright, G. H., *Explanation and Understanding* (London: Routledge & Kegan Paul, 1971).

Walzer, Michael, 'The Idea of Civil Society', *Dissent* (spring 1991).

Weingast, Barry, 'The Political Foundations of Democracy and the Rule of Law', *American Political Science Review*, 91 (1997).

Weintraub, Sidney, *Financial Decision-Making in Mexico: To Bet a Nation* (Pittsburgh: University of Pittsburgh Press, 2000).

Whitehead, Laurence, 'Tigers in Latin America', *Annals of the American Association of Political and Social Sciences* (Sept. 1989).

——'Democratization Studies', in Robert E. Goodin and H.-D. Klingemann (eds.), *A New Handbook of Political Science* (Oxford: Oxford University Press, 1996), 360–3.

——(ed.), *International Dimensions of Democratization* (enlarged edn. Oxford: Oxford University Press, 2001).

——'The Viability of Democracy', in John Crabtree and Laurence Whitehead (eds.), *Towards Democratic Viability: The Bolivian Experience* (London: Palgrave, 2001).

——(ed.), *Emerging Market Democracies: East Asia and Latin America* (Baltimore: Johns Hopkins University Press, forthcoming).

Wilde, Alexander, 'Irruptions of Memory: Expressive Politics in Chile's Transition to Democracy', *Journal of Latin American Studies*, 31/2 (May 1999).

Wills, Garry, *Lincoln at Gettysburg: The Words that Remade America* (New York: Simon & Schuster, 1992).

Wood, Elizabeth J., *Forging Democracy from Below: Insurgent Transitions in South Africa and El Salvador* (Cambridge: Cambridge University Press, 2000).

World Bank, *Helping Countries Combat Corruption: The Role of the World Bank* (Washington, DC: World Bank, 1997).

——*Global Economic Prospects and the Developing Countries* (Washington, DC: World Bank, 1998).

Wrong, Dennis, *The Problem of Order* (New York: The Free Press, 1994).

Yashar, Deborah, 'Contemporary Citizenship: Indigenous Movements and Democracy in Latin America', *Comparative Politics*, 31/1 (1998).

Znaniecki, Florian, *The Method of Sociology* (New York: Octagon, 1968).

INDEX